SEND FOR LEVENE

by *Peter Levene*

NINE ELMS BOOKS 2018

Published in 2018
by Nine Elms Books Ltd
Unit 6B, Clapham North Arts Centre
26–32 Voltaire Road, London SW4 6DH

E *inquiries@bene-factum.co.uk*
W *www.bene-factum.co.uk*

ISBN print 978-1-910533-42-0
ISBN e-book 978-1-910533-43-7

Cover illustration by John Penholder.
Cover and text design, typesetting and layout
by Lyn Davies Design *www.lyndaviesdesign.com*
Printed and bound by CPI Group (UK) Ltd,
Croydon, CR0 4YY.

CONTENTS

ILLUSTRATIONS

FIGURES

For Wendy
John, Nicole and Timothy
AJ, Dylan, Nicholas, Charley,
Thomas, Georgia, Jack
Luc, Amelie and Oscar

PREFACE

by Rt Hon The Lord Heseltine CH PC

I LIKE THE TITLE of this book. It indicates precisely the basis of my relationship with Peter. I established the 'prototype' in 1979, when as Secretary of State for the environment I had overall responsibility for housing. The major house builders expected regular access to the Secretary of State and used the informality of relaxed lunches to enable their spokesman, Tom Baron, to rough up the incumbent. Tiring of the process after the first couple of experiences, I eventually fought back and said that if he thought it was all so simple he had better come and work for me as a Special Adviser. He did, and the Department was much enriched by his presence.

Little surprise therefore that on arrival at the Ministry of Defence in 1983 and facing the daunting challenge of injecting competitive discipline and value for money accountability into the eight billion pound procurement budget my first question to officials was designed to find the name of the sharpest private sector man whom I could try to convert from poacher to gamekeeper. 'Send for Levene' assumed its first relevance as he describes it in Chapter 3. He came initially on a short-term secondment that not only introduced him to the public sector but was to form the basis for much of his future career.

His story, told with a refreshing simplicity and frankness, will resonate with anyone who has started their own business, or sought to get a grip on the complexities of management in the public sector or troubled private sector projects. His achievement in the Defence Ministry and later as advisor to John Major created his reputation as the 'go to' trouble-shooter. Docklands Light Railway, the Jubilee Line, the review of Canary Wharf, the saving of Lloyd's of London, are landmarks on the journey he describes. He brought his unique experience to the Mayoralty of the City of London and he enjoys, as a director of the China Construction Bank (Asia), a ringside seat as modern China emerges on the world stage. He tells his story with practical common sense devoid of generalisation or theory. This is a 'how to' guide to management by an experienced entrepreneur and exceptional public servant.

INTRODUCTION

WHILE I WAS compiling the
material for this book, and I was
rummaging through old photographs and other memorabilia, I
came across a small, worn piece
of card amongst the papers which
came from my late father's business when Martin, my nephew,
moved out of the shop in Brompton Road. Helpfully dated 1879
on the back, the card records an

1. Appeal card, Norwood Orphanage

appeal to the Governors & Subscribers of the Jew Hospital & Orphan
Asylum in Norwood for them to vote to take on the care of Pierre
and Alfred Levene, aged 9 years and 5 years, two children of the late
Maurice Levene who left a widow and nine children.

Pierre was my grandfather.

This extremely poignant tiny piece of card caused me to reflect on
how my family at that time would regard what for them would have
been the unimaginable future of a great-great grandchild who became
a Permanent Secretary, was awarded a knighthood and then a peerage,
was elected Lord Mayor of London and then the Chairman of Lloyd's.
I think they might have regarded such a tale as a modern and highly
fanciful version of Dick Whittington!

So it makes me pause for thought to reflect on how incredibly fortunate I have been and how my family today have been able to share in
the opportunities I have been granted.

CHAPTER ONE

Family, Childhood & Adolescence

M Y FATHER never really told me much about his family. Long after he had died, I decided to consult a genealogical research company. I knew that his father, Pierre Levene (1870–1938), had grown up in the Jewish orphanage at Norwood. Pierre's father, Maurice (c.1835–1879), died when he was nine years old, and his mother had been forced to place two of her nine children there. My father later spent a good part of his spare time in helping the orphanage by raising money for it, and over time it became very much part of his life.

When I commissioned the genealogical research, I found out that my father's family, the Levenes, were established in this country by the early nineteenth century. My great-great-grandfather, Lewis Levene (1807–1867), was born in Whitechapel, in east London. His wife, my great-great-grandmother, Caroline Levy (c.1803–1869) was born in Great Yarmouth in Norfolk. Another of my great-great-grandfathers, John Nathan (c.1800–1861), was a master butcher, and lived in Middlesex Street in the City of London Ward of Portsoken. They all lived in that part of London for generations, mostly poor and residing in what could probably best be described as crowded tenements.

In 1997, when I became a Life Peer, I was told that I had to choose a place-name to add to my title in order to avoid confusion with the existing Lord Leven.[1] So I chose Portsoken, the City of London Ward where I had been elected as Alderman in 1984. But when I chose it, I had no idea that so many of my ancestors had been born or lived there, nearly two hundred years earlier. I don't suppose that they ever

---

1 The current holder of this title is Alexander Ian Leslie-Melville, 15th Earl of Leven (b.1984).

imagined that their great-great-grandson would become Lord Mayor of London in 1998.

My grandfather, Pierre Levene, was sent from the orphanage to the People's Palace to train as a watchmaker. The People's Palace was founded with Drapers' Company funds to give educational facilities and night classes for students of all kinds. Its technical schools were formally opened in Mile End Road by Queen Victoria in 1887. I still have one of their bronze medals, which was awarded to my grandfather. The People's Palace was later incorporated into Queen Mary College in 1934 and merged with Westfield College in 1989. Many years later, in 1995, when I was running Canary Wharf, I was invited to become a Fellow of Queen Mary and Westfield College. While we were having drinks before the presentation ceremony, I noticed a glass case on the wall, with silver and bronze medals exactly like my grandfather's. And when the ceremony took place to award me my fellowship, I later realised that we had been standing on the same stage where he would have been awarded his medal.

In 1899 my grandfather, by then trading as a watchmaker at 174 Mile End Road, married Cissie Abrahams, a 24-year-old girl from

2. Pierre Levene – the original 1907 shop at 166 Fulham Road, London (later destroyed during the Blitz).

Newcastle. I don't know how they met. Her father had been a successful pawnbroker and town councillor in West Hartlepool, County Durham. However, he had died in 1891, so the wedding was organised by her mother. I have a copy of the wedding invitation and a newspaper cutting that describes both the ceremony itself at the Synagogue in Newcastle and a party given the following day by the bride's mother, for the poor children of the town. Given that Pierre Levene had been an orphan, so didn't have any money of his own, it was clearly a very favourable match.

He must have prospered, because in 1907 he opened a shop called *P. Levene* at 166 Fulham Road, just west of where the cinema is now. It was a watchmaking, jewellery and pawn broking business. At the time of the 1911 Census, he was living above the premises with his wife Cissie; two children – Maurice, my father, and Frances, my aunt; and his mother-in-law, Frances Abrahams. They also had a shop-assistant and a domestic servant. My grandfather was one of the founding members of the local Victoria & Chelsea Synagogue in Smith Street, just off the King's Road, which opened in 1916. Although the present synagogue on that site was built in the 1950s, there's a plaque on the wall just inside the door that records his part in its foundation.

My father, Maurice Levene (1900–1970) grew up in a very English atmosphere in Chelsea. He told me that he went to the first-ever game of Chelsea Football Club at Stamford Bridge in 1905, by crawling under the fence. That support has passed on, to the extent that my late brother and I have been avid Chelsea fans, as have my children and grandchildren as long as I can remember. In August 1918, as the First World War was drawing to its close, my father was called up into the Army, under the terms of the Military Service Act of 1916, which had imposed conscription on all single men aged between eighteen and forty-one. He later served in the British Army of the Rhine, based in Cologne, which formed part of the post-war Allied occupation of the Rhineland in 1919.

My father met my mother, Rose Lewis (1909–1991), in the 1930s. Her family was very different from the Levenes for both her parents had been born in Russia in the 1870s and had immigrated to England. Married in the East London Synagogue in 1893, they lived in Spitalfields.

My mother was the youngest of their eight children, and when she was growing up they spoke mostly Yiddish at home. Indeed, in later years, she would talk to her sisters for hours on the telephone in Yiddish. But my father didn't speak Yiddish, and as his mother-in-law didn't speak any English, my mother always had to interpret for them. He had never learnt to read Hebrew either, although he'd had his Bar Mitzvah, so I don't know quite how he managed that. Anyway, I know that all my mother's family, my aunts and uncles, regarded him as unusual, although they liked him because he was so different from them and was also successful.

3. My father, Maurice Levene serving in Germany, 1919

In 1926, while my grandfather was still alive, my father opened a second shop called *M.P. Levene Ltd* at 5 Thurloe Place, opposite the Victoria & Albert Museum. He specialised in silverware and rare postage stamps. After his father's death in 1938, he continued to run both this and the original shop in Fulham Road. When my parents married in 1935, they had bought a house in Willesden. This was fortunate, as in 1940 the Fulham Road premises, where my father had lived, were destroyed by a bomb during the Blitz. I can remember my mother saying how angry she was with my father, because they had a large stock of very valuable porcelain in there which he had not moved to safety and so all of it was lost.

My father's antique silver business in Thurloe Place was carried on by my brother, Colin Levene (1936–2014). He bought a new fifty-year lease, at a rent of about £1,000 a year, but when that was due for renewal, they wanted about £100,000 a year, so the premises had to close. Now my nephew, Martin Levene, continues to run the business by mail order and over the internet. Although I didn't go into the family business, I learnt quite a lot about postage stamps and silver as a boy. During the school holidays, I would go up to my father's shop on the bus, and he would send me out on errands. Whenever there was antique silver to repair, I would take items, backwards and forwards on the tube, mostly to a silversmith in the City called C.J. Vander. We had quite a selection of silver at home, but I remember it kept changing, because my father would come home and tell my mother he'd sold something we had in the house, and off it would go, to be replaced by a different piece.

It was interesting for me, with all this silver coming and going, and I think I must have absorbed some knowledge, because I can still usually identify English silver when I see it. Many years later, when I was Lord Mayor and on a trip to Brazil, I spotted some very attractive pieces in an antique shop in Rio de Janeiro. I contacted my brother and explained what I had found, and he said: 'How much do they want?' When I told him, he replied: 'Just buy it!' The haul included a set of English silver-gilt dinner plates with the heraldic crest of the Curzon family and their motto, *Let Curzon holde what Curzon helde*, which Wendy and I still have at home and use when entertaining.

Going back to the Second World War and the Blitz, my parents decided that living in Willesden was too close to the centre of town, so they rented out their house and moved to Pinner. And there I was born, on 8 December 1941, the day that Pearl Harbour was attacked by the Japanese and the Americans came into the war. Although historically this action is always recorded as having taken place on 7th December, if one considers the time difference, it was actually 8th December in London when the attack took place.

I was born after the Blitz on London, which took place between 7 September 1940 and 21 May 1941, but my parents had not escaped its consequences with the loss of their shop in Fulham Road. We had a bomb-shelter in the garden at Pinner, which we never used, but we also had an Anderson Shelter in the garage. I can remember my father and mother whipping us out of bed one night and taking us out there. We must have been in the shelter for about half an hour, when my mother said: 'What on earth are we doing out here? This is ridiculous, we're going back to bed.'

However, when the Germans started launching the V1 and V2 flying bombs in the summer of 1944, my parents decided that my brother and I should be evacuated from Pinner. We were sent, with our nanny, to stay for a few weeks with a fisherman and his family in

Filey, on the Yorkshire coast. When the flying bombs stopped in the spring of 1945, we came home to Pinner again.

Shortly after the Second World War, my parents moved back to their original house in Willesden. From there I went to my first school in Cricklewood, called Westcroft, where I was very happy. Initially, I travelled there with my mother; but by the time I was seven or eight, I was deemed capable of making this journey on my own, although it involved a trip on one bus and a change onto a trolleybus. The school was effectively a preparatory school for Haberdashers' School, now located in Elstree, but then also based in Cricklewood. I took their entrance exam and, being reasonably bright, was disappointed when I didn't get a place. I then learnt that Haberdashers' had a quota for the number of Jews they would allow in the school at any one time, which may have been why they had declined to take me. It was the first, and probably the only, time that I was confronted with anti-Semitism.

I then took the exam for the City of London School, passed it, and was accepted. My father said: 'Well, that's great. It's a good school, you'll like it there and, as one of their pupils, you will have the first qualification to become Lord Mayor of London.' Of course, strictly speaking, that wasn't true, but perhaps he had a premonition. I also remember attending Prize Day in my first year, and being fascinated when the Lord Mayor and the Sheriffs turned up with their retinues. It was all a foretaste of what was to come. And I certainly did not know then that more than thirty-five years later, in 1986, I would become a governor of the school, or that thirty years after that, we would donate a new library, which was opened in 2017 as the Levene Learning Centre.

When I started at the City of London School I was just nine years old, and was terrified of a number of things. Firstly, I had to travel alone from Willesden, which involved going by bus to Notting Hill Gate to catch the tube, then disembarking at Blackfriars, where a subway emerged close to the school on Victoria Embankment. It was a daunting journey for a small boy, but after about a week I picked it up and soon became an expert and knew exactly which carriage doors opened directly opposite the station exits.

At that time, in the early 1950s, there were slot-machines on the platforms that had previously dispensed chocolate, although of course they were all empty owing to post-war rationing. I can remember travelling with friends on the tube, on the way to school, and saying: 'Can you imagine? There's a machine here which used to give you a bar of chocolate if you put money into it.' Sweets had initially been de-rationed in April 1949, but it caused mayhem. Everybody went mad and emptied the entire nation's stock, and after just four months they were rationed again, and stayed that way until February 1953. My aunt, my father's sister, would, as a treat, take me to watch cartoons, and she used to give me some of the sweet coupons from her ration book. We all had ration books, although during the war, and in spite of the submarine blockade, we never went hungry. The food was very basic, and nothing like what is available now, but we had vegetables, we had chickens in the garden, and we were fine.

I vividly remember my first day at the City of London School. There were 800 boys there and, compared with my little prep school, it was enormous. We were taken into the Great Hall, where all the new boys were sent up onto the balcony. Then we were given a set of School Rules, in a yellow book, which said: 'Discipline: Six-Formers can report ill-discipline to Form Masters; Sub-Prefects can give detentions; and Prefects may cane.' Of course, today caning would be illegal, but at the time I was absolutely terrified. Our uniform included a cap, which you had to raise if you met any of the masters, while walking to school from the station. To be caught by a Prefect or a Sub-Prefect outside school without your cap on was considered a heinous crime. They were compulsory wear for everyone until you got to the sixth form, or, unless you were over six-foot tall, then only because they thought boys over that height would look absurd wearing a cap.

I had a number of contemporaries at the City of London School who later became well known in their fields, including the captain of the England cricket team – Mike Brearley, Michael Apted – the Hollywood film producer, and Lawrence Collins – now Lord Collins of Mapesbury – who had also been with me at Westcroft. He was the first solicitor to be appointed a High Court Judge direct from private practice, in 2000; and only the second solicitor to achieve that position, after Sir Michael Sachs, who had previously sat as a circuit judge for nine years. When Laurence reached the compulsory retirement age of seventy in 2011, he was appointed as a judge at the Court of Final Appeal in Hong Kong.

7

4. With my City of London School contemporaries. I'm on the middle row, second from the left. Film director Michael Apted third from left. Front row, third boy from right is England cricket captain Mike Brearley.

The City of London School was huge, with a swimming pool and a gym, but the classrooms were very old fashioned - several of them had a coal fire. We all wrote with pens, which we dipped into inkwells, a prized job in the class being that of the inkwell monitor. The ink was made from powder and water. We all went home with inky fingers.

The headmaster was Arthur Barton, a very tough Yorkshireman. Many years later, when I was Lord Mayor, I went on a visit to Israel. I knew that quite a lot of Old Citizens, as former pupils of my school are called, were living there, so I asked the British ambassador, Francis Cornish, with whom we were staying, if we could invite some of them for a drink at his residence. When he agreed and asked which school it was, and I said it was the City of London School, he told me that his uncle had been its headmaster. 'You don't mean Arthur Barton?' I said. 'That's the one,' he replied. 'I see,' I went on, 'so you must be one of the nephews.' 'Absolutely,' said the ambassador. Then I asked: 'Have you ever been to Saas-Fee in Switzerland?' 'Yes,' he said, 'how did you know that?' So I explained. Arthur Barton had no children. At the end of every term, he would give an address, which was always the same, to the point where we almost knew it off by heart, including: 'I took my nephews to Saas-Fee recently.'

When I was at school at the City of London, one of its best-known alumni was Prime Minister Herbert Asquith. He is on record as having said at a John Carpenter Club Dinner in 1892: 'Each of us here this evening, when he comes to interrogate his own inner self, must be constrained to confess that he owes the best, the highest and most stimulating influences which guide and which inspire him to the training which we one and all received at the City of London School.' I would thoroughly endorse that comment and recognise the enormous amount that I gained from some outstanding teachers. One or two in particular come to mind, notably those who worked to teach me both French and German, not just in getting the grammar correct but in learning to speak the languages with a true accent. There was a French teacher called Nicky Field, who was one of the most eccentric people you could meet and whose classroom was surrounded with boards to instruct you how to speak the language properly, and his insistence in getting it right was never-ending. The other two language teachers were Dr Patrick Whitmore, who also taught French and had been also a remarkable soldier who had fought in the Battle of the Bulge, and Dr Harry Law Robertson, a Scotsman who was a great German teacher who had graduated from the University of Giessen in Germany. His mastery of the German language and his outstanding knowledge of Germany led to his recruitment to work at Bletchley Park during the war, a subject which he never mentioned and which I only found out about much later.

I went on to study French and German for my A-Levels, during two years in the Sixth Form, but decided not to read languages at university but rather economics. I didn't win a place at Cambridge or the LSE but, fortunately, I was offered a place at Manchester University to read Politics and Economics.

Apart from my brief stay in Yorkshire as an infant during the war, I don't think I had ever been as far north as Manchester. I moved into Woolton Hall, a hall of residence named after Lord Woolton, the wartime Minister of Food between 1940 and 1943, who had studied at the university and became its chancellor in 1944. Woolton Hall had only been open for a year, everything was brand-new, and with its central heating it represented the utmost luxury. Being thrown up there alone, becoming my own boss, and learning about life was the best thing that could have happened, although I didn't realise that until I came home from Manchester at the end of my first term. During that holiday, I went out one night with my friends and came back at two o'clock in the morning. The next day my father said: 'And what time do you think you came in last night?' I replied: 'About two o'clock, so what?' He gave me a look, as if to indicate that he knew the world had changed, and I never heard any more about it.

At school, I had discovered that I excelled at running as a sprinter. I was in the under-fourteen and under-sixteen athletics teams, and ended up as captain of the school's athletics team. My hall of residence at Manchester was fifty yards from the athletics track, so I immediately joined the university team, and went on to become secretary of the athletics club and then its captain. I wasn't, by any means, the best athlete in the team, but I was a good administrator. While I was there, we won the British University Championship, the first time since the war. We had four or five international athletes in the team, including John Whetton in the 1500 metres and Ron Hill in the marathon who went on to represent Great Britain in the Rome Olympics in 1960. I remember bringing the trophy back on the coach and taking it into the track pavilion the next day. The groundsman, who had worked there since the place was built, recognised the magnificent trophy and said: 'My God, you didn't win it, did you?' He was amazed when I said: 'Yes, we did!'

I had a wonderful time at Manchester and, in spite of spending all my time running the athletics club, I somehow passed my degree with a 2:2. I found the economics pretty boring but the politics was much more interesting. We had some very good professors, including Richard Rose, the psephologist and Jim Ball (later Sir James Ball) who went on to become professor of economics at the London Business School and the Chairman of Legal & General. Our connection is immortalized in a later painting on the wall of the RAC in Pall Mall, depicting us both having a drink in the bar – somewhat implausibly! They also brought in teachers from outside the university, like Vladimir Dedijer. He had fought with Tito during the partisan struggle against the Nazis in Yugoslavia, and talked to us about communism. The French Fifth Republic had only just been instituted, with Charles de Gaulle taking over as its first president in 1959, so we also learned about what was going on in France.

It was an interesting time, politically. I remember travelling with the athletics club to a match against Liverpool University, right at the time of the Cuban Missile Crisis in 1962. We were all convinced that nuclear war was about to break out. As we were travelling along in the coach, I saw that a section of the motorway had been cordoned off, where a man was repainting the lines in the middle of the road. I can remember thinking: 'What the hell is he bothering to do that for? This place is all going to be rubble in twenty-four hours' time.'

CHAPTER TWO

United Scientific Holdings

B EFORE I LEFT university, I had two vacation posts, the first with Unilever and the following year a couple of months with Court-aulds. At Unilever I was asked to compile a report on the different languages of South-East Asia, so they could decide which languages to use on their packaging which would be understood by the largest proportion of consumers. Although Unilever subsequently offered me a job, I turned it down to look for something else. My parents had given me a Mini for my twenty-first birthday, and initially I actually considered becoming a driver.

At the end of each term at Manchester University, I would return to London for the vacation. I have to say that this often involved partying, rather than any attempt to continue with my studies. At one of these parties which had been organised by a charity, I met some old friends and was then struck by a very attractive young girl to whom I rapidly attached myself for the rest of the evening. This was none other than the then Wendy Fraiman whom I assiduously courted for the next four years, until I finally persuaded her to marry me. When we first met, Wendy was only 15 (!) and I was 20, but when we married in 1966, she was 19 and I was 24 – when I tell this to our grandchildren, they are incredulous!

By the time of my twenty-first birthday, Wendy and her family were helping me look for a job. Both her father and her brother knew a Scotsman called Bennie Linden, who had set up a business in the 1950s, originally called Scottish Distributors and with a number of subsidiaries – United Technical Supplies, United Scientific Instruments, Optical Instruments Balham and later Lindair, selling war surplus supplies, either by mail order or from his shop in Tottenham Court Road. At that time, the Royal Navy, the Army and the Royal

Air Force would hold regular sales, at which they sold off stock at very low prices. For example, a pair of binoculars, which might originally have cost £20, could be snapped up for five shillings, because they were auctioned off in bulk lots.

Bennie had a huge warehouse, full of racks of this military equipment. He sold countless watches and binoculars in his shop, and customers also bought telescopes from tanks and periscopes from ships, so they could extract the lenses to build their own items. But gradually, Bennie had noticed that strange individuals were turning up to buy things in bulk. He quickly realised that these people were purchasing on behalf of foreign armed services who were still using this equipment. When he took me on in 1963, he said: 'Look, we've got all this equipment, which we sell over the counter for £2. I can sell it to these foreigners for £20, maybe even £100, but we need to list it all in a proper military catalogue.' So, as a very inexperienced twenty-one year-old, I started work on compiling this catalogue. Initially he explained what was what, and gradually I taught myself more about all the equipment. We kept on buying additional stock, and had to find more warehouses, and I soon realised that he was absolutely right and that this was potentially a great business.

Bennie was brilliant, but extremely difficult and totally paranoid. He didn't trust anyone, and thought everybody was out to get him. As he had convinced himself that I was robbing him, he used to get to the office very early so he could steam open my mail before I arrived. In 1964, I had been with him for a year and, at that time, I was being paid £1,000 a year, which was a princely sum compared to my university contemporaries, who were on a more standard rate of £750. But I thought I was due a pay-rise and, after giving it some thought, Bennie agreed to an annual salary of £1,200. However, at that time he was being particularly beastly to me, and one day, while reading *The Times*, I saw a small advert on the front page which said: 'Well-established City Company looking for Director of Purchasing'.

I applied but didn't hear anything. Then, about four or five weeks later, I received a letter from a company in Chiswell Street in the City, which turned out to be the paper manufacturer Bunzl, inviting me to go and see them. So off I went, in great secrecy, knowing absolutely nothing about where I was going. As it happened Bunzl was originally a Jewish owned company, initially based in Vienna, which was the largest manufacturer of cigarette filter-tips in the world. They had fled the virulent anti-Semitism in Austria in the 1930s and relocated to London. I was interviewed by an extremely elegant, refined and charming Austrian gentleman called Mr. Fortgang. Two days later, he rang to say he wanted to see me again. When I arrived in his office, he said: 'Look, we'd like to offer you the purchasing post, but I think you'd be wasted in that job. Instead, I'd like to make you my personal assistant. I am the largest buyer of jute in the world. Under me, you will learn the trade, and eventually you will be able to take on my job. If you are interested, we're prepared to give you £2,000 a year.' This, of course, was almost double what I was then earning.

I went back to work and said to Bennie: 'I don't quite know how to tell you this. You remember a few weeks ago I asked for a pay-rise, and you gave me an extra £200?' 'Yes,' he said, 'and that was very generous.' I agreed, but then went on to explain that I had now been offered another job with a salary of £2,000 a year, at which he retorted: 'Well then, go. Nobody in their right mind would pay you that much. But you must finish the catalogue first.' That took a few weeks, but once I'd completed it, I told him that I proposed to leave at the end of the month. 'What are you talking about?' he said. When I reminded him of our earlier conversation, he replied: 'You're not really going, are you?' 'Yes,' I said, 'of course I am.' 'No, no, you don't want to do that,' said Bennie, 'you're being very hasty. How much are they going to pay you?' When I told him again that I had been offered £2,000, he responded by saying: 'Alright, I'll give you £3,000 a year to stay.'

At that stage, I didn't know what to do. However, I had already agreed to join Bunzl, so I felt I had to go back and talk to Mr. Fortgang again. When I arrived in his office, I explained what had happened, but assured him that, as I had accepted his offer, I would honour my word if he insisted that I take up the new job. He replied: 'When I was your age, the same thing happened to me, and I decided to stay where I was. So I want to tell you this: if you feel you can do well staying where you are, do it. There will be no hard feelings. You've behaved impeccably.' So that was that, and I went back to my office at United Scientific.

*   *   *

I soon started travelling all over the world. One of the first things I did was to go on a tour of Africa, because many of those countries were using our stock of slightly dated military equipment. I went to Nigeria, Ghana, South Africa, Tanzania, Kenya, Zambia, and – as it was then – Southern Rhodesia. With the help of the British Embassy or High Commission in each of these places, I asked to be put in touch with the government representatives responsible for their armed forces, and I would try to sell them some of the products in my vast catalogue. Of course, I was looked at slightly askance in most of these locations, because I was basically a kid. But, as was the norm in those days, we then started to attract people who could become our local agents, some of whom were more respectable than others.

The first place I went to, in the 1960s, was Nigeria. I hadn't been there very long when, through an intermediary, we secured the help of the finance minister, Mr Festus Okotic-Eboh. This all went very well until the first *coup d'etat* in Nigeria in January 1966, when he and the Prime Minister were assassinated. But, undeterred, we carried on. Back in the 1960s, the only decent hotel in Lagos was the Federal Palace which, as hotels go, certainly wasn't great, but was a lot better than its competitors and was managed – to my surprise – by an Israeli who offered to introduce me to senior Nigerians who frequented the hotel. On one occasion, I sat down in the restaurant there to order lunch, and having read the menu, called over the waiter and said: 'It says here "Horse Tail Soup". Is this horse-tail soup? Or do you actually mean ox-tail soup?' 'No, no,' he replied, 'it's horse-tail; you know, clippety-clop, clippety-clop.' It was also very difficult to get hotel rooms in Lagos, and on one visit, when I couldn't get into the Federal Palace, I had to book elsewhere. When I arrived at this alternative hotel and was shown up to my room, the porter opened the door and asked: 'Is this alright?' I said: 'Well, yes, it would be, except that it doesn't seem to have a bed.' That was not unusual.

Then I went to Ghana, which I found much less wild than Nigeria, because it still retained quite a lot of the British way of doing business. There I worked with Edward Boohene, a charming man, who went on to become chairman of Ghana Airways. I also went to South Africa, but because of the embargo, we were restricted on what we could sell there. Frank Dickens was our agent there, and soon Bennie was accusing me of conniving with him in order to steal money from the company. We had proposed that all our agents would get a percentage as their commission. I had offered them 7½ per cent, Frank asked me to put it up to ten, which I agreed, and Bennie thought that the extra 2½ per cent was going in my pocket.

By 1968 the military-equipment sales, based on my catalogue, were making a lot of money, particularly when compared with the shop in Tottenham Court Road. At this point, Bennie decided to float the business on the Stock Exchange. The flotation was handled by merchant bankers, Edward Bates & Sons. By this time, my relations with my boss had reached an all-time low, and I found out he had told these people that I was syphoning money out of the company, which was totally untrue. Being an ultra-cocky kid, then a mere twenty-six years old, I said to the bankers: 'Look, you may or may not know this, and I don't really care whether you do or not, but I just want to tell you that the successful part of this business is now me. And I'm not working for Bennie Linden anymore. So, if you want to float this business, it's either him or me.' It was a terrible thing to have to do to the man who had created the company, but the bankers soon found out that I was right. We then agreed that they would handle the flotation, I would be appointed as the new managing director, and Bennie would be paid out with £450,000 and would keep the retail business. He was also required to sign a written apology for accusing me of theft and to promise never to repeat the accusations again.

At that stage, a company floated on the Stock Exchange had to be showing a minimum profitability of £100,000, which we were just below. But the merchant bankers said that we could go ahead, although they also insisted that I would have to buy a lot of shares in this new firm. When I explained that I didn't have much money, they said: 'Don't worry, we'll arrange for a bank to lend it to you.' I was sent to see Alan Waterhouse, a bank manager at Barclays in the City, who agreed to the loan, but also warned me: 'You are signing away your life, and if this goes wrong, you will lose every penny you've got.' I responded by saying: 'I'm running this business, so it's not going to go wrong.' Fortunately, I was right, but at that time I had borrowed £250,000, which was far more than I could afford. Even three or four years later, when I realised what I had done, I thought I must have been mad. As it was, it all worked out very well. Later on, Wendy said to me: 'I've got a little money my father gave me, and I want to buy shares in your company.' At that stage, the stock market had gone into a slump, so I said: 'You don't want to do that; they've gone down from five shillings to one-and-sixpence. I've got hundreds of thousands of these shares, we could paper the walls with them, and they're not worth anything.' But she was adamant: 'No, I know what you're doing, I know you're working hard, and this is going to be good.' Years later, her shares were worth a lot of money.

*   *   *

When we decided to turn United Scientific into a public company in 1968, we did it by buying what was called a shell company, which was a firm that already had a Stock Exchange quotation, but was either not trading or dormant. The company we bought was called Cookson Bates Ltd, the name Bates being Ken Bates,[1] of Chelsea Football Club fame, who came from Lancashire. Although we bought this company as a shell, it actually retained a few odd assets, including a property in Burnley, which consisted of a parade of nine or ten shops at the bus station. Although they brought in a small income, it wasn't a lot of money and we decided to sell them. Unfortunately, we then discovered that when the local lawyers had drawn up the leases with the shop owners, they had specified the annual rent, but had omitted to put in a rent review clause, which meant effectively that the rents were fixed for the length of the leases. It was therefore impossible to value this property, because nobody would buy it under such conditions. To add to the complications, the freeholder, to whom we paid ground rent, was Burnley Corporation, who *did* have a rent review clause in their lease with us, so while we would gradually have to pay more, the shop owners wouldn't.

Our lawyer considered all this and said: 'Look, don't do anything. With a bit of luck, Burnley Corporation will forget to enact the rent review.' So we waited, and sure enough they forgot. He then said: 'Right, we're going to write to them to point out that as they have

---

1   Ken Bates (*b.*1931), businessman and football executive, who bought Chelsea F.C. for £1 in 1982 and sold it to Roman Abramovich in 2003 for £140 million.

missed their date, they cannot now bring in a rent review for another umpteen years, and that the lease is therefore void through uncertainty.' When they refused to accept these points, we took them to court and won the case; and when they went to appeal, we won the appeal. They then decided to take it to the House of Lords, at which we were staggered, because the whole case hinged on about £2,000 or £3,000 a year. We found out afterwards that they were being backed by a big property company, who were trying to develop an immensely valuable site in the City, where a similar problem had arisen. It's actually the site where Deutsche Bank is now located, and as the successful resolution of this issue there was going to reap serious money, they were prepared to fund the Burnley Council in a test case. When I asked our lawyers what chances they had of winning, they said: 'Zero.' It went to the House of Lords and, believe it or not, we lost. The United Scientific Holdings v. Burnley Borough Council Case of 1978 subsequently became the precedent for similar rent review issues throughout the country, and has since been cited in at least fourteen other cases. My son-in-law even came across it years later in his textbooks, when he was studying estate management.

We inherited various other properties that had belonged to Cookson Bates, one of which was a bowling green in the small Lancashire town of Rawtenstall. It had become overgrown and disused, and was totally devoid of value, because it was surrounded by other gardens and had no right-of-way to get to it. So we ignored it. In fact, we tried very hard to give it away. Then one day we received a letter to say that a landslip from our bowling green had fallen onto a neighbouring garage, which meant that we were required to pay for its new roof. Of course, like the rent review, none of this had anything whatsoever to do with the business of United Scientific, but we found ourselves dragged into these irksome unrelated property issues. I don't know what happened to the bowling green, I think we managed to give it away in the end.

*　　*　　*

Although Bennie and I totally fell out, I must give credit to him for my learning, as a complete ingénue, what business was really about from a very tough operator.

Soon after I joined United Scientific in 1964, I recruited my first direct assistant, Mick Cooper. He stayed with me throughout and is still with the spin-off of a much smaller niche business which he runs very successfully from the Midlands.

As the business grew, I was able to recruit some very able colleagues – two from the ranks of the military: Martin Proudlock, a young artillery officer who won an MC in Aden and Chris Joll, a Lifeguards' officer who is now both a successful impresario and author. We were also joined by Nick Prest who joined from the Ministry of Defence [MOD] Sales Organisation and who went on to become the Managing Director of United Scientific Holdings [USH] and now runs another very successful business Cohort plc.

By 1968 I was running USH, which was valued at £1 million, with twenty-five staff, exporting 90 per cent of our stock overseas to armed forces in Africa, Europe, the Middle East, and the Far East. Our range stretched from bomb sights to buoys, and from automatic pilots to mine detectors. Some was now also state-of-the-art equipment and we could sell it for huge margins, so something we had bought for shillings sold for hundreds of pounds. Profits had risen from £27,000 in 1964 to £90,000 in 1967, with an anticipated figure of £125,000 by 1970.[1] We leased an enormous underground warehouse from British Rail, which is now the booking hall and exit point for Eurostar at St Pancras Station. There we stored enough equipment for a small army. Under the terms of the lease, we paid only five shillings per square foot, on the basis that there were plans to develop the site and nobody else would take it, because you could be evicted with only three months' notice. As I viewed it merely as a warehouse, this didn't bother me, and in fact we were still there ten years later. It was a perfect place, run by three or four storemen, and one man in a workshop with a spray-paint booth, who refurbished equipment.

At first we were selling surplus second-hand equipment. We sold a wide range of spare parts for Centurion tanks, so we did a significant amount of business with countries using them. Even though I wasn't an engineer, I started to understand the workings of the tanks, so whenever there were tenders for Centurion parts the buyers concerned

1   Anon., 'Export king Levene is valued at £250,000,' *Daily Express*, mid-1968.

would come to us and we would bid to supply them. As a result, United Scientific became known as a support organisation of spare parts for British military equipment. But of course our source of supply was only what the MOD had decided to sell off. If somebody wanted left-hand sprockets and we had them, that was fine; but if they needed the right-hand ones, we often found we didn't have them. So we started to order new equipment from the original manufacturers. None of these companies had an export market, because their range was limited, and in any event they didn't have what we were building up from scratch, which was a distribution network around the world.

One of the companies we did business with was Helio Mirror, based in Erith in Kent. Tanks and armoured cars in those days, as they do today, have a cupola mounted on top of their turrets, which rotates. In the cupola there were a number of what the Americans called vision-blocks, known in the UK as unit-power periscopes. They consist of an upper and lower prism, which you look through, thus enabling you to see what's going on without sticking your head out. They were not terribly expensive, but you needed perhaps eight or ten per vehicle. The only people who could make these satisfactorily were Helio Mirror. The firm had been set up by two brothers, Dave and Stan Cowan, who had worked out an ingenious way of silvering the glass on these mirrors so that the silver didn't come off over time. The MOD liked this, bought huge quantities of these products, and although their company hadn't been set up as a monopoly, it had virtually become one.

By that time, in the early 1970s, I had decided that United Scientific should be not only dealers, but also manufacturers. We were looking around for businesses to buy, and I was told that the two brothers who owned this company might be prepared to sell. We could offer them export opportunities, because the last thing they wanted to do was go and sell things all around the world when they were quite happy making their periscopes and selling them to the MOD. I went to meet them and we got on rather well. Dave was the boss, his brother Stan worked with him. It was a highly profitable business. Anyway, we negotiated to buy it and agreed terms, and then gave it to the lawyers to sort out. At that time, there was a flu epidemic, and when both Dave Cowan and I caught the flu, the lawyers on both sides

5. Exhibition stand at Woolwich Barracks in the early 1970s with Dave and Stan Cowan, the founders of Helio Mirror.

managed to virtually ruin the deal. We had been on very good terms, and then they put in ridiculous conditions, to the extent that the whole deal began to fall apart. I phoned Dave Cowan from my sickbed, spoke to him on his sickbed, and said: 'These bloody lawyers! Let's give it a week, until we're both feeling better, and then we'll sit down and sort this out.' When we got together, we called all the lawyers in and said: 'Now look, don't say a word. We know what we've agreed, so either you do as you're told or you're fired.' So we went ahead, bought this terrific business and sold these periscopes all over the world. Then we started to broaden our horizons as our customers asked us if we could design the cupolas for their armoured vehicles. We rose to the challenge and Helio Mirror moved from being just an optical business to an engineering one, and this was our first venture into manufacturing.

Then we decided to look at another company called Avimo, with whom we had worked for a long time, which was based in Taunton in Somerset, and also built a lot of the equipment we supplied. Their name was short for *Aviation Moderne* and had been established by a Frenchman in 1936. They produced optical and electronic instruments that were used in aircraft, missiles, and armoured vehicles. We became a good customer of Avimo. Then we found that if there was something that people wanted, which we hadn't got in stock and which they hadn't made, once we got hold of the MOD blueprints, Avimo could make it for us and pay the MOD a royalty. Eventually, in 1971, we did a much bigger deal to buy that business.[1] Helio employed seventy or eighty people; Avimo had four or five hundred and was far more diverse. In 1977 we built a second factory in Taunton, this one being specifically for the development and production of laser range-finders. Whenever we had board meetings, I would drive myself down to Helio located at Belvedere in Kent, which wasn't very far. But for Avimo, we would go on the train from Paddington, and for a while we even experimented by flying down to Somerset in a helicopter.

*   *   *

I then decided to see what we could do in Asia, because so many countries there, including Singapore, Malaysia, and Thailand, were using British military equipment. I knew someone who was selling scientific equipment to schools through an agency based in Kuala Lumpur in Malaysia and in Singapore. Consequently I flew out to Singapore to meet him. It was the furthest east I had ever been in my life, and I had no idea how things worked out there. However, at that time, we were doing a lot of business with Israel, and on one of my trips there, their head of procurement had mentioned to me that they had a Defence Mission in Singapore. It's important to remember that the political situation in Singapore mirrored that in Israel, because both countries were either surrounded or bordered by somewhat hostile Moslem neighbours, in Singapore's case these being Malaysia and Indonesia. So the Singaporeans and the Israelis had found common cause. The other commonality was that both nations are very clever and innovative.

When I arrived in Singapore, I was told that the person I really needed to meet was Mr Ong Kah Kok, the Director of Logistics for the Singaporean Armed Forces. So, as I had done in numerous

---

1   Anon., 'Avimo take-over: jobs are safe,' *Somerset County Gazette*, 2 July 1971.

countries before, I rang up the British defence attaché and said that I would like to meet the head of logistics for the Singaporean Ministry of Defence. I was told that he was a very busy man, and it would be unlikely that he would have time to see me. I phoned the Israeli Embassy and asked to be put through to their defence attaché. 'We don't have a defence attaché in Singapore,' they said, 'we don't know what you're talking about.' At that point, I put the phone down, called back again, and this time I spoke to them in Hebrew. 'I'd like to speak to your defence attaché.' 'Certainly,' they replied, 'we'll put you straight through.' I was then immediately connected to a remarkable man, Ephraim Poran, more commonly known as Freuke. He said he would be delighted to help, and that Mr Ong worked very closely with him and he would introduce me. He did better than that. On the same day he organised a lunch between the Israelis, the Singaporeans and me, and from that point we never looked back.

Singapore and Malaya had been one country until 1965, when Singapore had broken away to become an independent republic. They were therefore very worried about their defences against both Malaysia to the north and Indonesia to the south. As the British had only pulled out in 1959, they had no army of their own, and had had to set up an entire military establishment from scratch. They decided to call on Israel for help. We had our lunch in a Chinese restaurant in Singapore, which for me was a challenge in itself because I was not used to eating with chopsticks. But, of course, everybody spoke perfect English, and after about an hour I suddenly realised that, if I closed my eyes, I wouldn't be able to tell which were the Israelis and which the Singaporeans, because they were identical in both their manner and their ability. Today you will find that the Singaporean defence manufacturing design base is very sophisticated, and they still work on projects with the Israelis.

Anyway, I went to see the director of logistics at the Ministry of Defence Singapore, Mr Ong Kah Kok, and showed him what we sold, much of which he needed, but he told me he couldn't afford our prices. Then he said: 'Look, we in Singapore are trying to develop our economy. Everybody here does national service. We have all these bright young kids. Why don't we set up a small plant to make these products here? They'll be much cheaper.' I didn't think he was being serious, but a couple of days later, before I left, he called me in and said: 'I've spoken to the Minister, here's the deal. You set up a factory here, to make this equipment for us. We'll go fifty-fifty with you on the costs, and we'll buy what you produce.' Then he produced a catalogue of factories and said: 'Which one would you like? A1, A2, A3? Or B1, B2, B3? This size or that one? One-storey or two-storey? Whatever you want, we'll build a brand-new factory for you.' When I asked: 'But what about the people? They don't know this business,' he replied: 'Well, I'll tell you what, you take a dozen Singaporeans to the UK and train them. We'll pay their travel and expenses while they're there. Then you bring them back and they will train the people here.' That wasn't all, for he went on: 'Once the factory is up and running, you will pay no tax on your profits for seven years, and we will lend you any money that you need to finance the place. Furthermore, your co-shareholder in this will be the Ministry of Defence Singapore.'

When I got back to London and explained this deal, my colleagues thought I had been sitting in the sun for too long, but I assured them it was all genuine. We weren't the first British company to consider setting up in Singapore. Plessey were the largest manufacturers of record-changers and they too had been offered a fantastic deal to move all production of these items to Singapore. I then phoned someone I knew at Plessey and asked what had happened on this venture. He replied: 'Well, at the end of the day, our board chickened out and we decided not to do it.' When I asked why, they said: 'Actually, it was the biggest mistake we ever made. If you've got any sense at all, and you've been made an offer out there, go for it.'

Because we didn't have any other overseas ventures, I have to admit that I was nervous about setting up in a small country on the other side of the world of which, at that time, I knew very little. When, however, I explained this to the people I had met in the Singapore Economic Development Board [EDB], they said to me: 'Well, please don't worry this can be covered under the UK/Singapore Government Guarantee Scheme.'

It turned out that this was a scheme which had been negotiated between the two countries when the UK Government were trying to help the nascent country of Singapore to develop its economy. The scheme provided, with a very modest premium – I think it was about

1% – a company-wide insurance for its whole operation in Singapore against political failure of the Singaporean Government or any attempt to sequestrate its assets by the Singaporean Government. USH then became the first to join this scheme.

We continued to pay this premium of 1% for a few years and the scheme, which at the time, was administered by the Crown Estates, seemed to be flawless. However, one day I had a call from the EDB who said: 'We would hope by now that you no longer have a fear of a political attack on your business in Singapore and, for that reason, do you really want to keep the insurance in place? To tell you the truth', they said, 'you are the only members of it and your annual 1% premium goes nowhere near just covering the administration costs of the scheme. We would like to suggest that we cancel the policy, refund all your premiums and save us both a lot of work and cost.' Unsurprisingly, I agreed immediately but it certainly proved what a good idea the establishment of the scheme had been.

We set up Avimo Singapore in 1974, with a brand-new factory, which was built on an industrial estate at Jurong, out to the west of the city. My first concern was where the employees were going to come from, because nobody lived round there. 'Don't worry,' they said, 'by the end of the year, in nine months' time, there will be flats all along this road to house 250,000 people.' 'Oh really?' I said, in some disbelief, to which they responded: 'If we tell you they will be there, they will be there. When you come back from the UK with the first twelve trained staff, the flats will be ready for you.'

My next question was how we would recruit these people. They told me that all young Singaporeans coming out of national service were vetted and recommended for future jobs. It was not unlike the system at the Norwood orphanage, which had set up my grandfather as a watchmaker. So, based on this advice, I took the managing director of our factory in Taunton, and one or two others, and we went out to interview some of these kids. We spent a couple of days doing this in a hotel, and then submitted the list of the people we liked which the Singaporeans then checked.

Then I had to find someone to run this factory. Dave Cowan, of Helio, had a daughter, Denise, who had just married a bright young engineer called David Fraser, so we despatched him and his wife to

Singapore to run the plant. However, he didn't know anything about optical equipment, and we therefore had to appoint somebody who could check that it was all top quality. I remember asking myself who our most demanding customer was, and of course it was the Israelis. I had become friends with a young Israeli captain, who came to do their inspections and used to give us a really hard time. His name was Avi Ayalon, and he's now one of my closest friends. We were all young then, and he didn't have a penny. So we told him what we were going to do, and the Israelis agreed, because they were working to help Singapore, that he could take leave from the army for a couple of years to move there.

We trained the first group of apprentices in Taunton, with the plan that they would then train the further recruits in Singapore and we would build up to a workforce of about eighty or a hundred. When I first informed the staff in Somerset that they had to take in these young men, they thought it was a ridiculous idea, but I insisted. They took in twelve trainees and, at the end of the year, I announced that we would be sending them back to Singapore. When I told Roy Mountain, who ran the factory in Taunton, he said: 'You can't take these people, they're some of the best workers we've ever had.'

Once we'd agreed to build the factory in Singapore, we started immediately looking for work to put into it. At that time, Avimo were bidding to the MOD in London to supply a new telescopic rifle-sight for all the British army rifles. It was a massive order. I remember Ong Kah Kok saying to me: 'If Avimo can get this contract and we make all the optical elements here in Singapore, it will make our bid very competitive, and the order would be a huge starter for this new factory. Why don't I, as director of logistics at the Defence Ministry in Singapore, write to the MOD in the United Kingdom to say that we're working to get ourselves off the ground, you've agreed to build this factory here and, if you can win the contract for rifle-sights and, if we can make the lenses and prisms here, it will be a wonderful deal for us and, incidentally, will also save the British government a great deal of money.' As a result, one night we went to his house and drafted this letter, sitting round the table, drinking beer and eating tiny dried fish, which were very salty. Once we had all agreed the text, our local business partner, Chan U Seek, who was also investing in the plant, said he would get the letter typed up on headed notepaper from the Ministry of Defence

Singapore. I proudly took it back to London, and sure enough we got the contract. From that point on, we had plenty of work in Singapore.

The factory there went on to produce a whole range of military optical products, including night-vision equipment, telescopes, periscopes, and fire control systems for tanks and armoured vehicles. When you're producing lenses, you have to be very careful not to touch them before they have been covered with a protective coating. One day, Avi phoned me to say: 'We've just developed this amazing non-transferable technology in Singapore. It's great, but you won't be able to use it anywhere else except here.' We already had very complex equipment that moved lenses around, so nobody touched them, but in Singapore they'd told him not to waste time because they'd had a much better idea. They used chopsticks!

The director of logistics, Ong Kah Kok, whom I had met through the Israelis worked directly for the Singaporean Defence Minister, Dr. Goh Keng Swee,[1] who was one of the founding fathers of the country, along with Lee Kuan Yew.[2] Dr. Goh was a fantastic man, and he came to open the new factory, within a year of our setting it up. He and I both made a speech. With anything like that, it always takes a while before you really get going, but the amazing thing about this factory was that we made a substantial profit within the first year, which was unheard of. It was at the time when we had a very left-wing Labour government in the UK, profit was a dirty word, and we had a three-day week and constant strikes in the UK. Dr. Goh's speech was filmed for television. He said how impressed he was with what we'd achieved in this factory, and then went on: 'In Singapore, profit is not a dirty word. We know that if businesses are not making a profit, they can't invest in the future. Thus, the more profit you make, the happier we are.' Of course, that went along with the fact that we didn't have to pay any tax, so this place became a goldmine – and, to this day, it still is. That was our first foreign operation.

Many years after we set up that factory, Lee Kuan Yew, the former prime minister of Singapore, came to London with his wife. We were invited to a dinner in his honour, where Wendy sat next to him.

1   Dr. Goh Keng Swee (1918–2010), Minister for Defence in Singapore, 1970–79.
2   Lee Kuan Yew (1923–2015), Prime Minister of Singapore, 1959–90.

Having said to her that he was aware that I had done a lot in Singapore, he then asked if anybody had presented her with her own orchid. When he found out this hadn't yet happened, he said he would arrange it. So, on one of our future trips to Singapore, she was invited to the botanical gardens, and they presented her with an orchid which is now known as *Dendrobium* 'Wendy Levene'. There's an orchid named after Queen Elizabeth, which she was given after a visit to Singapore in 1972, and one was dedicated to Margaret Thatcher, following her trip there in 1985, and now – following its official registration in June 2006 by the Singapore Botanic Gardens – there's a 'Wendy Levene' orchid too – Dendrobium Wendy Levene. Shortly after its presentation, they sent us a cutting. There are very strict rules on importing plants into Britain, so it had to have a health certificate and spend time in quarantine at Kew Gardens, but eventually we got our own plant. Wendy said: 'Look, we are likely to kill it within seconds if we get our hands on it.' The American ambassador's head gardener in London helps us with our garden in France, so Wendy rang him up and asked him if he could look after it for us. He took it away and put it in his greenhouse, whereupon it died, so that was the end of our 'Wendy Levene' orchid for the time being.

Just over ten years later, in January 2017, we were in Singapore and decided to call the botanic gardens to see if we could see Wendy's orchid. They told us that sadly it wouldn't be in flower until March. During this visit, we had dinner with Ong Beng Seng and his wife Christina. He is a business magnate, with a huge portfolio of hotels worldwide, and is one of the wealthiest men in Singapore; and she owns many of the fashion shops in the West End and Knightsbridge. They had invited us to dinner at the Four Seasons Hotel, but when we arrived we were told that he had actually meant the Hilton, which he also owns, so we were ushered through a passageway he had cons-tructed between these two hotels. Anyway, we told them about Wendy's orchid, and Christina said: 'Well, actually I'm the chairman of the Singapore Botanic Gardens.' She made an immediate phone call and said: 'They didn't give you the right information. Your orchid is there and it's flowering now. We're having one sent round, and you can take it home with you.' Well, I knew from past experience that it would be very difficult to get a plant into the United Kingdom without following all the official procedures, so I was a bit dubious about this. 'Don't worry,' they said, 'just take it. As you're getting off the plane in London at five o'clock in the morning, it will be fine.' But just as we were about to leave for the airport, the Singapore Botanic Gardens rang to say: 'We haven't got it packed up yet, and anyway we've got to get all the relevant certificates.' As it turned out we had to wait for that particular orchid to arrive in its own good time; but arrive it did.

*　　*　　*

By 1976 United Scientific had developed from having twenty-five members of staff to several hundred employees. Our pre-tax profits had risen from £470,000 in the previous year to £871,000, and we were anticipating in excess of £1 million for the first time in the company's history. Direct exports had also risen over the same period from £912,000 to £3.36 million, nearly half of which were going to Asia. The figures were so good that I was entitled to a £16,000 increase in my annual salary, although I was forced to forgo £12,000 of this under the Labour government's new pay restraint policy.[1]

Barclays were our main bankers. At that time, they were still run by members of the Quaker families, like the Trittons and the Buxtons, who had established the bank. Once a year, they would invite us for lunch at their head office in the City. It was an extremely formal affair, with liveried servants in attendance.

Once we had opened the factory in Singapore, I started to think about the biggest defence market in the world, which was the United States. In order to sell anything to the American armed forces, you had to overcome their overwhelming 'not-invented-here' factor, which was extremely difficult. For example, the US army evaluated one of our periscopes and found it superior to the one they were using in ten out of sixteen counts. But there was no way the procurement people could be persuaded to buy it, because they preferred dealing with American companies they knew. So I thought that if we couldn't beat them, we'd join them, and in 1977 we bought a company called

---

1   Anon., 'United Scientific director waives £12,000 pay rise,' *Daily Telegraph*, Monday, February 23, 1976.

Optic Electronic Corporation. It was based in Dallas, Texas, and designed and manufactured optical and mechanical fire control equipment for tanks, self-propelled artillery and guided missiles.[1] The price was $4 million (then about £2 million),[2] and although we had the money, there were strict exchange controls in place, so we had to obtain special permission from the Bank of England to buy the dollars for the acquisition. Barclays had offered us a lousy deal, but I had been introduced to the manager at the newly established London branch of the Republic National Bank of Dallas a charming and very helpful man named Horton Kennedy. He told me that they were keen to do business with us and asked me how much money we wanted. When I told him, he said: 'Piece of cake, sign here.' He then handed me a piece of paper, and that was that.

Of course, when Barclays found out about this, they were kicking themselves because they'd missed out on all the business. So, two or three years later, when we wanted to buy a second American company, called Nitec, who were making night-vision equipment for the US army, I phoned Alan Tritton at Barclays, and said: 'I just thought I'd tell you, we're going to buy a firm in Chicago for $3.8 million. As you lost out on the financing for the last one, would you like to bid for this?' He told me to get round to his office immediately. When I got there, he said: 'Look, whatever you want, it's yours; however much money you need, it's yours; don't worry about a thing, we'll do it.' He was, as always, surrounded by acolytes and one of them then piped up to say: 'Just excuse me a moment.' At which Alan exploded: 'Listen, I told you not to interfere. We're doing this business with Mr. Levene, he's a very good customer, and whatever he wants we give him. What's the matter with you?' 'I'm terribly sorry,' said the man, 'I only wanted to ask you the name of the company he's buying.'

There were complications in America. Both the companies we bought were suppliers to the US government, who were worried about the security implications of an overseas buy-out. This meant that neither I nor any of my other British executives were allowed to sit

1   Victor Felstead, 'Utd Scientific's £2m US takeover,' *The Times*, Tuesday, November 1, 1977.
2   Margaret Walls, '$4M defence deal by United Scientific,' *Guardian*, Tuesday, November 1, 1977.

on the boards of these companies. In order to get around this, we used a structure called a voting trust, which already existed in America, whereby we appointed Americans to act for us. In theory they weren't allowed to tell us what was going on, and it was the first time that a voting trust had been used in this way to facilitate an international deal, but we set the precedent and it all worked out very well.

*   *   *

In 1978 United Scientific received the Queen's Award for Export Achievement.[3] Our annual report recorded pre-tax profits of £2.7 million for the year 1976–77, up from £1.8 million for the previous twelve months.[4] At one point, shares in the company were valued at 293p,[5] which was a meteoric rise from 1975 when they had been changing hands at the equivalent of just 10p.[6] In 1980 we topped the British league of profitable companies, and were fourth in terms of growth out of the nation's top 200 firm.[7] In an interview with the *Financial Times*, I outlined the way we worked:

> We don't advertise. We knock on doors. A relationship with one man in each country is all we need. We have eight or ten commercial salesmen working out of the London head office touring the world. They have to keep on the move. If I see one of them sitting around here for more than a week I tell him to go out and get on a plane. There are not enough desks to go round – that is a deliberate policy[8]

Then, in 1981, I was reading *the Evening Standard*, and I came across an article stating that the state-owned carmaker British Leyland was

3   Peter Rhodes, 'The man who has bought Alvis,' *Coventry Evening Telegraph*, Friday, July 3, 1981.
4   Anon., 'Why we give good reports,' *Observer*, 26 February 1978.
5   Anon., 'United Scientific Holdings fighting fit,' *Investors Chronicle*, 3 March 1978.
6   Jim Levi, 'Those you wish you'd bought,' *Evening Standard*, Monday, September 19, 1977.
7   Alison Preece, 'Alvis sold,' *Coventry Evening Telegraph*, Thursday, July 21, 1981.
8   Terry Garrett, 'Quiet go-getter that bought Alvis,' *Financial Times*, Wednesday, July 29, 1981.

selling Alvis, its military vehicles subsidiary. Alvis was based in Coventry and manufactured Scorpion tanks, which it sold to the MOD and exported to eleven other countries. At that time, British Leyland was the basket-case of industry, with losses running at an annual rate of over £500 million.[1] I went to see their Chief Executive, David Andrews, and told him that United Scientific was interested in buying Alvis. 'What on earth for?' he said, 'everything we've got is losing money.' However, I thought it was a good business, and in the summer of that year we bought Alvis for £27 million.[2] It was the biggest deal I'd ever done, and effectively doubled the size of the company. Shortly afterwards, an article appeared in the newspapers, which said: 'Alvis is the only part of British Leyland that makes a profit, but now it is to be sold. This must be the new British Leyland policy: anything it owns which makes money must be disposed of immediately.'

* * *

At the time we were negotiating to buy Alvis, I went on one of my many visits to Nigeria. Having finished the business in Lagos, I needed to get back to London urgently, but was horrified to read an announcement that the Nigerians were planning a general strike for the following day. I said to our agent there: 'Look, this is terrible, I've got to get back to London tomorrow. How am I going to get there if they close the airport?' 'It's not a problem,' he replied, 'I'll get my driver to take you to Cotonou in Benin. There's an airport there, where you'll be able to get a flight to Paris. And there's a new motorway between here and Cotonou, and it will only take about half an hour to get there.' So that evening, the driver and I set off. When we arrived at the Nigeria-Benin border and I presented my passport, the Nigerian immigration officer said: 'You don't have a visa to go to Benin.' 'Well,' I responded, 'let me see what I can do.' I then approached his Benin equivalent, who only spoke French. He too pointed out that I didn't have the correct visa, to which I said: 'You didn't look in my passport

1 Anon., 'United Scientific: military adventure,' *The Times*, 3 July 1981.
2 Rupert Morris, 'BL sells Alvis and its tanks in £27m deal,' *The Times*, 3 July 1981.

very carefully.' Once he realised that I'd slipped some Central African francs inside it, he exclaimed: 'Ah ha, yes!' My passport was stamped and I was into Benin.

The driver then took me to Cotonou airport, where it looked as if half the population of Nigeria had decanted to catch the one available flight. I could see there was no way I was going to get on that plane, and I knew I would just have to go back to Nigeria. But it was getting dark and I was tired, so I decided to spend the night in Benin. I'd seen a big advertisement in the airport for the Intercontinental Hotel in Cotonou, so I told the driver to take me there. 'I can't,' he said, 'they haven't built it yet.' Instead, he took me to the Hotel du Port, which was small but actually wasn't that bad. As soon as we arrived there, the girl on the desk said: 'You can't stay here, you don't have a visa in your passport.' I assured her that it had been stamped. 'No, no,' she retorted, 'that's just an entry stamp. Where is your visa?' At this point, the driver said: 'Don't worry, I'll take you to the police station, and we'll get you a visa there.' Once we got there, the policeman assured me that I could have a visa, but it would cost several hundred Central African francs. Eventually it was issued and we returned to the Hotel du Port, where I said to the driver: 'Look, you stay somewhere nearby. Tomorrow morning we'll leave Benin and drive on to Togo, where there's another airport at Lomé. I'll get a plane from there to Paris.'

The next day we set off, and after driving through the jungle for about an hour-and-a-half, we got to the border with Togo. Once again, the immigration officer looked at my passport and said: 'You can't come in here, you haven't got a visa.' This time, the driver intervened: 'Don't worry,' he said, 'leave it to me; you go over there, and I'll fix it.' When he called me back, we approached the same official, and I urged him, as I had done in Benin, to look more carefully at my passport. He snapped back: 'Don't tell me that, give me your passport!' When I handed it over, he stamped it with a flourish, which I thought was a good sign, until I looked at the stamp which read, in French: 'Deported for absence of visa.' He then went on: 'If you try and bribe us again, you'll go over there,' and pointed to a jail cell that was full of incarcerated people trying to get out.

Of course, this was all before the era of mobile phones, I was now in the middle of the jungle, and nobody knew where I was or what I was doing. The driver had tried to help, so I told him to take me back to Cotonou, where I could apply for a visa at the Togo embassy. Actually, I had no intention of doing that. All I wanted him to do was take me back to Lagos, which although not always enjoyable, seemed to me at that moment the epitome of civilisation. When we got to Cotonou, I announced: 'You know what, it's going to be too late to get another visa. You'll have to drive me back to Lagos.' He said: 'Well, it will cost you.' 'Don't worry,' I replied, 'I'll pay you.' Normally, you only get single-entry visas for Nigeria, but by some miracle our agent there had got me a multi-entry one, so when we arrived at the Nigerian border, everything was alright and I was let back into the country. But this time they turned the driver away, on the grounds that he was from Togo and didn't have a visa. 'Look,' I implored, 'this is my friend.' After telling the Nigerian border guard the whole story and giving him a few Naira, they eventually let us both through.

While all this haggling was going on, I had looked past the guard and seen a newspaper in his sentry-box. Its headline read: 'Strike called off.' When I asked him what had been going on, he confirmed that the general strike had been cancelled. 'What happened at the airport?' I enquired. 'Nothing,' he replied, 'everybody went on time.' 'Right,' I said to the driver, 'take me to the airport.' When we got there, I discovered that the British Caledonian flight that I should have been on the previous night had left as normal. I had spent two days hurtling through three different countries for no reason. Although there was another British Caledonian flight that evening, I was advised that there were other planes leaving earlier for the UK. It was lunchtime, the departure lounge was deserted, but I started walking along to the various gates until I found a Nigerian Airways plane parked up. 'Where is this plane going?' I enquired. When they told me it was going to Heathrow, I said: 'Right, I'm getting on it.' 'Do you have a ticket?' they asked. When I produced it, they sighed: 'Ah, but that's for British Caledonian.' Fortunately, I was able to get it endorsed and when I finally got onto the flight, I said to the steward: 'Is this plane going to Heathrow?' 'Yes,' he replied, 'but we have one stop on route, at Ibadan,' which is another city in Nigeria. Eventually we took off and the pilot made the following announcement: 'Welcome on-board Nigeria Airways. We fly now to Heathrow. For people going to Ibadan, sorry, we are not going to stop there. They are on strike. So, if you are on the plane and you only want to go to Ibadan, I'm very sorry, but you are going to London.' When at last we landed in England, everybody said: 'Where have you been?' My reply was: 'If I told you, you wouldn't believe me!'

I had another novel experience with Nigeria Airways, when I was scheduled to take one of their flights from Lagos to New York. My plane was due to leave at two o'clock in the morning, and as our agent in Nigeria was catching a flight to London at midnight, he offered to take me to the airport. Once he'd left, I was sitting in the airport restaurant at about midnight, when I heard them announce the last call for passengers on the flight to New York. I thought this was odd, but I went along to the gate, where I said: 'I thought this plane didn't go until two?' 'Yes, yes,' they replied, 'but the pilot says that there are strong head-winds, so he wants to leave early.' Needless to say, there was hardly anyone in the departure lounge, so I got on the plane with only about twenty other people, and we took off. Then the captain announced: 'Welcome on board. We heard there are very strong winds over the Atlantic, which will slow us down. Everyone says that Nigeria Airways always arrives late, so we decide to leave early. And then we will get there on time!' And we did, but all the people who had booked on that flight and turned up at the right time, found their plane had gone – and there was only one flight a week!

*   *   *

In addition to having bought OEC (Optical Electronic Corporation) in Dallas, the purchase of Chicago-based Nitec, manufacturers of image intensifier tubes for the US Army, had one unexpected beneficial side effect. They had an extremely effective local agent in Egypt. Previously, United Scientific had been operating in Egypt through Mahmoud Zoulfikar, one of whose claims to fame was that he was a relative of King Farouk. This seemed plausible, as whenever he visited the erstwhile Royal Palace in Alexandria, the staff would prostrate themselves in front of him. He was a charming man and had an extremely charming wife, but his success for us was limited. The new representative we acquired from Nitec, Kamel Fattah, was a very different character. A former Brigadier in the Egyptian Army Artillery, he was a close friend of Field Marshal Abu Ghazala, who had become not only the Chief of Staff of the Egyptian Armed Forces but was also the Minister of Defence. Nitec had a large order for night vision equipment from the Egyptian Army, and this brought me into contact with the Field Marshal and Kamel's other good connections with their army.

In 1982 we set up a joint venture with the Egyptian government to build a new electro-optical factory near Cairo, on the basis that they would have a fifty-one per cent share in it and we would have the other forty-nine. The deal was negotiated through the Field Marshal. Our actual partner there was the National Service Projects Organisation [NSPO], which was, inter alia, responsible for investing pension funds for Egyptian army officers.

The first thing we had to do was set up an office in Cairo. In those days, it was very difficult to find office premises in Egypt, so I approached Abu Ghazala for help. He assured us he would find an office, and identified an army-owned villa in the suburb of Heliopolis, now an affluent area of the city, but then very much in disrepair. The villa was rat-infested and in a terrible state. 'Don't worry,' said Abu Ghazala, 'I'm sending in a penal battalion to clean the whole thing up.' They went in and did a very good job.

Then, two weeks before the office was due to open, Bill Meadows, our man in Cairo, rang me up from his hotel and said: 'Peter, I need to speak to you urgently.' 'What's the matter?' I asked. 'We've lost the office,' he replied. 'Don't be ridiculous,' I said, 'I'll speak to the Minister.' To which my colleague responded: 'I don't think that's going to help, you don't know what's happened.' It transpired that the elderly and frail General Muhammad Naguib[1] was being driven round Heliopolis and had seen our newly-refurbished villa. Naguib had served as the first President of Egypt in the early 1950s, following the coup to overthrow King Farouk. He had gone straight to the Field Marshal and said: 'My brother, my brother, I am a poor man fallen on hard times and I have nowhere to live. I was driving through Heliopolis and I saw this villa, which I know belongs to the army, and it looked

1   General Muhammad Naguib (1901–1984), President of Egypt from 18 June 1953 to 14 November 1954.

so beautiful. Is there anything you could do to help a poor old soldier?' And Abu Ghazala had replied: 'My brother, it's yours.' So that was it, we were back to square one, and had to find another office.

To celebrate the deal to build the factory, we all gathered at the Sheraton Hotel in Heliopolis for a dinner. The host was the Egyptians' principal negotiator, General Sardinha. Wendy, who had accompanied me on this trip, found herself sitting next to him. 'How do you like Egypt?' the general said to her. 'Oh, I love it,' she replied, 'the food here is so good. You have all these delicious fruits and vegetables.' 'Yes,' he said, 'we have big farms, we grow them all.' Wendy went on: 'The only thing I haven't seen here are avocados.' 'Avocados?' spluttered the general, 'of course we have avocados; we have a whole department in the army of nothing but avocados.' It turned out that he had misinterpreted what she'd said for the French word *avocats*, which means lawyers. There were other hilarious occasions in Egypt. Delicious Cape gooseberries in a fondant icing – called Harankash in Arabic – were served as petit-fours, and I innocently commented on how much I liked them. 'We'll give you some,' they said. When we got to the airport, I found they had delivered a whole crate of them for me to take back on the plane.

The day after the dinner with General Sardinha, I went to see Field Marshal Abu Ghazala again. He asked me if I was happy with everything. I replied: 'Yes, I'm very pleased we've got it done. But I've just heard that you're proposing that we split the management, with you appointing the Chairman and us the Chief Executive. And while I will be the deputy chairman, General Sardinha is to be the chairman.' 'Yes,' said the Field Marshal, 'that's right.' 'Well, he wouldn't be my first choice', I responded. And Abu Ghazala said: 'Yes, I suppose you're right, really.' Sardinha was never seen again, and by the next day we had a new general in charge, General Medhat Mustafa, who became a great friend. We also acquired four Egyptian army officers, who came to work every day in uniform and sat on our board. They were very effective and, whenever we wanted more orders for the factory, they would negotiate for the company.

Building the factory itself posed its own challenges. We had to spend a fortune constructing a huge wall around its perimeter, on this vast plot of desert land, just because every factory in Egypt has a wall around it. The site was not far from the airport, and shortly before construction was due to begin, we were suddenly told we had to move everything 1,200 yards from our original plot. When I asked why, the Egyptians said: 'Well, we didn't realise this when we gave you permission, but where you're planning to build this factory is actually on the spot of the main landing beacon for Cairo Airport.'

Back in 1958 Egypt and Syria had established a short-lived political union called the United Arab Republic, which actually fell apart following the Syrian *coup d'etat* in 1961. However, its aims had included founding the Arab Organisation for Industry, or AOI. The idea was that the Egyptians would establish a large defence industry in Egypt, making equipment under license. The project was to be funded by the Gulf States, and everybody involved would make money. Then the Gulf States had a row with the Egyptians and withdrew all their funding, so the Arab Organisation for Industry had never got off the ground. By the time we opened our new factory in Egypt, I decided to have a play on the initials and call it AIO, which in our case stood for Arab International Optronics founded in 1984. The factory is still there to this day, and, so far as I know, continues to do very well.

In Egypt I found that their best engineers, like their top doctors, were outstanding and as good as anyone we have here. But it was a different matter at other levels. The day after the official opening of this new factory, they sent a car to pick me up from my hotel. I was due to attend a meeting in Cairo, but as we were early, I told the driver that I wanted to go and have another look at the factory on the way. 'I don't think that's a very good idea,' he said. When I asked him why not, he told me we didn't have time. I insisted that we did. 'No, no,' he responded, 'you really don't want to go there.' At which point, I said: 'Look, stop arguing with me and just drive me to the factory.' When we arrived, it was about nine or ten o'clock in the morning, but the place appeared to be deserted and the offices were empty. Then I walked through into the main part of the site and found our 200 members of staff all fast asleep at their workbenches. The work ethic there was not paramount, and I had acquired a brand-new factory full of sleeping people, which even the driver knew about. I woke them up pretty quickly, and they never did that again.

* * *

During my tenure at United Scientific, we had developed a close association with the US company, Martin Marietta, as it was known at the time – it subsequently merged into Lockheed Martin. We had been negotiating with them over a new piece of night-vision equipment which they had developed in the Apache helicopter, which was known as TADS-PNVS. Eventually we agreed with them a licensing agreement that when that helicopter was brought into service in the UK, we would be the licensee to build this particular piece of equipment. In order to tie up the deal, a meeting was arranged at the Martin Marietta headquarters in Washington. I met the chairman, Tom Pownall, and it was a very friendly meeting. They had invited me for lunch and just before we went to eat, I asked them if (in US speak) I could use the restroom. So they showed me where it was. I walked in, the door closed, and I found myself in pitch darkness. I fumbled around in the dark for some time to find a light switch, but without success. Becoming somewhat panicky, I tried to feel my way around the door to find the handle, also without success. I thought I might be able to prize the door open from the bottom by

6. Handing over a large cheque for a licence agreement to Tom Pownall, Chairman of Martin Marietta in 1983, on the day I crawled out of the loo on all fours.

pushing my fingers between the carpet and the door. However, I found that at the bottom of the door there was a draught strip attached to it, ensuring that there was no gap. I managed to get my fingers around the bottom of the draught strip and started to pull. The fixing of the draught strip was, however, not very strong, and so the draught strip started to come away from the door. With one final tug, the door flew open and I was left on all fours crawling out of the door to be greeted by my hosts who were patiently waiting outside. That took a lot of living down.

CHAPTER 3

Adviser to Michael Heseltine

BY 1984 I HAD been running United Scientific for over 20 years. We'd moved from a staff of twenty and a turnover of about £200,000, to employing 5,000 people with an annual turnover of more than £130 million, in a company that was established on three continents. In 1983 our pre-tax profits amounted to £15.2 million, up from £12.5 million the previous year, and the group's order book for the future was in excess of £140 million.[1] But I was getting bored.

One day, my PA said to me: 'While you were out, I had a telephone call from the office of the Secretary of State for Defence. He wants to have lunch with you. You're to meet him at Wilton's, just off Jermyn Street.' Although I knew this post was held by Michael Heseltine, I was astonished by this summons, as I didn't know him, and nor did I deal with anybody at that level in the MOD. Anyway, I turned up at the restaurant at one o'clock, as instructed; at one-fifteen I was still alone, and by one-thirty I had convinced myself that the whole thing was a wind-up, when my host suddenly arrived.

Michael had been Secretary of State for Defence since January 1983, when Margaret Thatcher appointed him to replace John Nott, who had held the role during the Argentine invasion of the Falkland Islands and the subsequent Falklands War in the previous year. At that first lunch together, he was clear about the challenges he faced, saying to me: 'Look, I did National Service for a very short time in the Guards. I don't know anything about defence; I've been running my publishing business. Every week, my staff bring a file into my office containing yet another new contract that I'm expected to sign. The

---

1   Anon., 'United Scientific expands to £15.2m,' *Financial Times*, 16 December 1983.

sums of money are in the order of £100 million, £200 million, even £500 million. I reckon we're getting ripped off in spades. What do you think?' I replied: 'You know what? You're 100 per cent right.'

We then proceeded to have a very long conversation. I talked about the defence industry, particularly the export side of our business, and went on to express one or two of my ideas. At the end of the meal, I thanked him for inviting me and told him how much I had enjoyed our chat. 'Just a minute,' he responded, 'I didn't ask you here merely to have a good lunch. You've got to come and work for me.' When I explained that I couldn't do that, on the grounds that I was Chairman of a large public company, which was itself supplying the MOD, and that this would create an insurmountable conflict of interest, Michael replied: 'Oh yes, you can; we'll start you off on one day a week.'

I found out after our lunch that Michael Heseltine had been pointed in my direction when he asked in the MOD whether they knew anyone with a commercial background, in the industry, whom they could recommend to advise him. Although several people claimed to have been the one who gave Michael Heseltine the advice, it was in fact Lieutenant-General Dick Vincent (Field Marshal The Lord Vincent), who recommended my name to him.

The next day I was called into the Ministry to see Clive Whitmore, the Permanent Secretary, whom I knew well. Michael announced to him: 'I've decided I want Peter to come and work for us here on a part-time basis.' Not surprisingly, Clive's answer was: 'I'm terribly sorry, Secretary of State, but you can't do that, because there's a conflict of interest.' At which point, Michael said: 'Look, Clive, you're here to make things happen; go and make this happen.' So he did, and I was appointed in January 1984 for six months as Personal Adviser to the Secretary of State for Defence. Initially there was a terrible row, based on the fact that I was still running United Scientific and there was an assumption that the rest of the industry would complain about my new government role. So Michael decided to find something for me to do that would avoid conflict issues.

The Royal Naval Dockyards presented a perennial problem, and had been so since the time when Samuel Pepys was Chief Secretary to the Admiralty in the seventeenth century. By the 1980s there were two main sites, one at Rosyth in Scotland, and the other at Devonport near Plymouth. 'They lose money and never deliver anything on time,' Michael explained to me. Then he went on: 'I want you to go and sort them out. But this is all extremely sensitive, so just keep it very low-key.' So off I went to Devonport, where I was met by an admiral who had come to collect me in a helicopter. The first thing he did was to proudly show me the front page of the *Western Morning News*, with its leading article entitled 'The Hatchet Man Arrives.' The dockyard unions had already leaked news of my appointment to the press.

That wasn't my only problem. The Admiral, responsible for the Dockyard who had the title of Chief of Fleet Support [CFS], asked me what I was doing, and when I explained that the Secretary of State had sent me to look at the dockyards, he retaliated by saying: 'And what do you know about them? What are you trying to do?' I responded by saying that I was aiming to make them more cost-effective. 'What the hell is 'cost-effective'?' roared the Admiral. When I tried to explain, he said: 'Look, young man, we're here to fight the Russians, so just go away.'

The dockyards themselves were antediluvian. They employed about 6,000 people in Rosyth and 13,000 in Devonport. Furthermore, there were something like thirty different trade unions operating in the yards, so even a simple operation, like taking a cable from one end of a ship to the other, had to go through all these union members. Nothing was ever finished on time or on cost. The man who had leaked my arrival to the press was the chief trade union representative, and as he thought that I was the devil incarnate, it was all extremely difficult. But eventually we got to know each other and, after a while, he said to me: 'Look, I understand what you're trying to do, I think you're right, and I've decided that I'm going to support you. But I will deny it if you ever tell anybody that I'm doing this.' Shortly afterwards, there was another headline in the newspapers, this time saying: 'Union Boss calls Hatchet Man a disaster.' Consequently I called him in to see me, and he said: 'Sorry, I had to do that to keep them all happy.' In the end, he and I became good friends, and he was very helpful in getting things done.

I quickly realised that the dockyards were essentially large industrial operations that were being ineffectively run by the civil service, with an accounting system that was entirely meaningless in commercial terms. My suggestion was to adopt a concept I had encountered in America, called a 'go-co' which, in other words, is a 'government-owned, contractor-operated' business. This meant that we would not sell off the dockyards, because that would have caused too much of a row, but we would call in professional shipbuilding and repairing companies to run them on a proper commercial basis.

However, before we could do any of this, we had to sell my plan to the Royal Navy, and specifically to the Admiralty Board, which was a committee of senior naval officers, all of whom I believed were going to oppose me. Fortunately, the First Sea Lord at that time was an outstanding sailor, Admiral Sir John Fieldhouse (who subsequently became Lord Fieldhouse). He had commanded the Task Force sent to recover the Falkland Islands in 1982, was a great hero, and spoke – probably deliberately – like Winston Churchill. Somehow, he had come to like me, so I went to see him and told him what we were planning to do. He listened and then said: 'Look, since the time of Samuel Pepys, we have tried every way to run the dockyards. I have no idea whether this idea of yours will work, but nothing can be worse than what we've got now. So don't worry, I'll back you.' When we got to the Admiralty Board, and I outlined my plan, one admiral after another spoke up in opposition, until the First Sea Lord said: 'Well, I've talked to Mr. Levene, I think this is quite a good idea and we should try it.' At which point, they all said: 'Yes, sir; of course, sir; it's absolutely brilliant, that's exactly what we must do.'

It wasn't quite the end of our problems. Although my interim report on the docklands had only been circulated to a handful of senior staff, in March 1984 it was leaked to Gordon Brown, Labour MP for Dunfermline East. Michael Heseltine ordered a full investigation by the MOD police to find the culprit. Meanwhile, Gordon Brown called the report an 'unwarranted extension of privatisation into an area concerning national security,' and tabled seventeen questions for written answers in the House of Commons.[1] But

[1] Bridget Bloom, 'Private refits for warships proposed,' *Financial Times*, 20 March 1984; Rodney Cowton, 'Naval refits leak starts hunt for mole,' *The Times*, Tuesday, March 20, 1984

eventually the plan was adopted, and it was a major success. And although it wasn't the original object of the exercise, the staff numbers were dramatically decreased, which was something that had to happen. Today there are about 1,500 people working at Rosyth and 5,000 at Devonport.

While I was advising Michael Heseltine on the dockyards, the MOD had appointed a young Royal Navy captain, George Middleton, to help me, who did a brilliant job. When I left the Ministry, I left him behind to help with the implementation of the plan. Shortly afterwards, when I was appointed as Chief of Defence Procurement [CDP], I immediately asked the MOD if he could join my staff and they agreed. The following day, I received a summons from Admiral Sir John Fieldhouse, something which nobody would dare to ignore. When I arrived in his office, he said: 'What the hell do you think you're doing?' I replied: 'What do you mean? What have I done?' He proceeded to tell me: 'When you were sorting out the dockyards, I sent you this captain, knowing how good he was; and you agreed to leave him behind to help get on with the work. Now you get a new job, and the first thing you do is steal him. It's the most outrageous behaviour. How dare you behave like this? No, you certainly can't have him, and that's the last word on the subject.' 'Yes, of course, I do understand,' I replied. 'However,' he went on, 'I'm going to give you somebody else, who is at least as good, if not better. You are not going to interview him to decide whether or not you are going to take him, you *will* take him, and that's an order from me. Do you understand?' Of course, I instantly agreed, and he produced Rob Walmsley, who later went on to be one of my successors, as CDP between 1996 and 2003 – by then Admiral Sir Robert Walmsley – serving even longer than I had done.

When I first entered the MOD, my Deputy Secretary was John Bourn (later Sir John Bourn) who became the Comptroller and Auditor General. He was in every sense my right hand when I first joined the MOD, and then did an outstanding job for a very long time as Comptroller and Auditor General even though his entertainment allowance came in for some rather severe scrutiny before the end of his time in the post.

I could certainly never have achieved a fraction of what I achieved in the MOD without the civil servants and military officers who were assigned to work for me. One of the first of these was John Oughton, a remarkable and very shrewd man who certainly did not share the prevailing political views at the time when I joined and who had the tremendous knack for telling me, in no uncertain terms, that I did not know what I was talking about when I got it wrong.

CHAPTER FOUR

Getting stuck in at the Ministry of Defence

I WORKED AS Personal Adviser to Michael Heseltine, the Secretary of State for Defence, for six months in 1984, always with the understanding that I would never get involved in any kind of procurement, because that would have involved a conflict of interest.

However, as soon as I finished that job, Michael said to me: 'Look, procurement is in a terrible mess, I want you to have a look at it.' I said: 'I can't, you know I can't.' And he said: 'Nevertheless, I want you to have a look at it, and tell me what you think.' I then went to see Sir Derek Rayner (later Lord Rayner),[1] who had first been appointed to look at defence procurement by Edward Heath, back in the 1970s. Rayner had been an extremely effective managing director of Marks & Spencer, where he had imposed tight financial controls and strong management practices. Once at the MOD, he set up a new organisation called the Procurement Executive, of which he was the first Chief Executive. All three of the British Armed Services were then required to use this as their single procurement office. It revolutionized everything, but its success had clearly dissipated by the mid-1980s.

I went to see Derek in 1984 and said to him, 'Look, I've been asked to look at the problems with Ministry of Defence procurement. I know you did this. You wrote a report, I've read your report, and if I dare say so, you were absolutely right. But why didn't it work?' And he said, 'Well, I'll tell you why it didn't work. I went in there as a businessman for a year and sorted it out. But as soon as I left, the waters closed over and it went back to square one. You can go back and tell your

---

1   Derek Rayner, Lord Rayner of Crowborough (1926–1998): chief executive of Procurement Executive Management Board, Ministry of Defence, 1971–72; Adviser to Prime Minister on improving efficiency in Civil Service, 1979–2

Secretary of State that, unless and until they get a businessman to run defence procurement, it's never going to work.' I duly returned to Michael Heseltine and told him this, and he said: 'Well, you *are* that businessman. You're going to do it, and that's that.'

I remember going home and saying to Wendy: 'Look, I've decided that, having run United Scientific for twenty-one years, made a success of it, and met a lot of friends through it, I'm now going to chuck it all in to become a Civil Servant. But I am going to be one of the first Permanent Secretaries ever to have been brought in from the outside world.' Wendy said: 'You've got to be mad.' And I said: 'No, my business has been a great success and I've enjoyed it, but I'm bored and I want a new challenge.' I think Wendy still thought I was insane, but after I had been at the MOD for about a year, she said: 'I never usually tell you this, but I can see that you were right, and I know now why you wanted to do something else.'

The announcement of my appointment as CDP in December 1984 caused huge ructions. The First Civil Service Commissioner, Dennis Trevelyan, threatened to resign. He was then leader of the body that is responsible for ensuring the Civil Service is effective and impartial, and that appointments are made on merit. Worse still, the Secretary of the Cabinet, Sir Robert Armstrong (later Lord Armstrong of Ilminster), a very formidable man, who oversaw the appointment of all Permanent Secretaries, had not been consulted, so he too exploded. Everybody was threatening to resign.

There was also wider disquiet in Westminster, summed up by an article published in the *Daily Telegraph* on 20 December 1984:

A political storm broke last night over the appointment of Mr. Peter Levene, chairman of a company which makes military equipment, to be Chief of Defence Procurement in the Ministry of Defence at a salary of £95,000 a year. The salary is more than twice that of the civil servant moved to make way for him. ... There was scarcely-concealed anger among some civil servants at what they saw as the 'kicking sideways' of Mr. David Perry, the present Chief of Defence Procurement, to make way for Mr. Levene, who will have a five-year contract and will be paid well over twice Mr. Heseltine's salary of £38,910 a year. Mr. Perry will be paid £45,500 as the first Chief of Defence Equipment Collaboration.

Labour MPs attacked Mr. Heseltine, Defence Secretary, for appointing Mr. Levene, and for permitting Sir Frank Cooper, who retired as Permanent Secretary at the Ministry of Defence in 1982, to take his place as chairman of United Scientific.

A wide-ranging attack came from Mr. Gordon Brown, MP for Dunfermline East and a previous critic of Mr. Levene's work as a consultant to Mr. Heseltine and the Ministry on the future of the Royal Dockyards. He said that the twin appointments of Mr. Levene and Sir Frank were an 'outrageous abuse of public money,' and that they demonstrated 'the incestuous relationship between the Ministry of Defence and the arms world.'[1]

I countered this by telling the *Telegraph* (and all the other newspapers covering this story) that my new salary was significantly less than I had been earning, (which was £140,000), and went on to say: 'If you want somebody to control the spending of £8 billion a year, then you have to pay something at least approaching a commercial salary for the job. I think the spending of £8 billion of public money requires a lot of handling and, hopefully, with my background in the industry, I should be able to lend something to that position.' Fortunately, there was also positive coverage of my appointment in the press, as in the *Financial Times* on 21 December 1984:

Mr. Stanley Sheridan was until October 1983 the Major-General in the US army responsible for a big part of its defence procurement programme. He lunched with Mr. Peter Levene a couple of weeks ago and found him bubbling over with ideas about the whole business of defence procurement practices.

'We talked long and hard about how to save money in government,' said the retired Major-General yesterday. 'Mr. Levene is a very tough businessman, and he knows his business. I feel very pleased for your Ministry of Defence. I think they picked a good one.'[2]

---

1   Nicholas Comfort, 'Anger over £95,000 arms job,' *The Daily Telegraph*, Thursday, December 20, 1984, p.1.
2   Duncan Campbell-Smith, 'A tough businessman who knows his business,' *Financial Times*, Friday, December 21, 1984.

And their editorial on the same day went further, in outlining the principal reasons behind my appointment:

In defence procurement, there is certainly fat to be cut out through a determined attack on costs and prices. The civil service culture is perhaps not ideally suited to the hard and often unpleasant business of driving suppliers down to the lowest possible price. The savings that have been achieved when contractors have been exposed to competitive bidding – or even the threat of it – suggest that a more hard-nosed approach could pay big dividends. The Government's view is that a poacher turned gamekeeper – United Scientific is itself a major defence contractor – is likely to achieve results, and it is probably right. Even a 1 per cent saving in procurement costs would pay for Mr. Levene's salary many times over.[1]

By March 1985 I was due to take up my new job. However, this prompted yet another row over the form and terms of my appointment, and potential conflicts of interest. At this point I was told that it was all a terrible problem and that it might not be possible to appoint me. So I said, 'Well, hold on a minute, I've already resigned from running my business, and you have messed me about. Nevertheless, I am of course willing for my appointment to be considered under the existing Civil Service rules.' By this time, Michael was tearing his hair out. Enter Margaret Thatcher. I remember this like it was yesterday. She said, 'What is all this rubbish? I haven't got time to listen to all this nonsense. Tomorrow, Friday, I'm going to President Chernenko's funeral in Moscow. I shall be away for three days. When I come back, he will be installed in his office and working. Do I make myself clear?' End of story: by Monday I was working in my office.[2]

However, the Prime Minister was forced to admit, in a Commons written reply on 18 March, that my appointment had broken Civil Service rules, in that it had side-stepped the requirement for free and open competition for senior Civil Service posts. Nevertheless, she

1   [Editorial], 'Businessmen in Whitehall,' *Financial Times*, Friday, December 21, 1984.
2   Konstantin Chernenko, President of the USSR, died on 10 March 1985, and was given a state funeral in Moscow on 13 March. Peter Levene began his job as Chief of Defence Procurement on 18 March.

went on to support me by saying that the MOD had described me as 'exceptionally well-qualified by ability and experience,' and added that my appointment would be 'very difficult, if not impossible to undo.'[3] In order to meet the criticisms of the SDP and Labour leaders, David Owen and Neil Kinnock, Michael also had agreed that, for twelve months, I would not play any part in commercial dealings between the Ministry and the companies in which I had previously had a financial interest.[4]

*   *   *

When Michael first asked me to work for him in the MOD, the task of making this happen was given to Clive Whitmore (subsequently Sir Clive Whitmore) who was the Permanent Secretary. I had known Clive before, and subsequently we became close friends. Clive had anticipated correctly that my arrival might cause a terrible row. In order to get round all these potential problems, he came up with a brilliant plan whereby I would be seconded from industry. Thus, the businessman Lord Hanson was asked if he would take me on and pay me, so the MOD could then just buy in a service, rather than actually employing me directly. He agreed to do this, but in the end they decided not to go down that route.

Once I was appointed as CDP he said to me: 'Peter, you will look after procurement and the procurement vote and I will look after the rest. I trust you to get it right.' I learned a great deal from Clive and, through him and many others, developed great respect for civil servants and I realised how hard they worked.

Clive Whitmore's successor in the MOD was Sir Michael Quinlan. Michael had a long background in defence and was regarded as the leading expert in the UK on the nuclear deterrent. He was a pleasure to work with and a very wise and helpful colleague.

I am always irritated by those groups, particularly politicians, who criticise civil servants as being lazy and ineffective. In my opinion

3   Richard Norton-Taylor, 'Thatcher admits defence job was illegal,' *The Guardian*, 19 March 1985.
4   Margaret van Hattem, 'Curbs on Levene's role in contracts fail to satisfy MPs,' *Financial Times*, 19 March 1985.

they could not be more wrong and as Peter Hennessy (now Lord Hennessy), the most knowledgeable historian on the British Constitution, records in his book *Whitehall*, a comment which I had made: 'We have people within the MOD, within the Civil Service, for whom I would have given my right arm in industry.'[1]

So now I found myself in the MOD, really as an innocent abroad. Apart from my role in the Naval Dockyards, I had never worked in a Government department before, and though I thought I had a pretty good idea how they operated, my preconceptions proved to be completely inaccurate. I also had very little knowledge of the hierarchy. There were four Permanent Secretaries in the MOD, two listed as Grade 1 and two at Grade 2, and I was now one of the Grade 1s. I was only forty-three and I didn't realise how much authority I had. For a start, on my first day, I went into the office and found a letter on my desk from the Permanent Secretary of the Treasury, Sir Peter Middleton,[2] who happened to be a good friend of mine. It said: 'Dear Peter, You are now the Accounting Officer for Vote 2 (Procurement) at the Ministry of Defence, with an annual budget of £8.5 billion, which means you are personally responsible for this money. Please sign here. Now it's all down to you.' Also, there was an endless succession of four-star military officers – Admirals, Generals, and Air Marshals – all coming in to say, 'Well, sir, what do you want us to do?' At first it was all terrifying and quite difficult, though I got used to it after a while.

In order to find out what was going on, I summoned the twenty or thirty senior people in the Procurement Executive to an urgent meeting in my office. That in itself was an odd experience, as I discovered that whenever a group of staff gathered outside my Ministry office, they all had to enter in order of seniority. This meant that there was always a ridiculous jostle outside, with them saying: 'No, you go there … and you go there.' Anyway, eventually they all came in, and I said: 'Now look, guys, I'm new to this, I've just arrived, I really don't know anything about it, and I'm relying on you to tell me what's going on.'

1   Peter Levene interviewed for the BBC Radio 4's *Analysis* programme, 'Bangs to the Buck', 30 April 1987).
2   Sir Peter Middleton, GCB (b.1934), Permanent Secretary to the HM Treasury, 1983–91.

I will never forget it. My first day at the MOD was 18 March 1985, which is significant because the Government year runs from 5 April. We were therefore just three weeks away from the end of the financial year and having come from a business environment where at that time of year I was always trying to pull the figures together, I asked my new staff for an update on the finances at the MOD. The response was: 'It's alright.' To which I said: 'What does that mean? Come on, somebody tell me what's going on.' Someone piped up: 'Well, excuse me, Sir, but there is a bit of a problem. We think we're going to have a £500 million underspend.' 'And that's *bad* news, is it?' I asked. 'Oh, yes, it's terrible.' When I asked why, you could see them all muttering, as if to imply that I really didn't understand anything. Of course, it transpired that if the Ministry hadn't spent all its budget, the Treasury would reclaim any underspend. I remember saying: 'So you're telling me that if you haven't spent all the money, that's bad; but if you have spent all the money, it's good?' 'That's right,' they said,' to which I replied, 'This is like *Alice-in-Wonderland*.'

Anyway, once I had established that this was indeed exactly what happened, I walked across Whitehall to see Peter Middleton at the Treasury. Once I was in his office, I said: 'Look, Peter, I've been yanked out of my nice, comfortable existence, and put into this job to try and get some commercial sense into the MOD, so they get value for money. And yet, I hear we have this system whereby we have to spend *every* penny of our budget before the end of the year or we lose it. That can't be right.' He replied: 'Well, that's the way it works.' At this, I said: 'Yes, I know that, but if they want me to do what they've asked me to do, I can't do it with that background.' So he asked me what I wanted. Having already discussed my plans with my staff, I told him that I wanted an agreement whereby we could keep any annual underspend, up to 20 per cent of the total budget, to carry forward into the next financial year. Likewise, if we overspent, we would pay that back from the following year's allocation. Peter said he would think about it.

I went back to the MOD, told my staff what I'd done, and said that I wanted to write a letter to the Permanent Secretary at the Treasury outlining everything we had discussed. 'No, you don't want to do that,' they said. 'Why not?' I said, 'that is exactly what I want to do; go and write the letter.' After about three days, nothing had happened, so I demanded to see the draft. When it appeared, it bore no relation to what I had said, so I sent it back. After two further redrafts, I gave up and wrote the letter myself. One must remember that, at that time, I didn't speak the Civil Service language. The vocabulary of Government departments is completely different from the real world. They use, to me, previously unheard-of phrases like 'nugatory expenditure,' when 'nugatory' merely means 'unnecessary.' Anyway, in spite of the fact that I didn't speak their language, I drafted the letter myself, in English rather than in bureaucratic-speak. When my staff read it, they were deeply shocked and said: 'You can't say that.' 'I can,' I said, 'and I don't care, I'm sending it.'

Just before I went over for my next meeting with Peter Middleton, my staff warned me: 'Look, we've got to tell you, our mates in the Treasury have read your letter, they think it's nonsense, and they're all falling about laughing.' I replied: 'Well, I'm sorry to hear that, but I'm doing the best I can.' Back in Peter's office, he asked how I was. 'Fine,' I said, 'but did you get my letter?' And he said: 'Yes, but I have only one question. You came to see me four weeks ago. Why has it taken you a month to send me this letter?' 'That,' I said, 'is a very good question.' When I told him the reasons behind the delay, he said, 'That doesn't surprise me.' Fortunately, he then went on to say: 'Look, my staff here in the Treasury have told me that there is no way we can agree to your proposal. But I understand what you have been brought in to do, so although I won't give you a 20 per cent annual carry-forward, you can have a 10 per cent one.' That was in fact what we actually wanted, so we implemented it and managed to change the system. In the spring of 1987 we carried forward £600 million.[1] The MOD had often tried to get a carry forward arrangement in the past, but always via the usual channels of letters and low-level approaches. I succeeded because I knew the Permanent Secretary at the Treasury and discussed the issue with him personally. It showed the value of knowing people and using one's contacts in a perfectly proper way. Furthermore, the beneficial effects of the carry forward arrangements secured value for money for the Treasury as well as the MOD, because

1   David Buchan, 'Business meets bureaucracy: Interview with Peter Levene, the biggest buyer in UK industry,' *Financial Times*, Monday, November 30, 1987.

it helped to reduce the cost of delays in procurement. It was at about this time, shortly after I'd started the job, that I came home late, as I did every night, and found Wendy watching the BBC television series *Yes, Minister*. As I sat down, she laughed and said, 'Don't you think this is funny?' 'No,' I said, 'I don't think it's funny at all; I've just had a whole bloody day of this.'

One particular event sticks in my mind when Peter Middleton and I were sitting next to each other in the front row of the annual meeting of the Institute of Directors in the Royal Albert Hall, happily eating from our little picnic boxes with which we had been provided. The next morning a photograph of both of us appeared on the front page of the Morning Star with a caption: 'Two fat cats hard at work'. They could probably have produced a better caption had they actually realised who we were.

*   *   *

Shortly after I joined the Ministry, my Private Secretary said to me: 'Look, the Chief Constable of the MOD Police is coming to see you. There is a suspicion of corruption within your staff. He'll explain.' When this man arrived, he said: 'I've got a serious issue I want to discuss with you. Two of your senior staff flew up to Scotland to see a golf tournament. They were flown up by one of the MOD's contractors, who also paid for them to stay overnight and attend a golf tournament, with lunch provided. This is a very serious matter.' 'OK,' I replied, 'but nobody has actually explained this to me before, so perhaps we better start from scratch. Now, let's suppose I am invited to a golf tournament. Am I allowed to go?' 'Well, yes, probably,' was the reply. 'Fine,' I said, 'so let's say the company inviting me has laid on a bus to transport everybody. Is it OK if I go on the bus?' 'Yes, probably.' I went on: 'When I get to the golf tournament, there's a big marquee and everybody is having lunch, and they invite me to join them. Is that alright?' 'Yes, I suppose so.' 'OK,' I said, 'so we've determined that there's nothing wrong with being invited to a golf tournament; there's nothing wrong with getting transport to it – in this case a bus, rather than a plane; and there's nothing wrong with eating lunch. But you told me that my staff were also put up overnight. I went to see Shorts in Belfast recently, and they put me up in their company guest house.' The MOD policeman replied: 'Ah, but that's alright.' And I replied: 'Well, I don't quite understand what the rules are.'

Having discussed all this, eventually I said: 'Look, this is ridiculous. I understand exactly where you're coming from, so I'm going to start a new system. We're going to have hospitality books, and every one of the 36,000 people who work for us will have one. In these books, they will record all the invitations that they accept; invitations that are declined don't need to be listed, because they are irrelevant. Now, how are they to decide whether they are allowed to go to these events or not? This is the way we're going to do it. The presumption is that they can go. However, if they are not sure, they must consult their boss, and if he signs it off, they can accept the invitation. Thus every case of hospitality will be listed, together with a record of who gave permission for the member of staff to attend the function. These books will be examined quarterly by their boss, who in turn will have one which will be examined by his boss, and it will go all the way to the top, until it ends up with me.'

So that's what we did, and from that day on we didn't have a problem until I left, when some hair-shirted Permanent Secretary decided that, for example, it was alright for a four-star officer to go to Glyndebourne, but everybody else could only go to the local fish-and-chip shop. It was always a difficult issue, in that some of it was legitimate and some of it was corrupt. While I was in America, visiting General Electric, I took the opportunity to ask how they dealt with it. And they said: 'Ah, we have a compliance manual.' It was huge. I started reading it. It said:

> To make matters easy, we have examples which people can look at. Question 1: 'I work for General Electric and my brother is an officer in the US Airforce, which, of course, is a customer of General Electric. Would there be any problem to take my brother out for dinner?'
> Answer: 'No, you cannot do that – certainly not!'

It was absolutely absurd.

The rules imposed by the Americans were mind-bogglingly awful, so we didn't follow their example. However, we did have some of our own peculiar regulations at the MOD. Shortly after I arrived, my

Personal Secretary told me that I had my own allocation of a bottle of gin and a bottle of whisky, so if guests came to see me and wanted a drink, we could provide it. A few days later, the tea lady came into my office and said: 'You owe me £1.60.' When I asked her why, she said I'd had several cups of tea and coffee. So, I retorted: 'I don't drink tea or coffee, I only have water.' 'Oh yes, sir,' she replied, 'but you have to pay for the teas and coffees that your guests drink, and they are 8p per cup.' When she'd gone, I said to my office: 'Let me get this straight. I have a visitor, and I can give him tea or coffee, but I have to pay for it. But if I give him a gin-and-tonic, it's free?' 'Yes,' they said, 'that's right.' So when a friend of mine came round to see me later that afternoon, I said to him: 'Would you like a drink? Before you answer this question, I have to tell you that if you want a cup of tea or coffee, it's going to cost me 8p. But if you want a gin-and-tonic or a whisky-and-soda, it's free!'

* * *

Very early on, I was invited to the Paris Air Show. I had visited it quite often before commercially, but this time I was invited as CDP, and had therefore become an important VIP. In those days, things happened, in terms of hospitality, which would today break every rule in the book. I had been invited by Rolls Royce, to what they described as a 'seminar.' Actually it involved flying out to France on a Friday evening for dinner in the Moët & Chandon Chateau de Saran, then a lecture the next morning, another grand dinner hosted by Pomeroy champagne on Saturday night, followed by a day out in Paris. All of this had been laid on by Rolls Royce. In this day and age, you wouldn't be able to accept such an invitation, but at that time it was the norm. Even so, I said to my advisers: 'Look, is this alright? Is it ok for me to do this?' 'Yes,' they said, 'don't worry about a thing.' I accepted, for both myself and Wendy, who had also been invited and was very excited about the trip.

Then, about two days before we were due to leave, my staff told me that the departure time clashed with a very important meeting I had to attend. 'That's a pity,' I said. They replied: 'Don't worry. As Rolls Royce have organised an aeroplane to take everybody out there, we'll just get an HS 125 from Northolt and fly you out later to join them.'

'Are you sure?' I said. 'Yes, absolutely, don't worry about it,' they said. Wendy flew out to France ahead of me with the rest of the crowd, leaving me to attend my meeting in Whitehall. Once that was over, my staff said: 'Right, we can go now; we'll drive you up to Blackfriars Bridge.' At that time, there was a floating pontoon moored next to the bridge, on which was a helicopter landing-spot. We drove up to the pontoon, I got out of the car, and there was an RAF Gazelle helicopter, which whisked me to Northolt. As soon as I arrived there, the Base Commander appeared, saluted, and said, 'Good afternoon, sir.' This was a bit of a shock to me, although as it always happened on the many subsequent occasions that I used that airfield, I got used to that too eventually.

Anyway, I got into the HS 125 and found that it was flying just me out to France. We landed at Reims Airport, to find nobody there. Eventually, after about five minutes, a lone car drew up, carrying a senior French air force officer. '*Mon general*,' he said, 'I am so sorry we're late.' What had happened was that we'd landed on the military side of the airport, and he had been expecting me on the civilian side.

I was then driven to the Chateau de Saran, a most spectacular place, where I discovered, much to my amazement, that of the 100-odd people there, I was the top guest. Wendy, who had already arrived, whispered to me, 'Do you realise how important you are?' On the first night, there was a grand gala dinner. As we were going to bed, our hosts said, 'Would you like something to take up to your room?' I replied 'Well, can we have a bottle of Perrier or something like that?' '*Non*,' they said, 'we can only give you a bottle of Dom Pérignon, it's the only thing we have here.' That was it. For the next two days, we lived on champagne.

Following breakfast on the Saturday morning after the gala dinner, and because they had to be seen to be doing this thing seriously, Rolls Royce had organised a lecture on new developments in aircraft engines. While Wendy and the other wives were whisked off to enjoy themselves elsewhere, we all trooped diligently downstairs. This was only about ten o'clock in the morning, but after a very heavy night, and as the slide presentation progressed I realised, just as my own eyes were closing, that everybody else was fast asleep. And so it went on. That night, there was another gala dinner in Épernay, then a day in Paris with another dinner there. And all the time, Wendy kept saying to me, 'Why do they all want to talk to you? You must be very important.' And I said, 'Yes, I suppose you're right.' It was a real eye-opener, but I realised from then on that, wherever I wanted to go, I could call up a plane to get me there. Today, that would be strictly forbidden, but in those days you could do so.

*   *   *

Working in Whitehall threw up its own conundrums, as I explained in an interview with the *Financial Times* defence correspondent in October 1985: 'When I ran a business turning over £120 million a year, I expected to know every day what was happening. Now I'm running an organisation that's turning over £8.5 billion, I haven't the faintest idea. Well, I have *some* idea, but I haven't any of the basic information which I really need.'[1] So I set up a new cell. I knew that the large defence companies spent a lot of time and money analysing what the MOD was doing. Therefore I tasked the cell with an intelligence function of analysing how each of the companies in the Defence industry were performing, watching press comments and announcements – and their share prices. Shortly after I'd taken up the job, my staff told me that I was going to have to appear in front of the House of Commons Public Accounts Committee. They question all Permanent Secretaries on the validity of their expenditure, and as it is a cross-party body, I was advised that the Labour representatives would be out to get me. When I asked what specifically they would be asking me about, I was told that there was a designated topic for each session, and mine was to be the government profit formula for non-competitive contracts. I replied, 'Look, this is going to be the shortest-ever tenure for somebody in this job, because I don't know the first thing about any of this.' So they brought me a briefing book, which was several hundred pages long.

In desperation, I rang up Sir Frank Cooper, the former Permanent Secretary at the MOD, who had taken over from me as chairman at

---

1   Bridget Bloom, 'The big spender who drives a hard bargain,' *Financial Times*, Wednesday, October 9, 1985.

United Scientific and had been a legendary Civil Servant. I told him that I was going to have to appear in front of the Public Accounts Committee, that I hadn't a clue about how to handle it, and then asked for his advice. He said: 'Don't worry about a thing. Let me set the scene for you. There will be about fifteen people on this committee, split between the Government and the Opposition. It's highly unlikely that any of them will know much of the detail of what they're talking about, especially if it's a very complex subject. They will be briefed by their staff, and you will be briefed by your staff. Now, this is what you do. You will be asked a number of questions, which you can ignore. Write down ten topics which you want to talk to them about, and just tell them what you are doing.' 'What exactly do you mean?' I said. 'Let me explain,' he replied, 'they'll say to you: 'What are you going to do about this?' And you say, 'Well, that is an extremely interesting question. But, before I answer that, let me just tell you this.' Then you reel through your ten topics, and as they've only got five or six minutes each, you'll be able to talk them out.' Much to my amazement, I took his advice and it worked. It was yet more of Sir Humphrey Appleby from *Yes, Minister.*

*   *   *

When I first started at the MOD, there was a monthly meeting of the heads of the Procurement Executive, at which each of its four divisions – Royal Navy, Army, Royal Air Force, and the research establishments – was represented by senior officers. This monthly meeting was known, of course, by its initials – PEMB – Procurement Executive Management Board. I quickly got the impression that the most critical topic they discussed was the colour of the chairs in the meeting room. I put a stop to that, and insisted that in future each of them would give a report. When this caused consternation, on the basis that they were all four-star officers, I said: 'I don't care, they work for me, and this is what they're going to have to do.' I then found out that, whenever there was a query on something I didn't know about, sometimes on very large programmes, the Admiral or General submitting the report didn't know what the answer was and would have to bring in a young officer who understood the detail. I said to my staff: 'Look, I don't want all these senior officers in here. Bring me the Major or the Captain who's dealing with this, and who actually understands it.' 'You can't do that,' they said, 'because you're a four-star officer, so you can't meet on a level with them.' 'I can,' I said, 'and that's what I'm going to do.' And that's how I started to find out what was really going on.

One of the first challenges was to try to abolish the ubiquitous 'cost-plus' contracts that the MOD had tended to favour, in which the final price depended on what work over and above that originally proposed by the contractor was needed, in order to deliver what the Armed Services wanted. This meant that the Ministry vetted all the costs and paid them, plus an agreed rate of profit. There was therefore absolutely no incentive for the contractor to reduce his costs, in fact far from it. As his profit was entirely dependent on the extent of his costs, the more he spent, the larger his gain. Furthermore, there was every incentive to keep programmes going indefinitely. And the MOD felt no compunction about changing specifications as projects went along, because they had never been compelled to write precise ones in the first place. The 'cost-plus' contracts became the bane of my life. I remember saying to my staff: 'Don't you understand what this means? If we agree in advance to pay a percentage profit on a contractor's costs, the more they spend, the more they will make from us.'

The cynicism in some parts of the Defence Industry was exposed by none other than the then Chief Executive of British Aerospace, Admiral Sir Raymond Lygo. After retiring from British Aerospace, he admitted that the company routinely quoted unrealistically low prices for defence hardware, then put up the prices once the MOD had awarded it a contract. Sir Raymond said: 'It's a well-known fact, whether any-body admits it or not, [that] you'll never get any programme through government if you ever revealed the real cost,' he told the BBC in 2004. 'Whatever you want to get through government, you have to first of all establish what is the Treasury likely to approve in terms of money? And then you think, what can you offer for these terms within the parameters that have been set?' As a result, Sir Raymond said, British Aerospace would bid low and then inflate its prices after the contract had been agreed. 'And then the price goes up and they have a decision whether they are going to continue or cancel. The cancellation costs will be greater than continuing with it. So normally you say 'OK, we'll continue.' But that's life in Whitehall, I'm afraid.'

I was determined to get rid of these contracts. Also, when I first arrived, the MOD could still award contracts – without any competition – on the basis that there was a sole supplier and they claimed that nobody else could tender for it. In one case, this involved equipment that was being built for the Royal Navy by Racal, a fantastically successful business run by Ernie Harrison,[1] who was selling his military radios all over the world. But when there was a non-competitive contract, we didn't get sight of their costings, or what percentage profit we would be paying on those costs. So, under my new rules, Ernie's company appeared on a list of non-competitive contractors. As I knew him very well, I asked my staff to call him in for a meeting in my office. When he appeared, he said: 'What's your problem, Peter?' I replied: 'I'm told that we're placing a contract with you, but you won't reveal your cost or profit rates.' 'That's right,' he said. When I explained that we couldn't enter into such an arrangement, he retorted: 'Well, just a minute. Ask your guys how much of the development costs of these products you have paid.' When I asked my staff round the table, they said: 'Well, actually, unlike our other suppliers, Racal have done it all themselves at their own risk.' 'So how do we work out the price?' I said. 'Well,' they replied, 'they develop this equipment; we want it; we ask them how much it costs; they give us a price, and tell us to take it or leave it.' 'Are we buying a lot from them? And does it work?' I asked. 'Yes, and yes,' were the replies. So I said, 'What other choice do we have?' To which I was told: 'Well, anything else we've looked at is much more expensive.' At that, I said to them: 'So what is the problem?' And I had to say to Ernie: 'I'm very sorry we've dragged you in here, please keep up the good work.' On this occasion, the MOD just didn't get it; it was like somebody going to buy a TV and asking the retailer to provide the precise costs of making a television before agreeing to buy it.

Another early problem to emerge at the MOD was the fact that a great deal of money had already been paid out in advance on contracts that were not being delivered on time. I insisted that, in future, we would only pay for work that had been completed. For example, if we

1   Sir Ernest Harrison, OBE (1926–2009), Chairman of Racal, 1966–2000.

were four months into a programme, and the contractor had delivered 1 per cent of it, when they should have completed 15 per cent, we should only pay for the 1 per cent. Immediately, I was told that this was impossible, because the contracts stipulated the amount we had to pay by a specific date. I retaliated by saying: 'But it also says in the contract that, by that time, they must have done a certain amount of work; and if they haven't done that, they're not doing their job, they haven't delivered, and we're not going to pay them.' Needless to say, I quickly had various Chief Executives ringing me up, who said: 'What do you think you're doing?' To which I replied: 'Look, as and when you deliver what it says in the contract, we will then pay you, but not before.' The chairman of Ferranti, Derek Alun-Jones, went one step further by saying: 'That is outrageous, you can't behave like this; I'm going to put in an official complaint, and I'm going to make sure that a copy of it goes to the Prime Minister.' In answer to this, I merely said: 'That is a *great* idea.' I knew in advance that any such complaint would get nowhere, because when I'd first been appointed to my job, I had been called in to see Margaret Thatcher, and she had said to me: 'Look, you know why you're here. Your job is to procure the best possible equipment for the Armed Forces on the best possible terms, period. Your job is *not* to keep the British defence industry in the manner to which it has become accustomed. Do I make myself clear?' And I said, 'Yes, Prime Minister, you've made yourself very clear.'

Anyway, having established these new terms of payment, whereby we should only pay for work that had actually been completed, it quickly became clear that this still wasn't happening. In exasperation, I said to my staff: 'Look, this is ridiculous. What is the problem?' They were mystified, but eventually one of them came in and said: 'We've cracked it. It's all to do with their confidential reports.' The Procurement Executive's confidential reports were like the staff's report cards and were based on the extent to which their forecast of annual spending matched what they ultimately spent. Of course, they set their forecasts on what the contracts stipulated, so in order to match their reports, they paid out regardless of whether the contractors had actually delivered the goods. My response was: 'Great, thank goodness we've found out. We're going to change the rules. From now on, confidential reports will be written on the basis of how closely the money that is paid out matches the actual performance of the contract.' That made an instant difference.

None of this was rocket science, but it reflected the lack of business sense in the MOD. The staff there were highly intelligent, but they operated on the basis that the existing systems were how it had to work. They also normally had no commercial background. I remember saying to the Air Marshal who was running procurement for the RAF: 'Look, I've been here for a while, I'd like to fly a Tornado.' He replied: 'Alright, we can arrange that for you.' I then said: 'And by the way, I want to do it on my own, I don't want anyone else with me.' 'What on earth are you talking about?' he exclaimed. I went on: 'Look, I'll tell you what I'm talking about. I wouldn't have a clue how to fly a Tornado, as you well know, and you wouldn't let me do it anyway. But you've got staff here who are spending £200 million on a contract, with no financial or business experience at all. They've never bought anything more significant than their own car. We need to have people in here who understand what this is all about.'

Furthermore, the average tour length in the MOD, for military personnel, was about two years, three in exceptional circumstances. It takes anyone at least two years to learn about a job. It would be inconceivable, in the business world, to say that somebody who had been running Marks & Spencer had done it for two years, and therefore should be removed and replaced by someone else. And of course, from the point of view of the companies supplying the MOD, this was perfect, because they would find themselves dealing with someone who didn't know much of the history; and by the time they did, after two or three years, they could be absolutely certain that he'd be moved on. I also thought the system of promotions was very odd. For example, if you are a bright, up-and-coming RAF officer, you might become a Station Commander at an airbase. There you will get a nice house, with a driver, a gardener, and maybe a cook and a maid. All very attractive. Then, eighteen months later, you get promoted to a new post, which happens to be a desk job at the MOD, whereby you get nothing and go to work strap-hanging on the tube. I used to say to my military colleagues: 'Look, in the real world, people gradually move their way up to these perks. You don't give them everything, then remove it; then give it back, only to take it all away again.'

*   *   *

In April 1985, just a month after I had taken up my job, Michael Heseltine announced a major review of the future of the Royal Dockyards at Devonport and Rosyth, based on the report I had written for him a year earlier. The review was to include a number of options for the £400 million annual turnover of the dockyards. These included full priv-atisation, although the Government favoured my alternative of an agency

7. Landing by helicopter on HMS *Challenger*

system, whereby the dockyards would be operated under franchise by companies who had been chosen in open competition. This would secure healthy competition, while still maintaining British control over the national strategic assets involved. It also offered the prospect of outside work for the dockyards from customers other than the MOD.

By this time, the plans had the full support of the Admiralty Board, Admiral Sir John Fieldhouse, the First Sea Lord, saying, when approached by the press, that the Navy supported any moves which would help to save money.[1] However, the preferred option would require legislation, and the final decision was postponed for a six-month consultation period. In the meantime, the dockyard managements began separate negotiations with the trade unions to reduce inefficiency by cutting 2,350 jobs from the 20,000 workforce, of which 2,000 would go at Devonport and 350 at Rosyth.

The announcement of this review provoked a storm of protest in the House of Commons. The shadow Defence Secretary, Denzil Davies, called it 'completely cosmetic and quite a farce,' and went on

1   Desmond Wettern, 'Job losses as dockyards are privatised,' *Daily Telegraph*, 18 April 1985.

to describe my preferred option as 'a franchise suitable for a fast food burger bar, but totally unsuitable for the refit and repair of Royal Navy ships and submarines.' Gordon Brown went further and caused uproar when he 'claimed the review proposals were the disreputable plans of a discredited adviser, who had spent most of the last year hawking the dockyards around his friends in the private sector.' As Labour MPs cried 'squalid,' Michael Heseltine came to my defence by retorting: 'I deeply deplore the scurrilous language about Peter Levene. It is my responsibility to get a major increase in efficiency from the defence budget, and Mr. Levene can play a major role.'[1] He went on to say: 'I cannot ignore the fact that there are significant inefficiencies and overmanning in the dockyards. I cannot accept that that should be a permanent charge to the defence budget. If we can get a commercial approach within the dockyards, there are job opportunities which will be of significant benefit to the local economies.'[2] He also pointed out that staff absenteeism at the dockyards was running at 40 per cent above the national average, which was the equivalent of a month's extra time off for every employee. 'This,' said Heseltine, 'has got to stop.'[3]

* * *

By June 1985, three months after I had taken up the role of CDP, I was able to say that I hoped for savings of 10 per cent a year on defence equipment spending by the end of my five-year appointment, the equivalent of £800 million per annum at the then current prices.[4] However, even the Americans recognised the challenges I was facing. In the same month, I visited the US Navy for a meeting on ship and

---

1   Colin Brown, 'Role of Heseltine's aide ruffles Labour,' *The* Guardian, Thursday, April 18, 1985; Kevin Brown, 'Future of Royal Dockyards to be reviewed,' *Financial Times*, 18 April 1985; and Peter Pryke, 'Franchise plan for Navy yards is condemned,' *Daily Telegraph*, 18 April 1985.
2   Anon., 'Heseltine sets out options for dockyards,' *The Times*, 18 April 1985.
3   Desmond Wettern, 'Job losses as dockyards are privatised,' *Daily Telegraph*, 18 April 1985.
4   Sue Cameron, 'Levene hopes for cuts of 10% in defence equipment spending,' *Financial Times*, [day not recorded], June 1985.

weapon systems competition, and was told that my greatest problem would be an 'institutional bias against competition.'[5]

Meanwhile, the Prime Minister had not forgotten her instructions to me, and at about this time, I was called into Michael Heseltine's office to be told that Margaret Thatcher wanted to see me, that he would accompany me to the meeting, and that she would expect a report on what I had been doing. 'Have you ever done this before?' he said. 'What do you mean?' I replied. 'Well,' he went on, 'let me explain. We will go over there for a half-hour meeting. During that time, you *might* just be able to start and finish four sentences. If there's a ten-minute gap between the start of one sentence and the end of it, don't worry, because that's all normal.' 'Fine,' I said, 'I get the picture.' So we duly went to see her, and she said to me: 'I want to know what you're up to? With all the fuss over your appointment, how are you getting on?' I had prepared my presentation, so I talked to her for nearly an hour, during which time she didn't interrupt. Then she said: 'Well, that's fine. Carry on the good work and come back in a few months' time to update me.' 'Yes, Prime Minister,' I answered, and off we went. Michael Heseltine turned to me and said: 'That was absolutely amazing. How did you do that?' 'It's just my natural genius,' I replied.

Unfortunately, this tactic didn't always work. About a year later, the same thing happened. By this time, Heseltine had resigned and the new Secretary of State for Defence was George Younger,[6] who was also extremely shrewd, absolutely charming, and an excellent boss. Anyway, he called me in to say that the Prime Minister wanted to see me, and that he would be coming with me. He too said: 'Have you ever done this before?' 'Look, George,' I said, 'she's like putty in my hands. Believe me, we won't have a problem. Let me handle this; I know what to do, I've done it once already and it worked last time.' 'Well, if that's what you think,' replied George, 'I just hope you're right.' So off we went. I was quite busy at that time, but I'd told my staff to draft some notes for me, which I'd had a quick look at. 'How are you getting on?' said Mrs. Thatcher. I started quoting from the

5 Washington Staff, 'Tea and Sympathy,' *Aviation Week and Space Technology*, 1 July 1985.
6 George Younger, 5th Viscount Younger of Leckie (1931–2003), Secretary of State for Defence, 7 January 1986 to 24 July 1989.

script I had been given, only to realise that I was essentially giving her the departmental/party line, which was more or less drivel. Of course, she too noticed this after about thirty seconds. Suddenly, there was the equivalent of a nuclear explosion. 'What are you talking about?' she said. 'This is a load of absolute rubbish.' I sat there for about ten minutes, while missiles and bombs were thrown at me; at the end of which she finally said: 'Well, that's quite enough of that. Next time you come, you better know what you're talking about.' Then we all had a Scotch.

One of the earliest issues which I had to address was the growing concern over the future of Westland, the UK's only manufacturer of helicopters. This developed into something of a battle royal with Michael Heseltine on one side and the Prime Minister Margaret Thatcher with Leon Brittan and others opposing him. To my enormous surprise, Michael had gone to a Cabinet meeting at which Westland was to be discussed, and left the meeting part way through to tell the scrum of journalists waiting outside No. 10 that he had resigned. This, of course, came as quite a shock to me, and I was concerned to see how my effectively being cast adrift from my principal would affect the work that I had to do in the MOD. I believe that it is a great credit to the Department that they continued to treat me as if nothing had happened, which allowed me to get on with my job unhindered. Nevertheless, I was very pleased indeed to be able to link up with Michael once again when he rejoined the Government as Secretary of State for the Environment in 1990.

CHAPTER 5

Hard Graft at the Ministry of Defence

ONE OF THE main reasons for my appointment was that there had been so many scandals in defence procurement. The MOD either overpaid enormously or, when they got equipment it had ordered, it didn't work or was often delivered late. One of the biggest *causes celebre* in all this was the Nimrod AEW, which was an early warning aircraft, based on a Comet airframe built by British Aerospace, with radar and electronics supplied by GEC-Marconi. The MOD had ordered eleven of these aircraft in 1977, with the intention that the first would fly with the RAF in 1981, and a full squadron would be in operation by 1984–85.[1] This was in preference to participating in the NATO-funded Airborne Warning and Control System [AWACS] mounted on Boeing aircraft, which was by then in service in Europe.

By 1985, nothing had been delivered, and in February that year, Air Chief Marshal Sir John Rogers, who, as Controller Aircraft, was responsible for the project, had admitted that the mission avionics could take two more years to develop and that even then it would not meet the full standard required by the RAF.[2] The problem was that they couldn't get the radar to work. They set up trials, flying up and down the country, to see what they could detect. The only thing it picked up were the transmissions from radio taxis on the M1. After countless deadlines for delivery had been missed, Michael Heseltine told me that I had to sort this out. At that time, GEC was being run by

---

1 Bridget Bloom, 'UK Defence Procurement: How GEC was put on the spot', *Financial Times*, 22 October 1985.
2 Ibid.

Arnold Weinstock,[1] so I went to see him. Although I thought he was a great man, initially we had a sort of love-hate relationship, but later before he died we became much closer. Anyway, back in 1985, I said to him: 'Look, Arnold, we can't go on with this. I'm going to give you three months, and if you can make the radar work in that time, fine; but if not, we're going to pull the plug.'

In the meantime, three American companies were pitching for business, in the hope that the British order would get cancelled. One was Boeing, with their AWACS aircraft; the second was Grumman, who had developed a smaller aircraft, the E2C, which could land on an aircraft carrier and fold its wings up; and the third was Lockheed. I suggested that we also test these alternatives, to see what they could do. The Boeing system, which is what we should have gone for in the first place, was fine. But when it came to Grumman, my advisers said, 'Look, you can't even think about trying that one here. The frequency of the radar on it is such that, if it takes off in the UK and flies over the Channel, it will block out all television reception in France.' Nobody could see how it was going to be possible to test it. At this point, the Secretary of the US Navy, John Lehman,[2] said he would have the plane flown over from America, to which I said, 'You can't, we don't have permission.' And he said, 'No, you don't understand, I'm flying this over as a US Navy mission, and I don't need permission from anyone to do that. We'll fly it up and down the Channel, and it will be fine.' I said, 'Well, I hope you're right.' They then proceeded with the test, and actually nothing untoward happened at all. George Younger, the Secretary of State for Defence, personally went up in a Boeing AWAC one week and then the Nimrod AEW the following week. His comment at the end of all this was: 'Well, that's very interesting – either there's an airline strike we weren't told about, or I don't think it [the Nimrod] worked.'[3]

Finally, we ended up buying the Boeing AWACS planes, and the British Aerospace-GEC Nimrods were cancelled, at a huge cost of £1

1   Arnold, Lord Weinstock (1924–2002: managing director of GEC, 1963–1996.
2   John Lehman (b.1942): Secretary of the US Navy, 1981–87. First cousin, once removed, of the late Grace Kelly, Princess Grace of Monaco.
3   Interview with Sir Ian Andrews, quoted in David Torrance, *George Younger: A Life Well Lived*, (Birlinn, London, 2008), p.222.

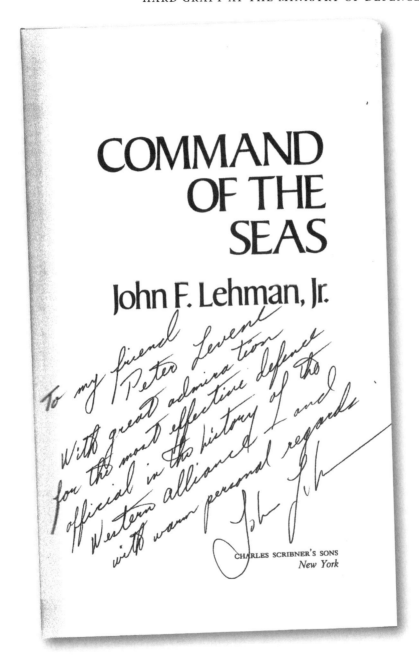

8. Secretary of the US Navy, John Lehman, later kindly endorsed my copy of his autobiography

billion.[1] This led to a very acrimonious exchange in the House of Commons on 18 December 1986. Once the decision had been made to buy the Boeing aircraft, rather than the home-grown Nimrod, we had to negotiate a contract. On a visit to Tokyo, I bumped into the Boeing executive who was handling the deal and somehow gained the impression that there would be negotiating room on the price that we would have to pay for these aircraft. I suggested that we should have a final negotiation, preferably at the eleventh hour. I asked George Younger to let me know when the Cabinet had given the green light to purchase these aircraft, with the maximum amount of advance notice before that decision became public. On the day in question, the Cabinet committee concluded at about noon and George told me that I would have about two to three hours in which to work. Twelve noon in London is 4 a.m. in Seattle. I remember him saying to me: 'Can you really call the chairman of Boeing at 4 a.m. in the morning?' I replied: 'I think that for an order of this size, he will be prepared to talk to me.' I had forewarned the Boeing chairman that he should expect this call and asked him if he could kindly arrange to be in his office, with his colleagues around him, as we would have some questions to ask. After a gulp, he agreed; and so, the minute I got the green light from the Defence Secretary, I telephoned him. 'Would you like the good news or the bad news?' I asked. 'Just tell me,' he replied. I then went on: 'The good news is that we have decided to buy your aircraft. The bad news is that we don't have quite enough money, so we will need a reduction in the price if we are to go ahead. I know that you have your colleagues gathered around you, but I only have two hours to negotiate with you, as the British Government has to make a final decision.' Happily, he did phone me back two hours later. They agreed to a keener price and we were able to proceed.

We got our new aircraft for a very good price. The contract had a two-year delivery period, but it came in on time, on cost, and delivered a product that worked. We also negotiated a unique arrangement whereby 130 per cent of the cost was to be offset by work placed by, and through, Boeing in the UK.[2] About a year after the Boeing aircraft

1   Bridget Bloom, 'UK Defence Procurement: How GEC was put on the spot,' *Financial Times*, 22 October 1985.
2   Torrance, op.cit., p.223

had entered service, I asked the Chief of the Air Staff how the AWACS aircraft were doing. He said they were 'absolutely fine,' and asked me why I was enquiring. I explained about all the problems we'd had, and how we had ended up buying this American system off the shelf. And he said, 'Well, it's been perfect since the day we switched the first system on.' In the long run, the deal we did to get it saved us a lot of money. But this whole business was a classic example of where politicians get procurement wrong. They get pushed into giving orders to British companies, because of the jobs involved, and then are extremely reluctant to cancel them, if things don't work out.

George Younger was refreshingly realistic on these matters. I remember, just before he arrived at the MOD in 1986, as Secretary of State for Scotland he had been fighting like mad to have some auxiliary replenishment vessels for the Royal Navy built in Scotland, and had been sending us aggressive letters. So, when he arrived in the MOD, I said: 'What do you want to do about these?' And he replied: 'Well, I'm not Secretary of State for Scotland any more, I'm at Defence, and it's clear to me – as you say – that building them in Scotland is not the answer.' I thought that was a very professional response and it illustrated the essential point that in our system it is Ministers responsible to Parliament who determine both the size and shape of the equipment programme, and which equipment is sold to countries overseas.[3]

There was an amusing side-line to our deal with Boeing for the AWACS systems. Shortly after it had been concluded, I received a call from the outgoing chairman of Boeing to say that their Chief Executive, Frank Schrontz, whom I knew well, was going to take over from him. He then asked if I could arrange for Frank to meet Margaret Thatcher. I said: 'Well, that's easier said than done, but I will try.' After a lot of negotiation with No. 10, I was told that a meeting had been arranged and a date had been set. At this point, Boeing said: 'Now look, we don't want any of this to get into the newspapers, because he hasn't actually taken over yet. He will get to meet her, but we don't want any photographers there or anything like that.' 'Fine,' I said. Frank arrived from America, and I walked him over to Downing Street. Much to his

3 Interview with Lord Levene, quoted in Torrance, op.cit., p.226.

absolute horror, when we walked into No. 10, we were met by a barrage of photographers. He nearly had a nervous breakdown, though fortunately it turned out that they were actually there to take photographs of the next visitor who was coming to see her. Anyway, we were ushered in to see Margaret Thatcher, who said: 'Very nice to see you, Mr. Schrontz; come and sit over here.' Once he had sat down, she let fly with both barrels about whatever was going on in America at the time. Furthermore, her friend, President Reagan, had not got things right, and Frank was asked to go back and tell him. This went on, at great speed, for half an hour, during which Frank never uttered a syllable. Finally, she said: 'It's been so nice meeting you,' and that was that. When we emerged, he said: 'Is it always like that?' and I replied: 'Yes.'

* * *

In the summer of 1986, just over a year after I had joined the MOD, I found myself back in front of the Public Accounts Committee. Fortunately, by this time, I had made significant progress, and was able to tell them that 65 per cent of all defence equipment contracts were now awarded on a competitive tendering basis, up from a mere 30 per cent a few years before; while the proportion based on the cost-plus method had fallen from 21 per cent in 1981–82 to 9 per cent in that fiscal year. The committee was also pleased to hear that pressure on the monopoly submarine-builder, Vickers, at Barrow-in-Furness, had led to a £25 million reduction in the cost of the first Trident submarine; and GEC, who had been effectively awarded a non-competitive contract to supply Stingray torpedoes, were now to be paid only under an arrangement tied to actual delivery of pre-tested finished products.[1] Overall, the MPs' report on the Ministry of Defence was optimistic and positive, although they regretted the fact that 'it had taken twenty years to reach this position.'[2]

* * *

1   David Simpson, 'MPs find value for money at the MoD,' *Guardian*, Friday, July 18, 1986.
2   Rodney Cowton, 'MoD spending controls 'a conspicuous failure'', *The Times*, Friday, July 18, 1986.

My original empire at the Ministry included all the research and development establishments, which actually accounted for the majority of the people who worked for me. One of these was the Atomic Weapons Research Establishment at Aldermaston in Berkshire, for which I was responsible and had to fund. Once I'd been in place for a while, they arranged for me to go to see it. The day before, I was given a copy of a brief about the visit. On the following morning I got up bright and early, was driven down to Aldermaston, and was greeted by the director of the Establishment. He asked if I had received the brief, and when I said I had, he queried whether it was OK. 'No,' I replied, 'it wasn't OK at all. It says: 'Arrive Aldermaston 0900; have tea or coffee in director's office; have presentation on this, then presentation on that, then more presentations; sandwich lunch; go home.'' 'Well,' he said, 'that's what we're going to do.' I responded: 'I understand that, but I've just driven down to Aldermaston. If you were going to give three or four presentations, you could have come and given them in my office. But as I'm here, I'd like to look around.' 'You what?' he cried. 'I said I'd like to look round. I do have security clearance for all this.' 'Oh yes,' he replied, 'we're sure you do, but if you want to look round, you'll have to put on a white coat.' And I said: 'Well, I think I can manage that.' So, very reluctantly, they took me on a tour. Much later, I got my staff to do an efficiency scrutiny on Aldermaston. One of the things that sticks in my memory was the fact that they employed fifty-six librarians, which gave me some understanding of the way in which the place worked.

At that time, they were building a new facility at Aldermaston, and by the time I got there – as with many other things – this project was costing a fortune and was way over budget. One of the costliest items was a vast ramp, which allowed everything to go in at first-floor level rather than via the ground floor. When I asked why we were spending so much money on this expensive ramp, I was told that we had saved a fortune by copying the identical designs of the new American plant at Los Alamos. Since we co-operated very closely with them on nuclear matters, the Americans had allowed us to use their design for free. I still didn't understand why this facility had to have an expensive ramp to the first floor, until I visited Los Alamos some time later, and then it all became clear. The American plant was built on a hillside, so in order to get into it, you had to drive up a sloped ramp. We, however, were building ours on a flat site, so not only was our ramp unnecessary, it was also very expensive.

Apart from the research establishments, I was also responsible for all the MOD production facilities, including the Royal Ordnance factories. One of these was at Enfield in north London, where they produced the famous Lee-Enfield rifles and the Bren gun. (The latter originated as a joint venture with the Czechs in the 1930s, as their factory was in a place called Brno and the British factory was in Enfield, they had combined both places to come up with a name for these new machine guns.) When I joined, Enfield had just secured a contract for the new much-maligned and hated SA80 rifle. It was a completely different design from the old rifles, which meant that the whole of the British Army had to change its drill. Once the first of these new rifles had been produced, they organised a ceremonial handover at Enfield, to which I was invited with the Minister for Defence Procurement and the then-Chairman of the Royal Ordnance factories, Brian Bassett. We went down there, to be greeted by the most extraordinary pantomime. They had arranged a sort of parade ground inside a hanger, and the centrepiece of the occasion was the chairman of Enfield driving on in his Rolls Royce and handing over these initial rifles. I think they had been contracted to provide 40,000 or 50,000, so I said: 'Presumably you've got all these rifles churning out like peas?' Well, it turned out in the end that they were virtually all hand-made, which nobody was very pleased about. Eventually, we sold all the Royal Ordnance factories to BAE Systems.

*   *   *

Shortly after I joined the MOD, I was invited to visit the SAS at their headquarters in Hereford. It was February on the Welsh borders, and when I arrived to see the commanding officer, he had all the windows in his office wide open. After a while, I said to him: 'Look, you may not notice it, but actually I'm freezing cold. Would you mind closing the windows?' 'Oh yes,' he said, 'I'm so sorry.' He then showed me round the whole operation, which was absolutely fantastic. Of course, the amount of equipment they use, compared to the rest of the armed forces, is *de minimis*. But he explained that every time they wanted to buy equipment, they were forced to go through an impossibly long and complicated procedure, given that they have to work instantly, and he wanted to know what I could do about it. Their budget was so small that I couldn't even find it. So I said: 'Look, I think you're doing the most fantastic job down here. As far as I'm concerned, whatever you want, you should have. From now on, the SAS can just have whatever it wants straightaway.' They were pleased about that, because it saved them a lot of work and they got their kit on time.

*   *   *

In my role as CDP, I made quite a number of overseas visits, particularly to France, Germany, Italy, and the United States. We tried hard to see to what extent we could coordinate our procurement activities and we had a lot of joint programmes. At first, they were called collaborative programmes, though after a while the name became a problem, because the word 'collaboration' has an unattractive association in France. We renamed them *'programmes en cooperation'*. On one occasion, there was a four-powers meeting (as they were called) in Avignon, with the French, Germans and Italians. All the ministers involved flew in from their different countries on very smart aircraft. But George Younger decided not to take a six-seater British Aerospace 125 corporate jet and opted instead to travel in a larger propeller-driven aircraft. As a result, a journey that should have taken about ninety minutes lasted nearly four hours. When we were leaving, at the end of the conference, one of the other ministers said to George: 'Where's your plane?' When George pointed it out, the other man said: 'You didn't come in that, did you? Don't worry, we'll give you a lift back!' 'No, no,' replied George, 'it's quite alright.' It was all very British.

   Not long after I became CDP, I went to the United States to visit one of the main missile companies, which was located on the west coast at San Jose in California. The trip was scheduled at the end of August, after our summer holiday at our house in Sea Island, Georgia. We had been recommended to Sea Island by our lawyer in Dallas – Dan Busbee. At first we stayed there in the local hotel. Then in the following years we rented houses until finally we bought our own which is still a favourite holiday destination for our grandchildren. I was to take a Sunday afternoon flight from Jacksonville and arrive at San Jose in the evening, ready to start work the following morning. It was the middle of summer and I had been on the beach. I went to Jacksonville airport wearing a T-shirt and shorts, with the rest of my clothes in my suitcase. As luck would have it, the plane was delayed due to bad weather; when it rains there, they instantly cancel half the flights. But eventually we took off and just made it to Atlanta in time to make the connection with a flight to California. However, I knew there was no way my luggage was going to keep up, and when we arrived at San Jose, I was still wearing my T-shirt and shorts from the beach. The resident MOD naval officer, who was supervising the programme I had come to discuss, came to meet me at the airport, wearing his uniform and a monocle. He took one look at me and thought, 'What the hell is this?' I explained to him what had happened and said I was sure that my clothes would arrive in the morning.

We then drove to the hotel in San Jose where I was staying. It was quite late and I wanted to go straight to bed, but just as I walked into my room, everything went black. There had been a major power-failure throughout the city. There I was, having just checked into a hotel I'd never been to before, sitting in my room in the pitch dark. It was no good opening the curtains, because all the street lights outside had also gone off. Fortunately, having stayed in many hotels in America, I was relieved to discover that, even in the dark, I could find virtually everything in the bedroom and bathroom, and then I got into bed. Of course, when the power supply was restored at about 3 o'clock in the morning, I was woken up abruptly when all the lights and the television came back on, and I was amazed to find that the room had three balconies!

The next morning, I still had no luggage. So I said to one of my colleagues and the officer who had met us at the airport: 'Look, between you, you're going to have to lend me some clothes, so I can be semi-respectable at these meetings.' They managed to cobble together a few items of clothing from various people, none of which fitted properly. But nobody had any spare shoes, so I had to stay in my beach shoes. We set off for our meetings and when we arrived, we found there was a big reception party. I felt very uncomfortable and tried to explain what had happened to my clothes. 'Don't worry about a thing,' they said, 'we're Lockheed, and if your luggage is in California, we'll find it by the time we have finished. All your meetings today are taking place here, so you'll be fine.' 'Fine,' I replied. But all that day I found myself moving from one lot of people to another, and each time I had to explain why I was wearing such a bizarre collection of clothes. Finally, at the end of the afternoon, I went back to the reception desk and said: 'You know I came here this morning and gave you my baggage check, so you could find my bags for me?' And the girl behind the desk replied: 'Oh gee, I forgot.' Consequently I remained without my clothes and I think I got them back eventually late on the second day.

On another trip to California, I visited Los Angeles with Donald Spiers who was at the time responsible for all the research establishments, and subsequently took over aircraft procurement. We were staying in a hotel near the airport and, finding ourselves with an afternoon off one Saturday, we went to sit by the pool. There we received a message that a visitor from the American nuclear industry was coming to see us. He would be flying in from Washington to talk about a very serious issue, which was so secret that it couldn't be put on paper, and he had to speak to us personally. When he arrived, he was shown to the poolside, where my colleague and I were having a drink. He then started to tell us a story that was so abstruse that neither of us really understood it. He also warned us that everything he had said would be exposed in the press on the forthcoming Monday morning, which – according to him – was going to be hugely embarrassing and difficult, and then asked us what we were going to do about it. I didn't understand the first thing about it. My colleague, who knew a little bit more than I did, said: 'So what?' We thanked this man for flying all the way out to see us and asked him what he was going to do next. It transpired that he had flown all the way to Los Angeles just to tell us this extraordinary story and was returning to Washington immediately. On Monday, once the weekend was over, I said to my colleague: 'Well, you better get onto your people about it.' Their response was: 'We neither know about this, nor care.' It was all most bizarre.

On the general question of hospitality in America, a country that I visited frequently both on United Scientific and MOD business, I remember going to see the aerospace and electronics company Martin

Marietta. We sat down to lunch in the director's dining room, and I was asked if I was prepared to pay $7 for the meal. I replied: 'Well, if you want me to, I suppose so.' They then explained that they had costed the lunch at $7 a head, and most public servants who came would pay so they could then say that they hadn't been treated to lunch. I said: 'Well, if I don't have to pay for lunch, then I'm not going to.'

On another occasion, the American aerospace company Lockheed gave a big dinner in my honour in a restaurant. The guests included US Air Force officers and our MOD project team, who were based in their factory and were overseeing the contract we had with them. We all sat down and had a very jolly, quite lavish dinner. At the end of the meal, I noticed that one of the MOD men was paying the bill. I said: 'Look, Lockheed have invited us, and they're the contractor. Why are you paying for this dinner?' 'Ah,' he said, 'I will explain. We've got US Air Force officers here, and they're not allowed to accept hospitality from a contractor. But if they can say that the hospitality came from a foreign government, in this case the British, then they can come. Thus, we pay the bill and that's alright.' 'That's not alright at all. I've never heard of anything so stupid in all my life' I replied.

In 1989 I went to China. Their defence industry was then very undeveloped, and I think I was one of the first senior western defence procurement representatives to visit the country. Wendy came with me. We went to Beijing, Shanghai and Xian, where we saw the extraordinary Terracotta Army. In Beijing we stayed in one of the first modern Chinese hotels, which I discovered afterwards belonged to the army. But in Shanghai there were no hotels, so they put us up in a government guest house, which actually was very comfortable. (Many years later, when, as Chairman of Lloyd's, I was signing a deal with the Mayor of Shanghai, I lunched in the same guest house, since renamed as part of a US hotel chain, although by that time there were many world-class hotels in China). On that first visit, we were escorted throughout by a female Chinese major, whom we called Rosa Klebb. It was fascinating, because it was well before China opened up, and we had to go everywhere with our interpreter. Actually, I rather suspected that, while they made no claim to speak English, some of the people we spent time with probably spoke it pretty well and could understand what we were saying. We didn't do any business with the

Chinese as a result of that trip, although I did realise that at that time their equipment was stone-age. Now, of course, all that has changed and they've caught up pretty fast.

We also went on a trip to India, where I insisted on taking a whole case of mineral water, because I was so worried about getting a stomach bug. As we were there over a weekend, our hosts announced that they were going to take us to see the Taj Mahal and the Red Fort at Agra. We found ourselves being driven round Agra in an ancient Morris Oxford by the senior military officer of that district, whose full-time job was to command the Indian parachute experimental establishment. Once we'd finished sightseeing, he said he'd like to invite us to lunch in the officers' mess. When we got there, drinks were handed round, and he started introducing me to a stream of Brigadiers and Air Marshals. It was very hot and I was tired. Suddenly I noticed that Wendy and my military assistant Fred Scourse were doubled up with laughter. I was furious and asked them why they were laughing. 'Do you know what you just did?' said Wendy. 'No,' I replied, 'what did I just do?' 'You shook hands with the waiter!'

*   *   *

I had developed a very good relationship with my French opposite numbers which led to frequent meetings during which some difficult problems were successfully resolved.

One of these visits had been arranged to take place over three days, starting at the French Underwater Weapons Research Establishment located, very attractively, in the South of France, and then moving on to Paris for further discussions. These meetings always had a social side which undoubtedly helped the relationship. Following a very good dinner on the first evening, I was awoken early the next morning to be told 'Your programme for this morning is cancelled, Moray (Stewart) (my deputy) will take over. An HS125 will be waiting for you at Nice airport to fly you back to Northolt. When you arrive, you will be driven to No 10 as Mrs Thatcher has called a high-level meeting to make a final decision regarding a go ahead for EFA (The European Fighter Aircraft - subsequently called Typhoon). When it is finished you will be flown back to Paris to rejoin the programme.'

I was whisked back to London, into the Cabinet Room in No 10 surrounded by a large group, each of whom had a very large dossier in front of them on the project. The meeting started by the Prime Minister addressing Dick Norman (Sir Richard Norman, the MOD Chief Scientific Adviser), for a reason which I never managed to work out, the Chief Scientific Adviser was the Chairman of the Equipment Policy Committee [EPC] – the committee which approved equipment going into service. When I started I thought that I ought logically to chair it, until I discovered that I was not even a member! But this did mean that Dick Norman took the full thrust of Margaret Thatcher's microscopic evaluation of the huge dossier. The dialogue went something like this: 'Now Professor Norman – on page 73, para 186a it states 'xxxxx' but on page 235, para 425b it says 'yyyyy' in contradiction. How do you explain that?' And so it went on. I was very glad that I was not in the firing line. I got the impression that the Prime Minister was probably the only person present who had read the file from cover to cover – and, what's more, absorbed it!

Anyway, after about a half an hour, I thought that having made this lightning journey, I should say something. So I coughed, and interjected 'Excuse me Prime Minister...'. That was as far as I got, there was an immediate response 'I have read your contribution, It's OK.' That was my sole contribution to the meeting. Afterwards I was driven back to Northolt, flown back to Paris and rejoined everyone halfway through dinner. Just another day at the office!

Although I had had some experience with army programmes and, to a lesser extent, with aircraft systems, through my work at United Scientific, however I'd had virtually no exposure to the naval side of things. Early on in my tenure, I was invited to the French naval equipment exhibition at Le Bourget, which I attended with my Military Assistant [MA], Rob Walmsley (later Vice-Admiral Sir Robert Walmsley and CDP from 1996 to 2003). I saw a piece of equipment there called a towed array, which is a long cable that is pulled along behind a frigate to help to locate enemy submarines. I knew we had a similar system in the UK, so I asked Rob what the difference was between them. 'Not a lot,' he replied. Having realised how much it had cost to develop ours, I approached my French opposite number, a very congenial nuclear scientist by the name of

Jacques Chevallier, and said to him: 'Look, we spend a fortune developing something like towed arrays, in a fairly specialised area. You may buy eight, we might buy fifteen, but if we pooled our procurement, we'd both save a lot of money.'

When I embarked on trying to sell this idea to my colleagues in the Ministry, I realised that, at that time, even to suggest having any kind of joint programme with the French was regarded virtually as high treason. It would probably have been easier to do something with the Russians. There was a lot of suspicion about the French, particularly when it came to aircraft. Nevertheless, with my colleague Jacques Chevallier, and the ready agreement of the two Defence Ministers, George Younger and Andre Giraud, we started what we called the Reciprocal Procurements Programme. The idea was that we would both show each other what we were making, and then we'd work out which was the preferred product. Then, in an ideal world, they'd buy all their requirement from us for certain items, and *vice versa*.

This began in 1987 with a series of Anglo-French procurement conferences. The first two-day event, on army equipment, took place in September at Lancaster House in London, with a formal dinner at Hampton Court Palace. Two hundred delegates explored the scope for 'reciprocal purchases of equipment developed or produced in one country which could meet the needs of the other.'[1] Three or four products were immediately identified, including a piece of British equipment that was already in service. When the French produced a picture of what they were planning to have for their army, it proved to be almost identical.[2]

The following conference, in March 1988, tackled naval equipment, and took place in France, and a third was convened in November, on aircraft systems, back in London. The French event included a formal, black-tie dinner at the Musée National de la Marine in Paris, just opposite the Eiffel Tower. It was hosted by the French Minister of Defence. As we arrived, we were all given a little leaflet on the history of the French Navy. I was fascinated, because I wanted to see what it

1   Lynton McLain, 'Talks to extend arms equipment link with France,' *Financial Times*, 11 September, 1987.
2   Michael Evans, 'Arms 'common market' growing nearer,' *The Times*, Saturday, September 19, 1987.

had to say about events in 1805. And, sure enough, there it was: *La Bataille de Trafalgar: pendant laquelle l'Amiral Nelson est tué.* That's all it said! So, when we sat down to dinner, and I found myself sitting next to the French Defence Minister, I said: 'Look at this.' And he said: *'Mais c'est vrai, n'est-ce pas?'*

Anyway, we moved forwards in fits and starts, with the three Armed Services, but there was a problem. Eventually, my French counterpart said to me: 'Look, we've entered into the spirit of things and we've placed a few small orders with UK suppliers for our requirements, but there's virtually no reciprocity on your side.' When I looked into this, I discovered that, because we now had a competitive procurement regime and were no longer in the habit of just placing contracts with national champions, our industry had become very competitive. So when we went to seek bids for our requirements in France, their prices didn't look very attractive. They, on the other hand, were less competitive and worked on the basis of directed procurement. When I explained this to Jacques Chevallier, he said: 'Well, can't you just sort of push something in our direction?' I had to say: 'I'm sorry, I can't do that.' After I had left, it didn't move forward very much. It was also hampered from the start by the Department of Trade and Industry, who opposed it in favour of orders for British firms.

* * *

While I was CDP, one of the main programmes I was responsible for was Trident, which involved both the submarines and their missiles. At that time, the main base for these vessels on the east coast of the United States was just being built at a place called Kings Bay in Georgia, about forty miles from our home in Sea Island. When Dick Rumpf, who was then Assistant Secretary of the Navy in Washington, asked if I would like to visit this base, we invited him and his wife to stay with us for the weekend, and then drove down to see it. It was massive, the largest civil engineering project in the United States, and of course one of the most protected sites in the world. With all the nuclear missiles, there was enough ordnance there to wipe out the world about twenty times over. When we arrived, we were met by a young naval officer who said: 'Good morning, I'm here to show you round, and I'm going to take you to meet the commanding officer of the base, who has actually just come back from your submarine base in Scotland.' 'Fine,' I replied, 'I look forward to meeting him.' 'Well,' said the officer, 'just before you meet him, I think I should warn you, he has a rather unusual pet, it's a ten-foot python.' 'That's nice,' I said, 'does he take it out for walks?' 'Oh yes,' was the reply, 'he goes about with it wound around his neck.' So off we went to meet this officer, who fortunately didn't have the python with him, but I asked him about it. 'Well,' he said, 'I've just been in Scotland, so I had to leave it in the terrarium; but I threw in a few live rats before I left, which would have kept it happy and fed until I got back.' 'How wonderful,' I said, and in an attempt to make polite conversation, went on: 'Tell me, is it a girl python or a boy python?' 'It's a girl python,' he replied, 'and her name is Bernice.' When we left, I said to Dick Rumpf: 'I've got to tell you something. If we had a large naval base with enough munitions to destroy the whole world several times over, and it was being run by an officer who goes out with a python round his neck called Bernice, I would be a little bit worried.'

On a more serious note, while we were there, I asked Dick how quickly re-loaded submarines were able to submerge from this new base. When he explained that it took a long time because Kings Bay is located on one of the shallowest parts of the North American continental shelf, I asked why they had decided to build there. 'Well, that's simple,' he replied, 'it's in Georgia; when the navy decided to take over Kings Bay as a submarine base in the 1970s, Sam Nunn, who was a senator for the state, was also chairman of the Armed Services Committee.' Another example of politics and common sense make for uneasy bedfellows.

* * *

From 1988 to 1991, in addition to being CDP, I also held the post of UK National Armaments Director. Every country, particularly those in NATO, makes a similar appointment, and all us were responsible for defence procurement. We used to get together twice a year in Brussels, at the Conference of National Armaments Directors, always known as CNAD. Like all organisations in Brussels, although this was run under the auspices of NATO rather than the EU, it was enormous. At that time, I think there were sixteen NATO countries involved, all of whom sent their own delegations and they also had a large number of permanent staff based at the NATO headquarters in Brussels. We discussed collaborative projects, amongst other things.

I served as the chairman of the European National Armaments Directors from 1989 to 1990. CNAD would set up sub-groups on everything, from torpedoes to missiles, and from army rations to post traumatic stress disorder. One day Lord Carrington, who was then Secretary General of NATO, called me in and said: 'Look, do you know how many sub-groups CNAD has? You are responsible for 380 sub-groups. They meet all the time and produce reports at enormous cost, while travelling round and round Europe. This is what we call NATO-tourism. Up with this, I will not put. [Paraphrasing Winston Churchill.] You've got to do something about it.' When I asked him what he wanted me to do, he replied: 'You've got to reduce them immediately. I will give you one year, but I want them cut by half.' I summoned all the other European National Armaments Directors and said to them: 'Look, this is no good, the Secretary General says we're wasting time and money, and we've got to get rid of half the sub-groups.' I was then told that if we got rid of the group that discussed what happens if you eat too many cauliflowers for lunch before a battle, it would be the end of civilisation as we know it. I retorted: 'Right, you've got three months to produce a list.' Of course, nothing happened, so I then said: 'Fine, I'll tell you what we're going to do. I've got a list of these sub-groups in alphabetical order, and I'm now going to delete every second group.' So that's what we did, although given time nearly all of them crept back again.

I also found myself chairman of a body called the Independent European Programme Group, known as IEPG, which has since disappeared. We wanted to establish a permanent headquarters for this organisation. The Italians had hosted its initial *ad hoc* meetings in Rome, and were angling to formally establish it there, which caused the usual international row. I think the French and the Germans also wanted to take it on, although nobody else did. As a consequence of all this, we ended up in Lisbon, which is a very nice city but semi-detached from the rest of Europe, so the communications there were somewhat lacking.

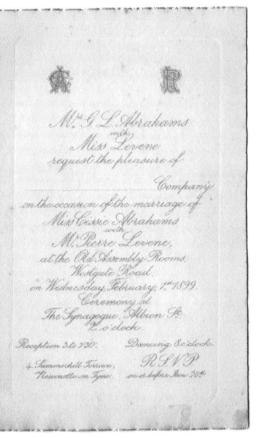

2. Levene family, 1909. *Left to right* Aunt Frances, my Grandmother Cissie Levene, my great Grandmother, my Grandfather Pierre Levene, and my father aged 8.

1. Invitation to wedding of my grandparents Cissie and Pierre, Newcastle, February 1899.

3. Report from the *Illustrated London News* of the wedding.

4. The first British troops pass through Cologne, where my father was serving, 1919.

5. Practising sprint starts at the Firs Athletic Ground, Fallowfield, University of Manchester, 1961.

6. In 1966, after four years of courtship, Wendy Fraiman and I marry. She was 19 and I was 24.

7. Receiving the Queen's Award for Industry at the Avimo factory in Taunton, 1978. *Left to right* self, Norman Ikin (Avimo Commercial Director), General Sir Noel Thomas (MGO), Roy Mountain (Avimo MD).

8. Disembarking from a test flight in EH101 helicopter, 1989. *Left to right* Sir Donald Spiers, helicopter pilot, self.

9. Four National Armaments Directors relaxing after a tough morning's meeting at Juan les Pins, 1989. *Left to right* Yves Sillard, John Betti, self, Wolfgang Ruppelt. Note the heavy protection floating behind us.

10. Signing the contract for the European Fighter Aircraft (Typhoon). *Left to right* self, George Younger, Air Chief Marshal Sir David Harcourt-Smith, Karl Schnell, Manfred Worner, German ADC, General Luigi Stefani, Italian Defence Minister, Italian ADC.

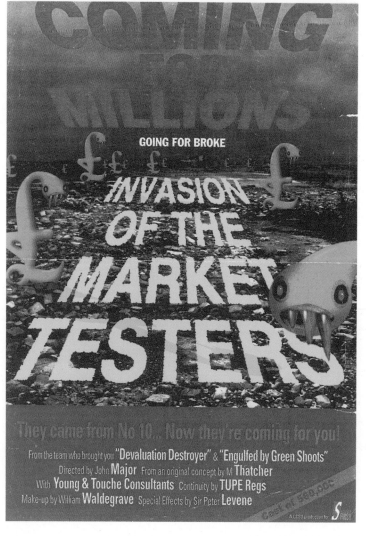

11. As the PM's Adviser on Efficiency, I am portrayed on a union poster as one of the villains behind Market Testing. As it turned out the poster actually gave our programme a huge boost!

12. I visit Israel's Prime Minister Yitzhak Rabin to discuss defence industry modernisation in 1993.

13. Meeting with the President of Lebanon, 1999.
Left to right Lord Hurd, President Émile Lahoud, self.

14. Meeting with Yasser Arafat in Gaza, 1998.

15. Wendy and I host a Mansion House lunch for the new King and Queen of Jordan, 1999.

16. In the Lebanon with Walid Jumblatt, leader of the Druze, in his castle admiring the painting of Russian Marshal Zhukov in 1945, trampling on Nazi banners in Berlin.

17. With former Spitfire pilot President Ezer Weizman of Israel.

All these organisations were known by their initials, as incidentally were all my colleagues. As a Civil Servant I quickly discovered that I didn't have a name anymore. I had become CDP. Although I initially thought this was a bit odd, eventually I found it was quite convenient, because it didn't matter if the CDS [Chief of the Defence Staff] or the PUS [Permanent Under-Secretary] changed. You didn't have to know their names, you just said you wanted to speak to the initials, whoever that might be. Even Wendy used to say, in the evenings, 'Hello, CDP's home.'

*   *   *

Of course, as CDP, I inevitably came under the scrutiny of numerous journalists. Some were better than others. One of our largest contractors had a department which was engaged on attacking me by endeavouring to plant all sorts of stories in the newspapers. I remember one day, when I'd read some particularly offensive article, I marched into Michael Heseltine's office and said: 'This is now too much. Read this article, it's disgraceful.' He had a look at it, and he said: 'Yes. Now, I'm going to tell you exactly what we're going to do.' He then took the article, screwed it up, and threw it in the wastepaper basket. And then he went on: 'All you need to remember is that today's newspaper is tomorrow's fish-and-chip wrapper. I suggest you do remember that, go back to your office, and get on with your job.' And that is exactly what I did. It was very good advice and I've often passed it on to other people.

Having said that, there were times when I was compelled to speak out if I felt I or others had been seriously misrepresented, as in the case of my letter to the *Sunday Telegraph*, which was published in that paper on 22 November 1987:

I am writing in connection with the article which appeared on the front page of *The Sunday Telegraph* dated November 15, headed 'Marconi Raid Plea by Prior angers MoD'. The article in question contains a number of statements which are entirely untrue.

You state that Lord Weinstock has had a series of meetings with Defence Ministers and officials, in which he expressed his anger and concern about the damage being done to GEC's image by allegations currently being investigated by the police on the instructions of the Director of Public Prosecutions. Since the start of this investigation, no meeting has been held on this subject between Lord Weinstock and Ministers or officials for some months, although he and I keep closely in touch on a whole range of issues as a matter of course.

You go on to describe relations between Lord Weinstock and myself as 'very poor.' This is untrue. On the contrary, relations between Lord Weinstock and me are very good, and perhaps an illustration of this is the fact that only two weeks ago I performed the public opening ceremony of a new GEC facility at their factory in Rochester, at which time I paid tribute to the excellent work being done there. The statement in question is as untrue as the following one which you saw fit to print, that 'they are at each other's throats.'

The Procurement Executive of the Ministry of Defence is managed on the basis of obtaining the best possible equipment for HM Forces on the most favourable terms possible. This requires a properly commercial relationship between the MOD as a customer and industry as suppliers. It is an approach which is well understood by industry in general and by the GEC Group in particular which is the largest single supplier to the MOD. Such a relationship, however, does not require personal animosity of the kind alleged in your article.'[1]

*   *   *

In my early days, I had introduced what I called the 'Levene law,' which meant that every potential contract was sent back to the negotiating table three or four times. By 1988 this had produced several cases where tender prices had mysteriously dropped by up to 30 per cent in the bidding rounds and 70 per cent in one case. In another, the initial £80 million quotation for the UKAIR CCIS command-and-control system for the RAF ended up, after hard bargaining, as a £37 million contract.

In January of that year, at the Public Accounts Committee meeting, I also argued for severe penalties to be introduced for contractors

1   Peter Levene, 'Marconi raid and report and the Ministry,' *Sunday Telegraph*, November 22, 1987.

who deliberately overcharged, saying: 'At present they merely have to refund. In essence it means we are fair game. If they take us on and we don't find out, it means that they keep the money. The penalty should be so great that they won't even bother to try.'[2] But in spite of the good news, the cost-plus contracts continued to haunt me. In March 1988, the Public Accounts Committee raised the issue that, according to the Government's recent efficiency report, *Learning from Experience*, which had actually been compiled in 1987, about £4 billion of each year's military procurement budget might still be associated with overruns on 'costs which were not foreseen when projects started' or with additional expenses when they 'entered full development.'

I insisted that the 'villain of the piece' was the old-style cost-plus contracts, some of which were still working their way through the system.[3] I also pointed out that these figures were misleading and inaccurate. As there was only about £6 billion of my annual procurement budget left, after purchases of spare parts, if the MOD was really overspending by £4 billion, we would hardly have been in a position to buy anything at all.[4] Furthermore, on recent contracts over the last two years, we were able to show that £1.4 billion had been saved by opening the bids to competition: on one equipment order alone an initial budget of £73 million had been reduced to a cost of £21 million; and two other cases with similar initial estimates had actually come in at £25 million.[5] At last, in May 1988, I could see that my message was finally getting through, as reported in an article in *The Guardian*:

> After rigorous acceptance trials which would have short-circuited the guidance systems of a less robust model, Peter Levene, the Chief of Defence Procurement, yesterday emerged dripping with praise from his erstwhile critics after the publication of the defence estimates White Paper. The Labour MP, Mr. Dale Campbell-Savours, whose guns are

2   Roland Gribben, 'Top Gun at the MoD,' *Daily Telegraph*, January 4, 1988; and Mark Hewish, 'UK defense procurement: the way ahead,' International *Defense Review*, No.2, 1988.

3   Martin Fletcher, 'MPs angry at £4bn defence budget overrun,' *The Times*, March 10, 1988.

4   David White, 'Defence waste of £4bn denied,' *Financial Times*, April 20, 1988.

5   David Hencke, 'Purged MoD underspent by £800m.' *Guardian*, Monday, May 9, 1988.

calibrated to the Ministry of Defence, said: 'He's good news. He's shaken up the organisation and given a good kick in the pants to a number of contractors who have been having it too good over the years …

Members of the Commons Public Accounts Committee who came to bury him were disarmed by his candour and determination to cut through MoD bureaucracy.

Here was this small, dynamic poacher-turned-gamekeeper who knew how defence companies operated and had none of the taciturn arrogance of the mandarins they were used to questioning,' said a close observer.'[1]

Of the many other politicians who served at the same time as me in the MOD, two who particularly come to mind are Tim Sainsbury and Alan Clark. Tim Sainsbury, a member of the Sainsbury family, was someone with whom I could work easily because he had a very strong commercial background. On one memorable occasion, soon after he joined the MOD, Tim invited Wendy and me to a dinner party at his home and he said to Wendy: 'I am sitting you next to a very up and coming politician who you will probably have never heard of but, in my view, before very long will be Prime Minister'. This was none other than John Major. On our way home that evening, Wendy said to me: 'You know what Tim said to me – I am sure he is right.'

Alan Clark joined us at the Ministry in July 1989, as Minister for Defence Procurement. Six months later, he recorded in his diary:

> I am getting on well with the civil servants. They are clever, of high calibre, most of them and not irredeemably set in their ways. And I am lucky that the Permanent Secretary, immediately answerable to me, Peter Levene, is thoroughly congenial. A quick mind and – so important – a sense of humour.[2]

I got on very well with Alan. He was eccentric and very clever, but you had to keep him under control. By this time Tom King had succeeded George Younger as Secretary of State for Defence. He and

1 Stuart Wavell, 'Gunning for the MoD's old guard,' *Guardian*, Wednesday, May 18, 1988.
2 Alan Clark, *Diaries*, (Weidenfeld & Nicolson, London, 1993), p.263.

Alan did not get on, and Alan used to plot to get round him. I often found myself in the middle of all this. 'Peter, I've had the most fantastic idea,' he would say, 'this is what we're going to do.' 'No, Alan,' I would reply, 'you can't do that.' 'Why not?' 'Because I would have to sign it off,' I said, 'and I'm not going to.' In fact, although he said that I was answerable to him, I was not. I was only answerable to the Secretary of State.

Wendy and I once went to stay with him at Saltwood Castle, where he kept his two Rottweilers, Hannah and Leni. Michael Howard and his wife were guests at the same time. In the evening, Wendy and all the other ladies ended up helping with the washing-up. Alan also refused to eat meat from any animal that had been slaughtered in an abattoir; everything had to have been hunted and killed. At the MOD we did a lot of entertaining. On one occasion, Alan hosted a dinner for the Norwegian defence minister at Admiralty House. When we sat down to eat, I discovered that Alan had chosen hare for the menu. I was sitting next to the guest of honour, who looked appalled when I told him what it was. 'Might I guess that you don't really like it?' I asked. When he agreed with me, I assured him that I would make sure we were served something else and happily ended up with some cold roast beef.

During the whole of my time at MOD, Margaret Thatcher had been Prime Minister and her rule was absolute. When programmes in which I was involved were referred to the Cabinet, I would receive the record of the Cabinet discussion. It had a familiar format – Ministers would discuss it one by one, until it came to the Prime Minister who would express her view either in favour or against and that would conclude the discussion. It was a somewhat rude awakening when, shortly after John Major took over, I saw another record, following the usual pattern, the Prime Minister expressed his view, but then . . . there was a further intervention by a Minister who disagreed! The world had surely changed!

From the first days, I had realised what extraordinary control Margaret Thatcher had exercised over the affairs of the nation with a remarkable record of success. But towards the end of her Premiership, it started to become clear that her firm grip and judgement was rapidly failing. One of her greatest supporters throughout had been Alan Clark, whom I saw daily. He could see no wrong in Margaret Thatcher and firmly believed that she would triumph in the leadership contest and continue as PM. He told me that he had just staked a large bet on her success, and that it would be the easiest money he would ever make. How wrong he was.

The British Empire Medal was awarded to salt-of-the-earth people like drivers and cleaners. It is rarely presented by the Monarch in person, but is more normally handed out by the Lord Lieutenant of the relevant county or local authority. When we had about ten recipients of this honour in the MOD, the task of handing out these medals fell to Alan as a minister. But he didn't just read out the citation he had been given. He made a personal address to these ten people. 'I want you to know,' he said, 'the work you do is amazing, and without you the Ministry of Defence would not be able to function. We owe you an enormous debt of gratitude.' Alan could be terribly cynical about some things, but he took that event very seriously. He did the most phenomenal job with those people; he made them feel ten feet tall, and I've never forgotten that.

*   *   *

When I joined the MOD I was a total outsider, having been appointed against all the rules, and was effectively Michael Heseltine's person. So as soon as he resigned in January 1986, I became very exposed, although actually this did not become a problem. Years later, I said to my colleagues, who by then had become pretty good friends of mine: 'Look, you saw this kid come in and start telling you all what to do. Why didn't you just chew me up and spit me out?' And they replied: 'Well, the Department and procurement was in a hell of a mess. We had no idea what to do, so we said: 'We don't know if this guy can help or not, but we might as well give him a chance. If he does OK, fine; and if not, then we'll get rid of him.' And that is what happened. It was an amazing experience, for a relatively young man running a medium-sized business, suddenly to be yanked out of his company and put into this position of enormous authority. I also found myself working with extremely senior people, whom I got to know very well, and who ended up as close friends; and I discovered that, in spite of my earlier perceptions, Civil Servants and Military Staff actually work very hard indeed, and many responded very well to the leadership that I tried to give.

Several examples of this spring to mind. On one occasion, we needed legal advice on various contractual issues, but what we were served up with proved to be quite inadequate. It seemed that we would have to employ a professional City firm. Then the youngish number two or three in the Treasury Solicitor's Department came to me and asked for the chance to show what he could do. If he failed, we would resort to the City. I gave him his chance, he got new staff on the job, trained them, gave them some quick experience, and then said to them: 'This is our chance to show CDP that we can provide the service he needs.' They succeeded, and after that we got much better legal advice.

On another occasion, while visiting an Army unit, I was introduced to a soldier, who had discovered the exorbitant cost of a spare part that he handled, and drew this to my attention. As a result, I introduced a scheme to show the costs of all spare parts and components, in order to encourage those who handled them to reveal these excess costs and thereby help to save money. In spite of the obvious merits of tapping into the knowledge and experience of those at the sharp end, who were keen on the idea, it was opposed by many in the MOD hierarchy and the companies they dealt with, who did not want excess costs revealed, thereby exposing their costing failures and the profits being made. All kinds of 'technical' problems about the scheme were invented, and, after I left, it too gradually died a death.

Writing in 1989, the historian Peter Hennessy summed up his perception of my role:

> His experience was rich, his drive singular and his aptitude for the pursuit of value for money remarkable. Once in the job his zest for competitive tendering won reluctant plaudits from defence contractors whose profit margins and delivery dates had suffered at his hands. Mr Levene's patron, Mr Heseltine, went so far as to claim in his political testament, published in the spring of 1987, that he 'will have saved, by now, hundreds of millions of pounds for the Defence budget. If he has saved 8 per cent of the equipment programme – and he has said that he expects to save 10 per cent – he will have paid for the Trident programme single-handed.'[1]

1   Peter Hennessy, *Whitehall*, (Secker & Warburg, London, 1989), p.372.

As CDP, my responsibility was for Vote 2 of the Defence Budget – that is the Equipment Vote, but that did not usually include expenditure on buildings or construction. However, there was one occasion when I was asked to intervene, and that was in respect of the Defence Crisis Management Centre known as 'Pindar'. This was being built deep underneath the MOD, indeed in the very building in which I worked. As with most MOD building projects, it was being managed by the PSA – the Property Services Agency – which was responsible for building and managing the majority of the Government's real estate.

Pindar was running very, very late and so, unusually I was asked to try to sort it out. When I looked into it, I found that there were many different contractors working on it, but the prime contractor seemed to have let it get out of control and there were totally inadequate and badly managed resources on site. After a huge row with the PSA and the prime contractor – Balfour Beatty – they agreed to mend their ways, and to ensure that, from that moment on, there would be literally hundreds of workers onsite to get the project finished.

Mission accomplished therefore? Not quite. Two weeks later I said to my Private Secretary Stephen French, that we should go down to the basement and see how the hundreds of workers were getting on. But Stephen said, 'Well they won't be expecting us, so do you think that is a good idea?', to which I replied 'That is precisely why I want to go now.'

We went down to the basement, tramped around the whole of the enormous site, and encountered in total no more than a dozen workers! There followed an even bigger row with the PSA and Balfour Beatty which in turn engulfed a number of their subsidiaries, but finally the project got going.

However, this was not my last encounter with the PSA. When Michael Heseltine returned as Secretary of State for the Environment, he said to me that he wanted me to help in finally resolving the many problems which had surrounded the PSA, and we succeeded in privatising part of it and eventually closing down the rest – none too soon.

I was initially supposed to do the job as CDP for four years, but ended up doing six. By that time, the Secretary of State for Defence was Tom King,[1] and in 1991 I told him that I thought I ought to leave at the end of that year. He replied that I was doing a good job and he wanted me to stay on. I said: 'Look, when I first came here, I was the only outsider and the most junior member of the Defence Council. Everybody else was a General, an Admiral, an Air Marshal, or a Minister. I didn't know about anything, let alone the things you were supposed to know about, and because of that, I was able to turn the whole place upside-down. Now, I'm the longest-serving member of the Defence Council, longer than any senior officer, and I know the book inside-out and back-to-front. Furthermore, I've trained quite a few of my younger staff to question everything. As a result, they now come to me and say: 'Look, this isn't right, we should be doing it in a different way.' To which, I find myself replying: 'You can't do that, this is the way you *have* to do it.' I realise that I've gone over to the other side, and I'm therefore no good to you anymore. You need somebody who is going to question everything.' So that was when I left, after six years. It had been a great job, but I'd done it for long enough.

On one of my trips abroad, I'd got to know my Australian opposite number, Dr. Malcolm McIntosh,[2] with whom I got on extremely well. When the MOD was searching for my successor, I suggested that Malcolm might be a good choice. This met with a certain amount of incredulity among my colleagues, who said: 'You do realise there's a lot of very sensitive information involved, which you are privy to?' I replied: 'Well, that may be, but if you think about it, The Queen's Private Secretary, Sir William Heseltine,[3] is Australian, so why not?' Anyway, after a certain amount of to-ing and fro-ing, Malcolm was indeed appointed as my successor and did a brilliant job. There was a question about where he would live, because coming to London from scratch was going to be very expensive, but in the end they put him in one of the beautiful houses at the Royal Naval College in Greenwich. He was instrumental in carrying forward a move that I had wanted to make, which was to

1   Tom King, Baron King of Bridgwater (b.1933), Secretary of State for Defence, 24 July 1989 to 11 April 1992.
2   Sir Malcolm McIntosh AC (1945–2000), UK Chief of Defence Procurement, 1991–96.
3   Sir William Heseltine, GCB, GCVO, AC (b.1930), Private Secretary to the Sovereign, 1986–90

put all the procurement under one roof. He found a site in Bristol and had an excellent building constructed, part of which is named after him, which is very appropriate because he was later diagnosed with cancer and died in 2000, at the age of 54. Early in his career in Australia, he'd worked in nuclear laboratories, and I suspect he picked up a dose of radiation at some point. He was a really great man, and I'm glad that he was awarded a Knighthood in 1996, when he left the MOD.

* * *

During my time as the CDP, we did a lot of business with GEC and its managing director, Arnold Weinstock. It was a phenomenal company with a renowned cash mountain. I knew that they had been charging very high prices to the British government for years, and when it became my job to stop that, Arnold initially tried very hard to stop me. However, our relationship improved over the years, and GEC became rather more forthcoming in giving us a good deal. After I had left the MOD, Arnold called and asked me to go and see him. When I arrived, he said: 'Look, our defence business is not being run the way I would like, so I want you to take over and start running that side of things here.' I replied: 'Well, Arnold, that is an amazing offer, and if it was up to me, I'd obviously say yes. But you know I'll never be allowed to do that.' I was, of course, bound by rules that imposed a two-year cooling-off period, during which time I could not be involved with defence manufacturers supplying the British government.

Arnold waived this aside. 'Look, don't worry about that,' he said, 'GEC is very important to the UK economy. I'll talk to the Permanent Secretary and the Prime Minister. I know that you're the right person to run our defence business, and I think that in the national interest they may let you do it.' He did go to see Robin Butler, who was then Cabinet Secretary, who in turn spoke to John Major, although he was adamant that it was not something they could agree to under any circumstances. However, within three or four days of my conversation with Arnold, I received an unexpected visit from Jim Prior,[1] who was

1   James Prior, Baron Prior (1927–2016); Conservative MP, 1959–87, when he became a life peer; chairman of GEC, 1984–98.

the chairman of GEC. His message was blunt: 'I know Arnold has asked you to come and run our defence business, but I just want to tell you, the deal is off and we have no interest in you doing the job.' When I asked him why, he replied: 'I'm sorry, we just don't think it's the right thing to do.' Then he turned and walked out.

Within a few years, GEC had been destroyed. Arnold Weinstock was forced to resign as managing director in September 1996, and was replaced by George Simpson, who embarked on a number of high-tech mergers and acquisitions. He and his colleague John Mayo pushed Arnold into a tiny office, and proceeded to sell the defence manufacturing businesses and spend his huge cash mountain on a series of overvalued information technology companies. I remember going to see him and being very upset by what I saw and saying to Wendy: 'This is like *King Lear*, they've shoved him into a cupboard.' When I asked him why he had allowed this to happen, he said: 'I had no choice.' His only son Simon, whom he had once hoped would succeed him at GEC, had died of cancer aged forty-four, just months before his forced resignation. By 2002, when Arnold died, shares that had been worth £12.50 at GEC's peak had fallen to four pence, and his own stake in the business, once worth £480 million, had been reduced to £2 million.[2] It was a Shakespearian tragedy that should never have happened. I knew that business and I know I could have continued its success if I had been allowed to run the military side of GEC.

*   *   *

Ironically, GEC had benefitted many years earlier from the demise of Ferranti, another electrical engineering company that supplied the MOD. The defence industry is an important one, but there are not that many large players in it, which means that everyone knows everybody else. I was therefore astonished when Derek Alun-Jones, the managing director of Ferranti, came to see me in 1987, when I was still CDP, and announced: 'Peter, I thought you'd like to know, we've done a great deal. We're merging the whole of Ferranti in a joint venture with a company called International Signal & Control.' 'What?' I exclaimed,

2 'Obituary: Lord Weinstock,' *Daily Telegraph*, 24 July 2002.

'Derek, do you know anything about that business?' He assured me that it was making lots of money. 'That wasn't my question,' I replied, 'Do you know where they're making their money?' International Signal & Control [ISC], of Lancaster, Pennsylvania, was run by a man called James Guerin. He had appeared out of nowhere and claimed to be making a fortune selling night-vision equipment and laser range image intensifiers, which was exactly the business I had been involved with at United Scientific. I found all this very odd, because nobody that I knew in the industry had ever heard of ISC, and none of the existing suppliers had ever lost any of the contracts that Guerin claimed to have won. I advised Derek to look at it all very carefully.

As Ferranti was also a strategically important business in the UK, and one that did a great deal of business with the MOD, I decided that if they were going to sell out to people we really didn't know anything about, we too needed to do some digging. Eventually we discovered that ISC claimed to have an enormous contract in Pakistan. Derek Alun-Jones flew to Islamabad, to meet ISC's military contacts and discuss this contract. They flew out and were ushered into the presence of a man they thought was a Pakistani general. When they asked for more information, he explained that they were asking about Pakistani national defence, and there was not much that he could or would be allowed to tell them about. However, he went on, 'I can tell you that this is one of the biggest contracts we've ever negotiated. It's vital for our country. But if you want us to put anything in writing, we will refuse, because it's top secret.' In September 1987, Ferranti went ahead with its merger.

By this time, I was very suspicious, and had told Clive Whitmore, the Permanent Secretary at the MOD, that I had grave doubts about it all. We agreed that we should call Derek in and tell him that we thought he was being conned. 'How dare you?' he exclaimed, 'these people are my partners. This is outrageous, we'll sue you. How can you say such a thing?' About three weeks later, he came back to see me again, and said: 'You know what you said the other day? Can you tell me anything more?' When I asked him why he wanted to know, he replied: 'Well, we're a little bit concerned.'

It turned out that phantom contracts in Pakistan and elsewhere had been invented to inflate ISC's value at the time of the merger.

Guerin was eventually tried and sentenced to fifteen years in jail. But in September 1989 Ferranti had to write-off £215 million as a result of the fraud, and in January the following year it was forced to sell its defence business to GEC. Derek resigned shortly afterwards, and Ferranti finally went into receivership in 1993.[1]

*   *   *

In those days there were various perks to being a Permanent Secretary. On one occasion, I walked into my office and found a quarter of a deer wrapped in cloth on my desk. Every year they culled the herd in Richmond Park, chopped up the carcases and distributed them to Permanent Secretaries in the Civil Service. There were also more significant honours. Senior Ministry officials – or their wives, if they were a man – were sometimes invited to launch one of Her Majesty's new ships. In 1989 Wendy was asked to launch HMS *Argyll*, one of the new Type 23 frigates. We flew up to the Yarrow shipyard in Glasgow with George Younger, then Secretary of State for Defence. I recall him saying to me: 'Peter, just you remember, today you are Denis [Thatcher]; so you walk five steps behind your wife, rather than the other way round.'

It was a huge event and an amazing experience. The ship had been built inside a great hanger and had to be launched down a slope on rollers. Wendy said: 'I name this ship *Argyll*. May God bless her, and all who sail in her.' Robert Easton, who ran the shipyard, had told her to hit a plunger, a bottle of champagne would then shoot across and smash on the hull, and she was then to give the ship a push. Of course, he had about 100 men down below who were actually launching the frigate. As the ship went down the ramp, the noise was indescribable because they have to weight down the hull with a huge attachment of old chains, to stop it scooting off across the River Clyde and hitting the opposite bank. There were lots of hymns and much singing. It was an incredibly emotional occasion, not least because all the dockyard workers there had been working on the ship for about two years.

Two years later in 1991, when HMS *Argyll* had been fitted out and

1   'Obituary: Sir Derek Alun-Jones,' *Daily Telegraph*, 7 February 2008.

fully equipped, she was formally commissioned at Devonport. Once you have launched a ship, you become her sponsor for the life of the vessel, so Wendy was of course invited to this event. The Royal Navy were very attentive to our Judaism, and as there was to be a short religious service at the commissioning, they told her they thought they should invite a rabbi. I got in touch with Malcolm Weisman, who was, at the time, the Senior Jewish Chaplain to HM Armed Forces, and told him what was happening. When he asked me what he was expected to do at such an event, I referred back to the Royal Navy for advice. They replied: 'Oh, that's easy. Just tell him to perform the usual Jewish prayers for the launch of a frigate.' 'Yes, of course,' I said, 'how silly of me to ask!'

Many of those Type 23 frigates have now been taken out of service but HMS *Argyll* has survived. In fact, she went into Devonport for her latest re-fit in 2015 and returned to sea in 2017 with a new principal weapons system called Sea Ceptor. As her sponsor, Wendy is usually invited to visit the ship once a year. They get her all dressed up like the Michelin man, fly her out to sea in a helicopter, and on one occasion they put her up for the night, the First Officer having, very gallantly, given up his own cabin. She takes gifts for the seamen and the captains write regularly to her. Following on from of all this, Wendy decided to apply for the Livery of the Worshipful Company of Shipwrights. Interestingly, because we have no naval connections in the family at all, her great nephew has just joined the Royal Navy. He went to Britannia Royal Naval College at Dartmouth, graduated, and is now at sea as a trainee weapons officer.

CHAPTER SIX

Adviser to the Prime Minister

W HEN I LEFT the MOD in 1991, after six years as CDP, I wasn't sure what I was going to do. Under government rules, I was debarred from going back into the defence industry for two years. So, in June of that year, I joined the American investment bank, Wasserstein Perella, as deputy chairman of their London office, at a time when the company was committing itself to developing its business in Europe.

In an interview with the *Sunday Times* in January 1991, shortly after my new job had been announced, I summed up my time as a civil servant: 'When I came to the Ministry of Defence, it was regarded as a soft touch. That is not the case now. It was absolutely necessary to try to go too far, to make sure we would go far enough. I was determined not to keep the industry in the manner to which it had become accustomed.'

I also went on to say that my greatest achievements there had come in the first eighteen months, when I had still been an outsider; and that as Wendy was now complaining that I had started to talk like a civil servant, it was definitely time to move on. In 1985, at the beginning of my time at the MOD, I had been described as 'a 43-year-old whizz-kid arms dealer'. Now, with my move into merchant banking, I was looking forward to the future: 'I shall be the old man at Wasserstein,' I told the *Sunday Times* journalist, 'but I shall enjoy being associated with the whizz-kids there; I understand the whizz-kid mentality.'[1]

By the time I left in March 1991, Michael Heseltine had re-joined the Cabinet as Secretary of State for the Environment. He immediately

1   Fiona Walsh, 'Levene sets sights on takeovers,' *Sunday Times*, 6 January 1991.

asked me to join his team of Special Policy Advisers, to help on commercial and financial matters, and in particular on the proposed privatisation of the Property Services Agency, which handled government real estate. It involved working in the department about two days a month and was unpaid.[1]

In November, I was sitting in my office at Wasserstein Perella when I had a call from Michael's Private Secretary. 'The Secretary of State has decided that he wants you to do something else for him,' he said. When I asked what it was he replied: 'Railways,' I responded by saying: 'If he thinks I'm going to run British Rail, he can forget it, because I'm not!' 'No,' said the Private Secretary, 'it's not British Rail, it's the chairmanship of the Docklands Light Railway [DLR].' I told him that I had never heard of the DLR, that I had quite a lot to do, and that I thought somebody else could be found to take this on. The response to this was: 'There's no point in saying that. The Prime Minister is going to announce your appointment at the Lord Mayor's Banquet on Monday. Have a nice day.'

In fact, the Docklands Light Railway [DLR] had been built between 1985 and 1987, over an initial eight miles with fifteen stations. The first phase of an extension to Bank had opened in July 1991, a further extension to Beckton was due to open in 1992, and an additional line to Lewisham was expected to be operational by 1996.[2] But there were serious problems. The trains didn't run on time and people found themselves abandoned on the station platforms. In fact, when The Queen came to open it in November 1987, even her train broke down; she was stuck inside it, and they couldn't get her out.

However, at that stage, I knew nothing about railways or Docklands, but I said to Michael Heseltine: 'Alright, if the Prime Minister tells me I've got to do this, then I will do it.' However, I also told him that I couldn't do it on my own, and that I wanted to take three people from the MOD, whom I had worked with before and knew to be really good. With the Prime Minister's backing, he agreed. The first was Major General Malcolm Hutchinson, who I appointed as

1   Michael Dynes, 'Docklands rail chief to work with Heseltine', *The Times*, 13 November 1991.
2   Michael Dynes, 'Docklands rail chief to work with Heseltine', *The Times*, 13 November 1991.

managing director. When I was at the MOD, he had run what I called the Red Team, which tried to pull any proposed procurement to pieces in order to see where the flaws were. Malcolm had spent his army career in the Royal Electrical and Mechanical Engineers [REME], and was President of the Institute of Electronics & Electrical Incorporated Engineers. I told him that I needed his help because I knew a lot of the problems on the DLR arose from the software, which meant that the signalling didn't operate as it should. He agreed to join me. What I didn't know at the time was that he was a great train buff, whose main interest and hobby was railways. I also recruited two other members of staff from the MOD: Stephen French became my new planning director, and Stephen Gibbs took on the projects organisation role. The team was completed with Anthony Jackson, who left his job as finance director at my old company, United Scientific, to take on the same role at the DLR.[3]

My appointment as chairman of the DLR coincided with the decision by Malcolm Rifkind, then Secretary of State for Transport, to strip London Transport of its powers to run the railway, and to transfer ownership and control to the London Docklands Development Corporation.[4] Within a week of Malcolm Hutchinson and his team taking over, Malcolm came to see me and said: 'I've found a solution for you, at least a short-term solution.' I replied: 'Great, what is it?' 'Well,' he said, 'the idea at the moment is to have trains running every three minutes, but they don't. They all get fouled up, and the whole system grinds to a halt every hour or so. But I have discovered that, if we said we could run the trains at six-minute intervals, there's no problem. So, if you were standing at the station waiting for a train, and it doesn't come after three minutes, you're not very pleased; but if you know it will definitely turn up every six minutes, that's fine.' When I asked him how quickly he could start this new system, he replied: 'As soon as you tell me to do it.' Within a few weeks, the DLR was fine, and it continues to work very successfully to this day and now has a new moving block signalling system allowing trains to run at three minute intervals or less.

3   Anon., 'Military precision for Docklands railway', *Financial Times*, 2 April 1992.
4   Michael Dynes, 'Docklands rail chief to work with Heseltine', *The Times*, 13 November 1991.

We also had to get to grips with contractors responsible for supplying track and trains, some of whom were performing extremely badly. The staff at the DLR said to me: 'We've written to them and asked them to do better, but they're just not responding.' My response to that was to say: 'Well, let's stop paying them then.' 'You can't do that,' they cried, 'they'll sue.' To which I replied: 'Let them.' In the end, some sharp words were exchanged, but the performance of those contractors changed overnight.[1]

Once we had succeeded in getting the initial stretches of the railway working properly, we turned our attention to the planned extension out to Beckton. The viaducts and tracks for this had already been built, but we still needed additional financing to get it up and running so we decided that we needed to engage Bechtel, the American engineering giant, to enable us to get the extension to work. By this time, Michael Howard had succeeded Michael Heseltine as Secretary of State for the Environment, and he declined our request for more money. In the end, I had to say: 'Look, do you realise that we've got all this elevated track and we've already bought all the extra trains which are sitting on it in full public view? If you refuse this final funding, we're going to have a ghost railway with trains going nowhere, forever. Is that what you really want?' After that, we got permission to go ahead, and the new extension opened in 1994.

Rather to my surprise, there was an unexpected perk to being the chairman of a railway. In the past, chairmen of railway companies, such as Great Western, had carried a gold fob on their watch chains, which entitled them to free first-class travel on everybody else's railway. By the 1990s the fobs had dropped out of use, but the travel privileges remained the same. Thus, I was told that – as chairman of DLR – I had now joined this special club. I decided to try this out. The most expensive tickets I could find were first-class returns with our car from Euston to Edinburgh. Wendy and I went up on the sleeper, which wasn't too bad, although I can never sleep on trains. We then spent a few days in Scotland and re-joined the train for the return trip to London, as planned and booked, at Inverness. The journey from Inverness to Edinburgh took twice as long as our leg from London to

1   Richard Tomkins, 'A fast track to efficiency', *Financial Times*, 12 March 1993.

Edinburgh; we were on that train for hours and hours, and I remember thinking that would teach me a lesson!

* * *

I served as chairman of the DLR from 1991 to 1994 and continued to work for Wasserstein Perella during the same period. In January 1992 I also acquired two part-time advisory roles to the government. The first was a seat on the panel of advisors appointed to implement the Citizen's Charter, which had been established by the Prime Minister, John Major, in order to guarantee citizens the right of redress on occasions where a public service failed to meet certain standards. The second was the chairmanship of the Treasury's Public Competition and Purchasing Unit, which aimed to extend the contracting-out of public services.[2]

Following the general election in April, which returned the Conservatives to power, John Major also appointed me as his Adviser on efficiency and effectiveness in May 1992. In this role, which I held from 1992 to 1997, I reported direct to the Prime Minister on the progress of securing substantial improvements in the management of public services following on from Lord Rayner, Sir Robin Ibbs and Sir Angus Fraser[3] As I was acting with the direct authority of the Prime Minister, with whom I got on very well and have great admiration for, I would periodically report back to him. After a while, I said: 'Look, Prime Minister, you've got far too much to do; I can't keep on coming back to tell you about all this stuff.' And he replied: 'I agree. If anyone wants to query anything, just tell them that you'll talk to the Prime Minister and get back to them. Then go back the next day, say you've spoken to me, and I've said it's OK.' 'But how will you know it is OK?' I asked. 'Because I trust you,' he said, 'and you had better not get it wrong.'

The remit for my new role was enormous and included the National Health Service, the Civil Service, and all nationalised industries. In an interview at the time, I explained my new task: 'I will be focusing

2 Anon., 'Council tendering adviser appointed', *Financial Times*, 11 January 1992.
3 Ivor Owen, 'Sir Peter Levene appointed to Major's personal staff', *Financial Times*, 16 April 1992.

on the efficiency of the running of government right across the board. They wanted someone who understood how both business and Whitehall works. Perhaps it's easier for someone who has spent several years running a government department as a Permanent Secretary to be able to do this. It's certainly a job that needs doing.'[1]

The task began by meeting the Secretary of State and Permanent Secretary of every government department, in order to look at what they were doing and to suggest how they might improve their performance by acting more commercially. This was a natural progression from my work as the chairman of the Competition and Purchasing Unit, and indeed my earlier role at the MOD, because it involved pursuing quality through competition. My message to each department was unequivocal: 'Whatever function you're carrying out, with the probable exception of policy, we want to be sure that you are competing this between the in-house team and potential outside suppliers. You will nominate who the in-house team is, they will then be cut off from the final assessment, and we will thereby have a competition between them and any outside suppliers who pitch for the work. We'll then see which one actually comes up with the best results.'

Initially, many of the government departments said that nobody would be interested in bidding for the work they undertook. And when I offered to organise a bidders' fair at the Queen Elizabeth II Conference Centre in Westminster, they thought nobody would turn up. In fact, this event was so successful that we had to lay on another two. That was the genesis of two of the most successful companies, Capita and Serco, which took on huge amounts of government business but who subsequently have experienced a very bumpy ride.

Unsurprisingly, the Civil Service Unions were dead set against the market-testing programme and produced a magnificent poster, as illustrated, but which had the opposite effect to that intended in that it encouraged far more companies to bid.

These 'efficiency scrutinies' were carried out by small groups, made up of two or three bright young people from within the relevant department, who were usually thought to be non-conformist, backed

1   Anon., 'Prime Minister calls on banker to advise government on efficiency', *Jewish Chronicle*, 24 April 1992.

up by a couple of members of my staff from the efficiency unit. They had tight timetables and were expected to produce their reports within ninety days. Fortunately, I had been able to recruit several extremely bright civil servants to help me, including Una O'Brien and Helen Ghosh, both of whom later went on to serve as Permanent Secretaries. I also asked for – and was given – John Oughton, whom I had first met when he was appointed as my Principal Staff Officer, when I became a Personal Adviser to the Defence Secretary, way back in 1984. John then took over as Head of the Efficiency Unit.

Susan Scholefield, who had worked as my Private Secretary in the MOD, was a very remarkable lady who, in addition to being an *énarque* and therefore spoke fluent French, was also a semi-finalist on Mastermind. In our many dealings with our French opposite numbers, Susan and I had been able to charm our French colleagues by conducting the meetings in French, which was a new experience for them and it made our negotiations a lot easier. I was given, within the Efficiency Unit, some outstanding secondees to join that very small group, who were a mixture of both civil servants and those on loan from the top ranks of industry, and I asked if Susan could join also the team, which she did, and was an invaluable member. I like to think that the Efficiency Unit played a key role in the development of some of our most senior and effective civil servants.

The object of the exercise was to save money right across the Civil Service. At the end of the first year, the results were as I had expected: about fifty per cent of the competitions were won by the outside supplier, and the remaining half by the in-house team. Then it became more interesting, because the savings on these vast contracts – whether won by the in-house team or an outside supplier – were in the region of twenty to thirty per cent. I said to all the Permanent Secretaries: 'This is a great achievement, but I have just one question. If you can save up to thirty per cent, with your own in-house team, what on earth have you been doing for the last few years?' The answer was unsurprising: 'Nobody has ever asked us to do such an exercise.'

I particularly remember my visit to the Home Office, with a team of five or six people. Ken Clarke was then Home Secretary and the Permanent Secretary was Clive Whitmore, who had been my original boss at the MOD. As soon as we got there, Ken Clarke said: 'Look, I know what the Prime Minister is doing with this programme and I'm right behind him. It's a great idea and just what we need. But you will of course understand that there's nothing we can do about it at the Home Office, because we don't have any functions which we could possibly compete.' This was exactly what I thought he was going to say, so I retorted by saying that I had a suggestion to make. When he asked me what it was, I explained: 'Actually it's the prisons. If you think about it, what do they do? Prisons need heating, lighting, buildings, maintenance, food, and security. What is the difference between that and running a hotel? Put basically, it's the standard of the food and the level of security, so we should be able to get private companies to run the prisons, and to do it rather more effectively than has been done up to now.' From that initial conversation we set up the first privately-run prisons, some of which are better than others. The privatisation of the prisoner collection and delivery service was less successful at first, because a number of the prisoners escaped, but – like all these things – you have to work on them to get it right in the end.

There was a similar example with passports, which were all prod-uced in-house. When I asked if we could contract that out, the civil servants said: 'How can you suggest such a thing? Passports are the ultimate test of somebody's nationality.' I did manage to get them to concede that we were already buying in paper to create passports, as well as printing and binding services. I suggested that we employ a specialist company to implant the security elements into new passports, in the same way that credit-card companies produce their products. I also argued that we could implant a number of staff from the passport agency, so that ninety-nine percent of the passports could be issued automatically, but there would be people there to deal with the odd query. And if there was such a query, it could be over-ruled by the Home Office. In the end, that was a battle I didn't win, and the Passport Office still issue all passports.

However, we also did a study on the NHS, called 'Patients, not Paper', which involved interviewing doctors who were having to fill out millions of documents. Then we did one for the Ministry of Agri-culture, Fisheries and Food, where we found farmers who owned three cows were being obliged to complete hundreds of pieces of paper-work. We worked successfully to reduce all that. And in March 1997 we issued a report telling cabinet ministers that the 'ever-increasing archives of government papers and documents should be cut back to save the taxpayer £7 million.' I went on to say that 'failure to tackle the problem would mean twice as much space being needed within eight years,' and pointed out that seven billion pieces of paper were already taking up 900 miles of space in warehouses and government departments, at a cost of £35 million a year.[1]

Once I had been the Prime Minister's Efficiency Adviser for a while, I suggested to John Major that we should publish league tables on all the government departments, to indicate how they were doing. The Welsh Office came bottom of our first table. John Redwood, who was then Secretary of State for Wales, had taken little interest in our efforts. But when his department was bottom of our league table, he drove his department into action.

The Efficiency Unit kept going until the General Election in 1997, which John Major lost. The then Cabinet Secretary, Sir Robin Butler, suggested to Tony Blair that he might want to keep it going but he decided against it. The post was abolished and John Major and Michael Heseltine generously recommended me for a life peerage in the 1997 Birthday Honours' List. I developed the deepest respect and was able to work very closely with Sir Robin Butler (now Lord Butler of Brockwell) who became Cabinet Secretary and was instrumental in recommending to John Major that he should appoint me as the Prime Minister's advisor on efficiency. Robin was and remains a man of great wisdom and charm and, in my view, represents one of the finest examples of the best of the British public services.

I got to know John Major reasonably well. He is a remarkable man and, in my opinion, was able to manage a very difficult political situation very well and I believe was greatly underestimated by the media and the public at large. It is very interesting that of all politicians in the years since he left office, he has behaved with the greatest dignity and in every sense can now be rightly considered as a quintessential elder statesman.

*   *   *

1   Valerie Elliott, 'Cabinet told to save £7m by tackling paper mountain,' *The Times*, 12 March 1997.

In 1995, while I was acting as the Prime Minister's Efficiency Adviser, Michael Heseltine was promoted from President of the Board of Trade to become Deputy Prime Minister and First Secretary of State. The Millennium Commission, set up the year before by John Major, now became Michael's responsibility, and in February 1996 the Greenwich Peninsula was selected as the site for the Millennium Exhibition. This derelict land had been seriously contaminated by toxic sludge from the Greenwich Gas Works, which had operated there from 1889 to 1985, and the clean-up operation by British Gas was seen as a chance to regenerate that part of east London. In the early stages of planning all this, Michael told me that the Millennium Commission had allocated a grant of £200 million to the project. This would come from the National Lottery Millennium Fund, but it would only be handed over if the sum was matched by private-sector investment. So I was given the task of obtaining £300 million in commercial sponsorship for the Millennium Exhibition itself, which I set about doing with its Chief Executive, Jennie Page.[1] The idea was to pull in all the main British companies, but this proved extremely difficult because none of them were eager to do it. As one of the City institutions we approached put it: 'What we are being asked to do is stump up millions of pounds for a project that will last twelve months in a building we do not have and on land we do not own.'[2] However, by June 1996, I was able to announce that the project was viable, on the basis that sixteen big companies had pledged money towards it, including British Airways, British Telecommunications, British Aerospace, BskyB, BAA, BP, GEC, London Electricity, Marks & Spencer, Siemens, Ford, Royal Mail, Hanson Energy, and Reuters.[3]

The Millennium Commission engaged a company called Imagination to pull together plans for the exhibition. Early schemes put forward included a giant clock-face, a winter skating rink, and 'twelve pavilions devoted to the theme of time past present and future.'[4] Each

1   Russell Jenkins, 'London's team seeks £500m for exhibition,' *The Times*, 29 February 1996

2   Anon., 'In the City', *Private Eye*, 24 January 1997.

3   James Blitz, 'Greenwich to get go-ahead for millennium exhibition,' *Financial Times*, 17 June 1996.

4   Anon., 'Time is running out,' *Evening Standard*, 13 May 1996.

pavilion was to be funded with £12 million from a sponsor. Imagination was run by a very unusual character called Gary Withers. At one point he decided to set up an exhibition in the Cabinet Office, when Michael Heseltine called an emergency meeting of thirty-six leaders of British industry in June 1996, as part of our hunt for sponsors.[5] This resulted in a terrible row after Gary's workmen spent twenty-four hours sawing and hammering to create all these installations in the main conference room for which I received a rocket. On another occasion, we had a meeting in Michael Heseltine's office, and when he refused to countenance some of Gary's more grandiose ideas, Gary burst into tears. He then opened his briefcase very carefully, took out a bottle of mineral water and a glass, poured it out, drank it, and then went on with his plans.

In the late-1990s, the extension of the Jubilee Line from Charing Cross to Stratford was an important part of the regeneration of east London. It was also essential as the main source of access to the Millennium Dome and the only realistic way to get there on New Year's Eve. By the time of the 1997 General Election, work on the new railway was running years late, and when Tony Blair defeated John Major, I was called in to see the new Deputy Prime Minister, John Prescott, in May 1998.[6] He knew that I had sorted out the DLR, so he asked for my help. I told him that I had sat on the management committee for the Jubilee Line in the early-1990s, when I was chairman of Canary Wharf, and we had put money into it, although my recollection was that it wasn't doing well at that time. He said: 'Well, it's a big mess now, and I've been told that you're the only person who can sort it out.' I replied that I would be happy to try, but that as I hadn't looked at it for a couple of years, I would need time to assess what sort of state the project was in.

Fortunately, I was able to get back some of the team who had helped me with the DLR. We discovered that things were really bad. When I asked them what we were going to do, they said: 'Look, we need three months to assess everything, and then we'll be able to tell you if there is any way this can be salvaged.' I repeated this to John Prescott, who

5   Anon., 'Light a torch for Britain,' *Evening Standard*, 7 June 1996.
6   Nigel Rosser, 'Jubilee line move to avert Dome disaster,' *Evening Standard*, 13 May 1998.

agreed that we should get on with it. At that time, Sir Richard Mottram was Permanent Secretary at the Department for the Environment, Transport and the Regions, which was overseeing the Jubilee Line extension. I had first met Richard at the MOD in the 1980s, when he was Michael Heseltine's Private Secretary, and he was a good friend. He now explained that the situation was so serious that, although I was responsible for the group looking into how the problems could be resolved, they had also decided to appoint a minister with responsibility for the Jubilee Line, whom I was to work with. This turned out to be Glenda Jackson, the Labour MP for Hampstead and Highgate. I agreed to talk to her.

At our first meeting, she said: 'I've been told that you've got a group working on this, and that it's going to take three months to see what, if anything, can be done.' 'Yes,' I replied, 'that's right.' 'Well,' she went on, 'I've got a really good idea. How many people have you got on your group?' When I told her there were six of us, she said: 'What I want you to do is get twelve people in your group, and then you'll be able to get it done in six weeks.' I had to explain that it didn't quite work like that. Then she announced that she wanted to join the group. When the Permanent Secretary explained that, as the minister in charge of the Jubilee Line, it wouldn't be appropriate for her join my group, she retorted: 'Well, then I'll set up my own group.' So we ended up with Peter's group and Glenda's group.

After three months, I decided to recommend that the government should call in the American company, Bechtel, one of the most respected global engineering, construction and project management companies in the world, which, as mentioned previously, we had employed them to sort out the problems with the DLR. But when I suggested them for the Jubilee Line, the management of London Underground didn't want to know. In the end, I said to John Prescott: 'If you want to get this fixed, I'm not telling you Bechtel can do it. But they're the only chance you've got that it *might* get sorted out, so I suggest that you call them.' Fortunately, he agreed, we brought them in, and the Jubilee Line extension opened successfully in December 1999, just in time for the Millennium.

By 1997 the Millennium Exhibition, originally intended to be set up in twelve pavilions, had developed into what became the Millennium Dome, which was divided into fourteen zones. We gradually recruited companies to sponsor them. Among the main supporters were Boots for the Body zone; BAE Systems and Marconi for the Mind zone; Tesco for the Learning zone; and the Ford Motor Company for the Journey Zone. By that time, I knew that I was going to be appointed as Lord Mayor of London in November 1998, so I said that the City of London would take responsibility for the Money zone. We commissioned Bob Baxter of Amalgam, who worked with a firm called Caribiner. They created a fake newscast, which was presented by the newsreader Trevor McDonald. In this film the British economy had collapsed, financial systems had broken down, there was rampant inflation, and the whole country resorted to mayhem, with looting on the streets and buildings on fire. Everything was in flames and it all looked very realistic. Then, of course, the film explained that this was *not* what happened, because along came the City of London, this great financial centre, which had organised everything for hundreds of years, so all was sweetness and light. I saw this film and thought it was rather good. During the 2008 banking melt down, I realised that the premise of this film was ironic and was glad that no one unearthed it to show publicly at just that time.

On the night of 31 December 1999, Wendy and I were invited to the New Year's Eve party at the Dome, to celebrate the new millennium. We feature in the famous photographs and films of The Queen having to link hands with Tony and Cherie Blair to sing *Auld Lang Syne*, as we were sitting immediately behind them. Many of the people attending that event, including VIP guests and press representatives, were kept waiting outside for hours, because all the Jubilee line trains were sent on to Stratford, where everybody had to disembark and then walk back through prolonged security checks and endless ticketing problems. However, we went on a special train with the Prime Minister, the Archbishop of Canterbury, and various others. As it didn't stop at any of the stations on route, we saw hundreds of people on the platforms staring in astonishment through the windows as we passed by.

We were allowed to take two friends with us for this event. When we got to the Dome, I said to them: 'Look, you've read all this stuff in the papers about how awful this is. I can't tell you whether that's true, because I'm not responsible for it all; but I am responsible for the Money zone, which has been sponsored by the City of London, and that is superb.' So in we went, and up the escalator to the Money zone, and it was the biggest shambles imaginable. They just hadn't got their act together, so the only thing in the Money zone was a million pounds in cash, in a big glass box the size of a small room. Other zones were similarly ghastly. I could at least take comfort in the thought that I had had nothing to do with whatever had been put in there, but I had been involved – with Jennie Page – in getting the Dome itself built on time and on budget.

During the late-1990s there was much speculation that computers were not going to be able to cope with moving from 1999 to 2000, a problem which became known as the Millennium Bug. I had been working for Deutsche Bank since 1998, as London Chairman of Investment Banking, who had spent about $700 million on re-programming all our systems in the run-up to the millennium. At the end of the party in the Dome, Wendy and I got back on the special train to return to central London, and I said to her: 'What's going to happen? When we get home, the central heating will be dead, the burglar alarm will be ringing, the telephone won't work, and everything will be switched off.' We got home about two o'clock in the morning, opened the front door, went inside, and found everything was fine. Computer companies had pulled an enormous stunt against the whole world, for absolutely no reason.

In 2002, I was asked to take on responsibility for The Queen's Golden Jubilee celebrations. For whatever reason, I fell out with the civil servants who were running this and eventually quit – one of the few times that I threw in the towel. Happily, Jeffrey Sterling (Lord Sterling of Plaistow) took over responsibility from me and made a great success of it, for which I was always very grateful.

CHAPTER SEVEN

Canary Wharf

I FIRST HEARD of Canary Wharf during a visit to the Chelsea Flower Show, where I saw a model of the proposed Docklands developments. When I was told what it was, I remember responding: 'Don't be ridiculous, nobody is going to build a place like that in that area; and even if they do, nobody will go there.' Shortly after that, and as a direct result of my work on the DLR, I met Paul Reichmann, who was the Canadian developer behind these plans. Reichmann was a very strange but totally brilliant man who, as an Orthodox Jew, would not allow anyone to work on site after nightfall on Fridays or at all on Saturdays. By the time I encountered him in 1992, Canary Wharf had been largely completed, mainly through the efforts of George Iacobescu. George, now Sir George, later worked for me there and is currently Chairman and Chief executive of the Canary Wharf Group, which, through his efforts, has become a phenomenal success.

However, Reichmann had run into serious problems, as he explained to me: 'I've had huge successes in Canada with my company, Olympia & York, and I thought we could do the same thing here with this development at Canary Wharf. But having been in London for some years, I've realised that although we speak the same language, I have insufficient understanding of how things really work in the UK, and for that reason I've got things wrong. As I know there is so much that you do understand, I've come to ask if you will take over the project and run it.' I replied: 'Well, it's very kind of you to ask me, but word has it that you're going to go bust very soon' which, of course, he denied. But about a week later that is exactly what happened. By June 1992 administrators had taken control of the £1.6 billion project.[1]

It then took a year for Canary Wharf to come out of administration, with a refinancing package put together by twelve banks led by Barclays and Lloyds, and including Citibank, Morgan Stanley, Credit Suisse and Royal Bank of Canada. By September 1993 they had already sunk £568 million into the scheme and were prepared to lend another £278 million over five years, thereby securing the government's agreement to extend the Jubilee Line extension into the docklands. At this point the bankers asked me to take over as Chairman and Chief Executive of Canary Wharf Ltd., which would run the project on behalf of the banks' shareholders. The properties were placed in a holding company – Sylvester Investments, named after the cartoon cat that never managed to catch Tweetypie the canary.[2] I took up my new post in October 1993, with Patrick Garner, a chartered accountant and former director of the property development company Trafalgar House, as finance director.[3]

The first phase of Canary Wharf had been largely completed, but the main problem it faced was lack of occupancy. When the administrators took over in 1992, only twenty-one per cent of the office and retail space was occupied, and although they had managed to raise this to thirty-eight per cent by the time I took over, it was still very sparsely populated.[4] Furthermore, the servicing and running costs of this vast site meant that it was operating at a huge loss. George Iacobescu and I got to work immediately, our first task being to change the image of Canary Wharf and persuade people that it wasn't deserted. I called in the public relations expert, Tim Bell, who had advised on Margaret Thatcher's three successful general election campaigns, and he put some very bright people on the case. They put posters across London Underground, all situated on the side of the tunnels at stations, so people could read them while they were waiting for a

1 Ivan Fallon, 'Hanson raises hopes of Canary Wharf rescue bid', *The Times*, 1 June 1992.
2 Patricia Tehan, 'Banks agree to £1.1bn Canary Wharf rescue', *The Times*, 11 September 1993.
3 Patricia Tehan and Ross Tieman, 'Levene to head new team at revitalised Canary Wharf', *The Times*, 29 October 1993.
4 Patricia Tehan, 'Dream of a city on the water revived', *The Times*, 11 September 1993.

train. The posters posed basic questions: 'How long will it take to get from this station to Canary Wharf? How many shops and restaurants do you think are now at Canary Wharf?' Prizes were offered for anyone sending in the correct answers. It worked like a dream, and we were able to dispel a lot of the myths about the place.

By this time, the DLR was working properly, and the Limehouse Link road tunnel from Tower Bridge had opened in May 1993. However, initial problems which delayed the tunnel meant that businessmen who had been persuaded to go and look at premises in Canary Wharf often found themselves stuck in a taxi for over an hour, just trying to get there. Even taxi-drivers themselves, when asked to drive there, were known to say: 'You don't want to go there, it's a terrible place to try to get to.' To counter this, we decided to give a huge tea party at Canary Wharf for all the taxi-drivers, so we could show them all the good things that were happening. It caused an overnight transformation in their opinions. After that, they told everybody that Canary Wharf was an amazing place. We also lobbied secretaries, because I had contacted the chairmen of major companies whom I knew and asked them to do me a favour by coming down to look around and have lunch. Every one of them turned up half-an-hour early, because their secretaries had assumed that it was going to take ages to get there. When they all discovered that it didn't take that long, the mood started to change.

The next challenge was to encourage retailers, because very few shops had been occupied. I remember asking an optician, who had already opened an outlet at Canary Wharf, how his business was doing. He said: 'This place is amazing. These guys rush in, order another pair of glasses, and rush out again. The only thing they never bother to do is to ask how much it will cost.' So it then became much easier to persuade other retailers that the workforce there had an income way above the average London rate, and could spend money without thinking too much about it.

By the summer of 1994 we had let another eight shop units to upmar-ket brands, including the Jermyn Street shirt-maker Thomas Pink, and fashion retailers Austin Reed, Lords Formal Wear, and Suits The Business.[5] At the same time, Corney & Barrow opened one of their

5   Anon., 'Canary Wharf receives retail therapy', *Estates Gazette*, 4 June 1994.

modernistic wine bars, with stock market prices on wall-mounted tele-vision screens, clocks on the ceiling, and direct phone links to brokers.[1] The newsagent was doing very well selling sweets, chocolates, news-papers and cigarettes. Later on, I also persuaded Richard Felton, of Felton's the Florist, to open a branch. I knew him because he had a flower shop on Brompton Road on the corner next to my father's business. Once he had established himself, I asked him how things were going. 'It's won-derful,' he said, 'our shop is next to Boots, so on Valentine's Day all these guys rush in to buy flowers, and then go into Boots to buy condoms!'

One of the largest shops was an empty space facing the platform of the DL R station, which had been earmarked for Marks & Spencer. Then they announced that they didn't want to open in Canary Wharf. As I knew their chairman quite well, I made some progress in getting them to change their minds, and eventually they said: 'We're going to take it and here's the deal. You give it to us rent-free for seven years; you pay all the costs of the fit-out; and at the end of seven years, it's ours forever, for nothing.' And I replied: 'Well, you know what? That's such an amazing deal that I wouldn't go anywhere near it.'

The next day I had a phone call from the chairman of Tesco, Ian Maclaurin, who said: 'You know that we hear everything on the grapevine? I gather you've lost Marks & Spencer.' When I told him that was correct, he continued: 'Right, we've looked at that site, we're prepared to take it on, and we'll sign a lease now.' The rate he was offering to pay wasn't ideal, but it was great news that they were prepared to take the place. Tesco then made a huge success of that store. They installed cold-storage cabinets, so people working at Canary Wharf could do their shopping at lunchtime and leave it in store, ready for collection when they went home on the train. It became the only branch of Tesco in London that majored in Dom Pérignon champagne. After that, Canary Wharf quickly went on to become the huge shopping centre that it is now.

As part of my job to promote Canary Wharf, I invited everyone I knew, in the City and elsewhere, to come and have a look, in the hope that we could persuade their companies to take space there. Paul Reichmann's office, which I now occupied, included a very smart

---

1   Vanessa Houlder, 'Canary Wharf winning converts', *Financial Times*, 10 June 1994.

private dining room, in which I hosted lunch parties. At one of these events in 1994, we had the then Chairman of British Airways (Colin Marshall), the Chairman of London City Airport and Directors of the builders John Mowlem, as well as one or two of my colleagues. At the end of the dining room was a door leading to the kitchen. Halfway through lunch, and in the middle of our conversation, the door opened and our very efficient butler appeared, carrying a tray on which were plates with lamb chops on them. Then he tripped over the edge of the rug. In slow motion, he, all the plates and the lamb chops flew through the air and landed on the carpet. I remember everybody being terribly British about it, as if it hadn't happened. I stopped mid-sentence and then carried on. The butler didn't know what to say, so he solemnly went round picking up all the chops, and returned to the kitchen. A few minutes later, he came in again with the same tray, having dusted off the chops and put them back on the plates.

By May 1994, the main tower on the site – No. 1 Canada Square – had become a centre for the newspaper industry, with the *Telegraph*, *Mirror* and *Independent* groups either already relocated from Fleet Street or shortly to arrive. Speaking to a journalist from *The Times*, I explained that 'the combined benefits of environment, facilities, services, and cost at Canary Wharf cannot be ignored by anyone looking to make a sound business decision.'[2] Six months later, in November, Morgan Stanley confirmed that they would take 350,000 square feet of office space, in addition to the 450,000 square feet of existing space they already occupied;[3] and in April 1995 BZW, the investment banking arm of Barclay's Bank, announced that it would move 1,700 employees into 510,000 square feet of offices, in the biggest single office leasing agreement in Britain.[4] Both Morgan Stanley and Barclays had been among the eleven-strong syndicate of banks that stepped in to rescue Canary Wharf in 1993. By the end of 1994, occupancy of the site had risen to seventy-two per cent.[5] Unlike Paul Reichmann, who had

2   David Thurlow, 'Newsmen sent to the tower', *The Times*, 17 May 1994.
3   Anon., 'Canary Wharf plans rent rise', *The Times*, 4 November 1994.
4   Tom Stevenson, 'BZW headquarters to move to Canary Wharf', *Independent*, 5 April 1995; Roland Gribben, 'BZW prepares £200m move to Canary Wharf', *Daily Telegraph*, 5 April 1995.
5   David Sands, 'Docklands: Preparing for action', *Estates Gazette*, 26 November 1994.

been keen to attract only the head offices of companies, I had a different policy, as I explained to the *Financial Times*: 'It is my job to fill the place with good tenants. Beyond that, I don't really mind who comes here.'[1]

One of the companies occupying a building at Canary Wharf was advertising agency Ogilvy & Mather, which was a division of WPP led by Martin Sorrell, who was acting in a very litigious manner and had threatened us with all sorts of actions to try and improve the terms of their tenancy. In due course, he insisted in taking his action to Court and had told me that there was no way that they could lose the case. However, to my enormous satisfaction the Judge summarily dismissed WPP's case and it led me to question the very combative side of his character which has been to the fore more recently.

London City Airport had opened in 1987, but both the flights and destinations it served were fairly limited, and by 1993 it was still only handling 245,000 passengers a year. When Colin Marshall was at the 'lamb chops' lunch, I had told him that he should put more flights in. But he had replied: 'No, it's a waste of time, we don't want to do it.' Now, of course, all that has completely changed; the airport has its own DLR station, which opened in 2005, and in 2015 it served over 4.3 million passengers, which was an eighteen per cent increase on the previous year and British Airways is now a major user.[2] The airport had been built by the engineering company Mowlem, who decided to sell it in 1995. George Iacobescu and I mulled over whether we should buy it at the then asking price of about £20 million, but we decided not to and it went to the Irish businessman Dermot Desmond. He then sold it seven years later for £750 million, and it changed hands again in 2016 for over £2 billion. That was one of my greatest commercial mistakes.

When I was at Canary Wharf, there was a lot of talk about using the River Thames more as a means of transport. In the end, it turned out to be an unattractive proposition for a number of reasons. Firstly, the river is not straight, but goes through a succession of long bends; and secondly, the tides are extremely strong, so it can take up to twenty-five minutes longer going in one direction compared with the other. The idea of riverboat services sounded wonderful, and indeed, on a

1   Simon London, 'Canary Wharf wins vote of confidence as climate alters', *Financial Times*, 4 November 1994.
2   Statistics from the UK Civil Aviation Authority.

summer's day, it might have been nice to get on at Chelsea Pier and sail downstream to Canary Wharf. But we certainly couldn't envisage too many people wanting to do that in February, when it would be freezing cold, the river would be choppy, and the boat would probably be late. However, we did make some use of the Thames. We had a very fast launch at Canary Wharf, which could reach speeds of about twenty knots. As I still had to catch quite a number of flights from Heathrow, I would take this boat from the pier at Canary Wharf, jump out at Hammersmith, and then hop into a car for the short drive to the airport, which saved a huge amount of time.

When I arrived to run Canary Wharf, the banks who had rescued it were owed £850 million, and my job was to get their money back. They had given us fourteen years to achieve this, although actually we did it in two. The banks then decided to sell their holdings and recoup the £850 million. By that time, Canary Wharf was doing very well, so I advised them to wait for another eighteen months, by which time I thought it would be worth £1.5 billion. To which the banks' representatives said: 'We couldn't care less. Our job is to recover our loan. And much more important than anything else, our personal bonuses are attached to the recovery of the loan. We won't get any more money, even if we get back treble the amount we loaned, so we're going to sell it now, come hell or high water.' I told them I thought that was a stupid thing to do. Anyway, they went ahead, and Paul Reichmann, who had really lost a large part of his money by then, got together a syndicate of international investors who then bought Canary Wharf back from the banks. Two or three years later, they subsequently floated it for about £2.5 billion.

Once he was back at Canary Wharf, Paul asked me if I would stay on. But I knew him of old. He was a genius, but impossible to work with. I remember saying to him: 'Look, I think you've done a fantastic job and I'm a great admirer of what you've built here. But for the future, either I run this place or you do, and I don't want to fall out with you.' So I left. Speaking to the press at the time, I said: 'I think I've done what I wanted to do. I was never a property guru. Collecting rent is not what I want to do for the rest of my life. Canary Wharf was a disaster but it has been put back on its feet.'[3]

3   John Willcock, 'Rescuer of Canary Wharf gets ready to take wing again,' *Independent*, 2 January 1996.

There was also an unspoken under-current to my decision. When I took over at Canary Wharf, there had been significant disquiet in the Corporation of the City of London, because it was seen as the main adversary to the Square Mile in offering competitive letting space for the Financial Services Industry. I had repeatedly pointed out that this was a ridiculous argument, as Canary Wharf would be able to provide space for 120,000 people, and it would be physically impossible to put another 120,000 people in the City of London. However, there remained a lot of ill-will on this subject. By that time, in 1996, I was expected to become Lord Mayor within the next two years, and I was more or less told that if I wanted to do that, I should give up my job at Canary Wharf.

Paul Reichmann used to fly backwards and forwards to Toronto via New York on Concorde. It was so fast that he could leave London on Friday afternoon and be back in Canada in time to avoid travelling on the Sabbath, which would have been against his religious principles as an Orthodox Jew. Shortly after I had left Canary Wharf, I got a call from George Iacobescu, who said: 'Peter, you've got to help Paul. There's a problem at London Airport. All the flights have been delayed, he's sitting on the runway in Concorde, and they've now worked out that the delay is going to be so long that he'll end up flying on the Sabbath.' 'Well, what do you want me to do about it?' I asked. 'You've got to get him off that plane.' He replied. 'Alright,' I said, 'leave it with me; I'll see what I can do.' I rang up Colin Marshall at British Airways and explained that he had to get Paul Reichmann, one of his passengers, off an aeroplane that was sitting on the tarmac at London Airport. He not unreasonably asked me why. I replied: 'Look, I haven't got time to explain. Please just do me a favour and get him off that plane.' 'Is it important?' said Colin. 'Yes, it's very important,' I replied. An ambulance was sent out to the Concorde on the runway, evacuated Paul from the plane, and put him in the hotel at the airport terminal. Of course, once he got there, he couldn't eat anything but fruit and water for the next twenty-four hours, until the Sabbath was over and he could resume his journey.

CHAPTER EIGHT

Alderman & other appoinments

W HEN I WAS awarded a place at the City of London School in 1951, my father told me that I had obtained the first qualification to become Lord Mayor. Strictly speaking, that wasn't true, although in some ways it was, because it introduced me to the City of London Corporation at an early age.

However, it really began when I was chairman of Alvis, which was part of United Scientific. Our main product was the Scorpion tank, and we had received a substantial order for them from Malaysia. General Zain Hashim,[1] the Malaysian army Chief, who, incidentally, had been born in Hampstead, came over to the UK for a ceremony to take delivery of their first vehicle. The event took place at the Alvis factory in Coventry, where we also had a test-track. We travelled up to Coventry on the early train, the General accompanied by his young son, who must have been about ten, and I with my son, Timothy, who was about the same age. We all indulged ourselves with the wonderful, first-class breakfast on the train-journey to the Midlands.

We also had with us John Howard, who at that time held the role of City Marshal, which meant that he was one of the ceremonial officers working for the Lord Mayor. When we invited General Zain Hashim for the handover of this first tank, we had asked him if there was anyone in the UK whom he wished to invite to the ceremony. He had nominated John Howard because they had served together as soldiers when the British Army undertook operations in Malaya during the Emergency of the 1940s and 1950s.

Once we got to Coventry station, we all moved into a coach for the

---

1   General Tan Sri Dato' Zain Hashim (b.1930); chief of logistics, 1977; then deputy chief of the Malaysian army, 1978–80; and army chief, 1981–84.

drive to the factory, and I found myself sitting next to John Howard. I asked him what he did, and he said he worked in the Mansion House, and explained a little about the Sheriffs and the Livery Companies. When I told him that I had been at the City of London School, he said: 'Well then, you'll have seen it all.' He then asked if I was a member of a Livery Company, and when I said I wasn't, he said: 'You should join one, and you should also become a member of the Common Council and an Alderman.' I thought this sounded interesting, so I asked him which Company he thought I should join. He advised that the Armourers' Company would be the obvious choice, because they had been representing the manufacturers of military equipment since their foundation in 1322. He also offered to approach Sir Lindsay Ring,[1] an armourer himself and a former Lord Mayor, as my potential sponsor. Lindsay Ring's catering company, Ring & Brymer, served a lot of events in the City. I thanked John Howard and waited to hear from him.

After about a week, I hadn't heard anything, so I got in touch with John. He said he would chase the matter, but still nothing happened. I later discovered that Lindsay Ring was apparently prejudiced and didn't want to have anything to do with me. Anyway, John Howard assured me that he could find another sponsor, and introduced me to Sir Christopher Leaver,[2] also a former Lord Mayor, and a member of the Worshipful Company of Carmen. He helped me to get elected to his Livery Company in 1984, and subsequently helped me to become both Master of that company in 1992 to 1993 and then Lord Mayor in 1998 to 1999.

However, before I could start on the track to stand for election as Lord Mayor, I had to become an Alderman. Although it is possible to be elected to that position in one step, the preference is that it is first best to serve initially as a member of the Court of Common Council, which allows newcomers to familiarise themselves with the City of London and its governing bodies. I set about trying to get myself elected to one of the Council's twenty-five wards, most of which had annual elections at which the existing councilmen would usually be re-elected unopposed. Each ward has an Alderman and three or four

1 Sir Lindsay Ring (d.1997); Lord Mayor of London, 1974–5 (Armourer & Brasier).
2 Sir Christopher Leaver (b.1937); Lord Mayor of London, 1982–82 (Carmen).

councilmen, but, at the time, it was frowned upon to oppose them, so I had to look around to find a suitable vacancy. Fortunately, a councilman in the ward of Candlewick had just retired, and there was to be a by-election, so I decided to stand there in 1983.

Most of these City wards are small. Candlewick, I quickly discovered, had only twenty-two names on its electoral roll, and I remember thinking that was certainly manageable. In order to be eligible to vote, you had to actually live or lease a property in the ward, so I set out to visit the voters. Two of my key supporters were a caretaker and his wife, who lived in one of the office buildings. Another couple that I contacted had actually moved out of the ward by the time the election happened, but they retained the right to vote until the roll was next updated, so they also supported me. Nobody else knew these people were there, and they certainly hadn't visited them, so I knew I had already secured a few votes.

Standing against me were the chairman of the ward club, who knew everybody, and a third candidate, Richard Nichols,[3] who subsequently became a great friend and also went on to become Lord Mayor. As I had been to visit everybody on the electoral roll, I won by a landslide – as if you can ever describe winning a vote in a constituency with 22 votes a landslide. The chairman of the ward club failed to get a single vote, which was quite a surprise! Bearing in mind that, in order to stand for election, you have to have two voters to nominate you, it appeared that even the people who had nominated him had ultimately failed to vote for him. Richard Nichols got four or five votes, and I got the rest, and so was elected as a member of the Court of Common Council for the ward of Candlewick in 1983. The Court meets every month to deal with City matters, most of which are pretty mundane. The real work is done by various committees, to which you are assigned, and which handle things such as licensing, highways, planning applications, and property matters. It's like any other council, except that this tiny enclave of one square mile is worth more than almost all the rest of London put together.

Within a year of taking on this role, Tony Joliffe,[4] the Alderman of

3   Sir Richard Nichols (d.2016), Lord Mayor, 1996–97 (Salter).
4   Sir Anthony Joliffe, Lord Mayor, 1981–82 (Painter Stainer).

9. Just after I'm first elected to Candlewick Ward, Margaret Thatcher visited the Red Cross Market, which Wendy and I had chaired.

Candlewick, suddenly resigned. He had served as Lord Mayor between 1981 and 1982 and so a by-election for a new Alderman was announced, in which I was encouraged to stand. Although my two absent voters had been removed from the ward's electoral roll by then, I was confident that I knew all the other residents. So, on the basis of my large majority the year before, I didn't bother to visit them all again. Once again, Richard Nichols was standing against me, and the third candidate was Christopher Mitchell, who ran El Vino's wine bar in Fleet Street. By this time, the electorate had shrunk from twenty-two to just eighteen people, so every vote counted. But I was so certain of victory and cocky that I had done no canvassing, didn't turn up when they were voting, and merely arrived once it was all over, thinking that I had it made. In the final count, Christopher Mitchell got five votes, I got six, and Richard Nichols got seven, so I lost. I was very angry with myself, because I had taken it all so casually and the defeat was entirely my own fault.

Fortunately, shortly after that, I was told that another election was to be held in the nearby ward of Portsoken, in the eastern part of the City, near Whitechapel and Spitalfields. The Alderman there was Sir

Bernard Waley-Cohen,[1] a scion of the great Jewish families of Samuels and Waley-Cohens, families that had founded major businesses like Shell. He had been the Alderman in Portsoken since 1949, but had reached the age of seventy and so, by convention rather than any fixed law, was due to retire. At that time, Portsoken was the Jewish ward. Many Jews had settled there, going back to the time of my grandparents and great-grandparents, but their descendants had gradually died off, leaving only widows behind, so there were numerous old ladies living in Portsoken. They were all concentrated in Petticoat Tower and Petticoat Square, in what were the equivalent of council flats owned by the Corporation, and which were the successors of the tenement blocks that my ancestors had lived in. I was told that, with this huge population of Jewish widows, I would stand a good chance in the forthcoming election.

Each ward has an Alderman, a deputy, and three or four other members of the Common Council. The deputy in Portsoken was a lady called Iris Samuel, who was a legend in the City. She was a traditional 'cor blimey' Cockney, who didn't give a stuff about any kind of formality or playing according to the rules. Her husband had died and she had become the self-appointed and very effective champion of all these widows, who worshipped her. Whenever a window was broken or the heating didn't work in their block of flats, they would ring up Iris and she would say: 'Leave it to me.' She would then telephone the Corporation and give them absolute hell until the problem was solved. I was told to go and see her. When I met her, she said: 'Yes, you'll do. I don't like all those other po-faced people, we'll get you in.'

I then went to see Bernard Waley-Cohen, and said to him: 'Look, I know Portsoken is traditionally the Jewish ward, and that we've had Jewish aldermen for years, and I'd really like to stand to succeed you.' Unfortunately, he was already suffering somewhat from ageing so we didn't have much of a conversation. When I told Iris Samuel about this, she retorted: 'Don't worry. I'm going to take you round these flats and introduce you to all the old ladies.' There were hundreds of them. I decided to do it properly this time. Our kids were quite young

---

1   Sir Bernard Waley-Cohen (1914–1991): Alderman for Portsoken Ward, 1949–84; Lord Mayor, 1960–61.

then, so I sent them round with Wendy to visit all these Jewish widows. Whenever one of the children said: 'Will you vote for my daddy?' they'd say, 'Of course I will.' This went on for two or three months.

I also had to produce an election address. Even though there were a lot of elderly ladies living in the ward, there were also quite a lot of businesses in Portsoken – particularly law firms. As partners in these companies, many of the lawyers had become signatories on the leases of their buildings, which made them technically property-owners and thereby each partner was eligible for a vote. So I wrote two election addresses. The one for the law firms and businesses said that I was running a public company and worked for the government, and was illustrated with a photograph of me in my office. The alternative version for the residents said: 'I'm a nice Jewish boy, these are my children,' and had a picture of me on the beach with the kids.

Two of the Councilmen for the Ward decided to work against my election. They teamed up with an outgoing member of the Common Council who was retiring, and together they wrote a letter to all the residents, supporting another candidate. The other candidate was David Vermont, who had been Master of the Mercers' Company, and had been nursing the ward for years, in the hope that he would succeed Bernard Waley-Cohen when he retired. On the day of the election, I was pretty sure that I would win, especially with Iris's support. I secured 490 votes, David got far less and so I was elected as the Alderman for the Ward of Portsoken in 1984, a post I held until 2005.

*   *   *

As an Alderman, you immediately become a magistrate, which means you have to sit for a minimum of twenty-six sittings a year. There were three courts, one in the Mansion House itself and the other two at the back of the Guildhall, although they have since been moved into a single building. Each sitting in court lasts half a day, so that amounts annually to thirteen working days of your time. I found this quite demanding, although in one way it was helpful. In the MOD, I was dealing with contracts worth hundreds of millions of pounds. Then suddenly I would have to jump out of there to go and sit in court, where we would find ourselves fining someone £25, only to discover that they genuinely couldn't pay. It helped me keep my feet on the ground and was a useful conduit to the real world. Having said that, I remember several times flying into Northolt on an RAF jet at six o'clock in the evening, having attended meetings all over Europe, and then dashing into one of the huts on the airfield to change into costume for a City dinner. In hindsight, people used to ask me how I managed to do it all, because it seemed impossible, but at the time I just got on with it.

Fortunately, while I was at the MOD, I had a wonderful West Indian driver called Jimmy, who came from St. Lucia. He had worked at the Ministry for years, knew everything that was going on, and sold delicious corned-beef sandwiches to all the staff, which were much better than any other lunch you could get there. Jimmy would collect me every morning, in my army-issue Ford Granada staff car. One day, after I'd been in the job for a few months, he told me that it had to go in for a service. When I asked him if he would get it back in the afternoon, he said: 'No, they have to keep it for a week. The first day they check it over; the second day they write a report on it; the third day they do the work; the fourth day they road-test it; and the fifth day you get it back.' Whenever we did get it back, it was often in a worse state than when it went in for servicing. I used to say to him: 'Can't you get them to *de*-service the car?'

Jimmy was a delightful man who had previously driven Geoffrey Pattie, a Conservative Defence Minister and a good friend. Everybody loved Jimmy, and he would do anything for my family and me. One night I was invited to attend a mess night with the Royal Engineers at Chatham. I went with General Sir John Stibbon[1] who, as Master-General of the Ordnance, was responsible for procurement for the army, but reported to me at the MOD. Jimmy drove us both down to Kent. It was an extremely hot summer's night. We left Chatham at about ten-thirty or eleven o'clock to drive back to London. On the way back up the M2, Jimmy kept opening the window. When I said: 'Jimmy, for God's sake close the window, there's a terrible draught back here,' he replied: 'I need air.' Anyway, he got me home.

The next morning, I got a phone-call at about eight o'clock from

1   General Sir John Stibbon (1935–2014), Master-General of the Ordnance, 1987–1991.

my Private Secretary, who said: 'Look, I'm sorry but we've got some very bad news for you: Jimmy is dead.' I replied: 'What do you mean he's dead? He drove me home only a few hours ago, at seventy miles an hour up the motorway.' It transpired that he had suffered from asthma for years and had failed to tell anyone because he thought he would lose his job. When the final attack came, he had been rushed to hospital, but just dropped dead. I then started an enquiry to find out when he had last had a medical check-up, and was told that only the military drivers underwent that sort of test. When I pointed out that Jimmy might easily have died a few hours earlier, while driving John Stibbon and me at speed up the motorway, the exceedingly pompous head of civilian human resources at the Ministry merely retorted: 'Well, you don't have to worry about it, because we've never had a case of this happening before.' To which I replied: 'So bloody what!'

It was all very sad. Jimmy was a born-again Christian from a West Indian church in Stamford Hill, and they held the most amazing funeral. I was asked to give the address, so when Wendy and I arrived, we were given seats up at the front. There, lying before me in an open coffin, was Jimmy, dressed in a white dinner jacket, which I remembered he had just bought. I broke up. It was very, very difficult to make that address. Fortunately, it later turned into a wonderful party, a sort of West Indian wake, which was quite something. After that, it got more complicated. He'd been collecting the money he charged for his corned-beef sandwiches and storing it in his locker at the MOD. It amounted to about £500 or £600. He had been married and had children, and I think was divorced, but had been living with another woman. They all wanted to get hold of his estate, and as he had made no will, it took some time to sort it all out. I think Jimmy's proudest day had been when I got my knighthood in 1989. He requisitioned one of those old Daimlers that the Army use for ceremonial parades, polished it up, and drove us to Buckingham Palace, with his usual beaming smile. We missed him terribly when he died, especially as he used to look after our children. Sadly his replacement was no good at all.

In 1993 the IRA detonated a truck bomb on Bishopsgate in the City of London, killing one person and wounding forty-four others. The widespread damage cost £350 million to repair. The Bevis Marks Synagogue, the oldest surviving synagogue in England, was one of the buildings to be hit, although fortunately the damage there was pretty superficial. Bevis Marks was built by Spanish and Portuguese Jews in 1699 to 1701, to replace an earlier synagogue in nearby Creechurch Lane. At the time of the IRA atrocity in 1993, I was the only Jewish Alderman, so they asked me to help with arranging the funding of the repairs. Of course, the synagogue was insured, by the Ecclesiastical Insurance Company, who were the nicest people you could possibly imagine. One wall had been quite damaged but was certainly repairable. However, when I pointed out to these insurers that it would look terrible if we re-painted this one wall and not all the others, they agreed and gave us the money to redecorate the whole building. Then we decided that, as the synagogue was nearly 300 years old and looking a little bit worn at the edges, we would set up the Bevis Marks Synagogue Trust, which raised £200,000 for additional refurbishment and restoration work on the interior, with a very generous donation coming from the City of London Corporation.

A few years later, in 1996, we held our daughter Nicole's wedding in the Bevis Marks Synagogue, with the whole place lit by candlelight. The reception was at The Savoy. Unbeknown to my daughter, I had arranged for one of the horse-drawn coaches that the Corporation of London uses in the Lord Mayor's Show to take her and her new husband, Matthew Walsh, from their wedding to the reception. The Mounted Branch of the City of London Police gave her an escort of horses along the Embankment to The Savoy, and she arrived there in this Cinderella-like coach. Later still, in 2001, when Bevis Marks Synagogue reached its 300th anniversary, we held a special service attended by the then Prime Minister, Tony Blair.

Once you become an Alderman, you start slowly to move up the ladder towards becoming sheriff and then Lord Mayor. Progress is determined by seniority, in terms of the date on which you were sworn in and approved at the Court of Aldermen. When I joined, there was quite a backlog, so I knew it would be at least ten years before I became Lord Mayor (in fact it was 15 years). That suited me fine, because in 1984 I was still running United Scientific and had just taken on the role as Personal Adviser to the Secretary of State for Defence, so I was quite busy. Richard Nichols, as Alderman of Candlewick, where I had stood unsuccessfully, was just senior to me.

John Chalstrey[1] and I, on the other hand, were elected on the same day. He was one of the top surgeons at St. Bartholomew's Hospital, and was elected for Vintry Ward, which is just south of St. Paul's Cathedral and west of the Mansion House. By 1993 we had reached the top of the ladder, but it was deemed that I was senior, on the grounds that I had been sworn in half-an-hour before him. At this stage, John being ten years older than me, the City of London Corporation asked whether I would mind if they slipped him in ahead of me as the next Sheriff. With my other commitments that suited me fine, so I agreed and he was appointed that year.

In turn I too became Sheriff – 1995 to 1996. It was an interesting role, although a lot of my duties were ceremonial, which I don't have a lot of patience with. It involved a huge amount of dressing-up in outdated clothes, to the extent that the Sheriff – and indeed the Lord Mayor – might have to change clothes five times a day. All this was sacrosanct, but it was a bit like being in a school play. Sheriffs were required to open the courts at the Old Bailey every day, both first thing in the morning and when they resumed after lunch. In order to do this, I had to wear what they called 'Old Bailey', which consisted of a frock-coat and trousers, topped off with a sort of clergyman's collar with frills. As attendance at court had to be fitted in with going to the office, I would only have ten minutes to change.

I would arrive at the Old Bailey in costume to open the courts at 10.30, go straight back to the office and change into normal clothes, and then re-dress again in order to be back in time to host lunch at the Old Bailey by 12.30. Theoretically, the Lord Mayor was the lunch host, but as he was normally far too busy to attend, the Sheriff stood in for him. I found myself hosting lunch three times a week, with the other Sheriff, Ken Ayers, covering the other two days. Each of these meals was attended by about twenty people, made up of the Sheriff, the Secondary (who ran the Old Bailey), three or four guests, and the judges, all of whom came dressed up and ate lunch with their wigs on. They are fantastic people, who have invariably spent the morning trying extreme criminal cases and diabolical murders. I think they

1   Sir John Chalstrey (b.1931): Alderman, Vintry Ward, 1984–2001; Sheriff, 1993–94; Lord Mayor, 1995–6.

found the lunches a welcome break and a chance to talk to reasonable people, so we would often invite stars of stage and screen or politicians as guests, who in turn found the judges and their work fascinating.

The food was meagre. It was provided by the Lord Chancellor's department, on a budget of about £1.50 per person per day, for three courses. However, it was an incredibly efficient meal. You could invite guests for pre-lunch drinks at 12.40; then at 12.55 we would walk through to the dining room and sit down, interspersing the guests among the judges. Exactly an hour later, at 1.55, we would all rise from the table, and go out to open the courts again.

Opening the courts, either in the morning or after lunch, involved me, dressed up in my outfit, escorting each judge to their court. When we arrived, we would find waiting an official, whose job was to knock on the door of the courtroom, and then escort the judge to sit on the bench. I would bow to him as he went into court, he would bow to me, and that was it. Doing this three times a week at lunchtime was fine, as it didn't take up too much of my time and they were interesting events. But the same role in the morning became ridiculous, when I quickly discovered that the judges couldn't be bothered with all this rigmarole. They were arranging to arrive earlier, so by the time I was ready to take them in, they were already sitting in court. Eventually I said to the Recorder, who is the senior judge at the Old Bailey, 'Look, this is absurd. I'm busting a gut to get here in time to get you into court, but none of you want me to do this. Why are we doing it? Why don't we stop?' And he replied: 'What a great idea.' Of course, like a lot of things in the City, we were instantly told that we couldn't do that, so I responded by saying: 'Says who? I'm the Sheriff, he's the Recorder, and we have decided that's what is going to happen, so that's it.' After that we successfully ditched that morning ceremony.

There was a similar anomaly with the Sheriff's role at the Court of Common Council, which met on a Thursday once a month. All the Common Councilmen and the Aldermen would go to the Guildhall. The Lord Mayor would then process in, followed by the two Sheriffs. As soon as he had sat down, the Aldermanic Sheriff would have to leave immediately to rush back to the Old Bailey in time to open the courts again. This meant that the non-Aldermanic Sheriff, who wasn't actually a member of the Common Council, sat through the whole session, while the Aldermanic Sheriff who was a member, and should really have been there, was not present. In order to solve this problem, I suggested that perhaps the two Sheriffs should alternate the court duty every month. Everybody agreed this was a good idea, but they couldn't decide how this new plan was to be approved. So I said, not for the first or last time while I was in the City, 'I have just decreed it, so that's what we're going to do.' We implemented it immediately, and for six months nobody noticed that only one Sheriff was processing in with the Lord Mayor, instead of two. When they did notice and asked what had happened, and I explained that I thought the previous arrangement had been a waste of time, they said: 'But can you do that?' To which I replied: 'Well, I've done it, so that's that.' It has continued to this day and works fine. There was so much of that sort of logjam in the City.

In 1991 the former Lord Mayor Sir Christopher Leaver, who had first encouraged me to get involved in the City, asked me if I would consider taking over from him as Honorary Colonel Commandant of the Royal Corps of Transport. He had served as an officer in the regiment while doing his National Service. I told him that I would be delighted to succeed him. However, I was a little concerned as to how this would work, as I had never held a commission in the army, and my former military experience was limited to serving as a staff sergeant in the Army section of the Combined Cadet Force at the City of London School. As I was working at the MOD at the time, I went to see the Chief of the General Staff, General (subsequently Field Marshal) Sir John Chapple, whose office was next to mine, and put my problem to him. His response was: 'Anybody who has served for six years on the sixth floor of the MOD is well entitled to become the Honorary Colonel Commandant of the Royal Corps of Transport, and I shall certainly support this appointment.' I took up my new role in 1991 and continued in it until 1993, when the Royal Corps of Transport was merged with four other army corps to form the Royal Logistics Corps, and I became their Honorary Colonel Commandant, a post I held until 2006.

I enjoyed my role very much and would turn up at regimental events every so often, although I made a point of never wearing their uniform, because I reckoned I wasn't really entitled to it. When I was Lord Mayor, between 1998 and 1999, I often found myself involved in various military events, and the army kindly provided a young officer, Paul Holder, who acted as a military aide for me at the Mansion House. The Bosnian War of 1992–95 had caused terrible damage in that country, and Paul asked me if I would like to visit the Royal Logistics Corps, as their Honorary Colonel Commandant, to see some of the work they had been doing there. We went out for a few days, starting in the Croatian town of Split before we moved into Serbia. That trip was the one time I did wear uniform. It was a sad situation, where every second house had been destroyed. Where Moslems and Christians had formerly lived side-by-side for decades, they had now spent three years

10. Disembarking from RFA in Split harbour as Honorary Colonel Commandant of the Royal Logistics Corps.

blowing each other up. The XIV Olympic Winter Games had been held in Sarajevo in 1984, so I asked them what had happened to their wonderful ski slopes. They said: 'We'll never be able to ski here again, because they mined all the slopes, and we'll never be able to find all the mines.'

Many years later, in November 2016, I received a telephone call from Paul Holder, by then a Lieutenant Colonel. Since my days with him in Bosnia, he had worked on aid programmes all over the world, served in both Iraq and Afghanistan and he also spent a year as Master of my Livery Company, the Carmen. He rang to tell me that he had been given the post as defence attaché in South Sudan, which was a job he longed to do, but that he was unfortunately now in London Bridge Hospital having been diagnosed with incurable pancreatic cancer and had just months to live. I went to visit him, and he still looked as fit as a fiddle. He had married his long-term Dutch partner, Annemiek, and in December, just before Christmas, she gave birth to their son Frank. Paul died a few weeks later, on Sunday 5 March 2017, aged just fifty – a very sad loss.

CHAPTER NINE

Lord Mayor of London

IN NOVEMBER 1998 I was elected as the 671st Lord Mayor of London, for the customary period of one year. I was determined to change the mayoral image of being just a ceremonial figure riding around in his gold carriage at the Lord Mayor's Show. In interviews at the time of my election, I told journalists that 'whilst the pomp and ceremony plays a role, it is really just the top dressing, like the State Opening of Parliament.' I felt I was taking on 'a serious job, promoting the financial services industry in this country around the world.' My appointment also coincided with a crucial time for the City, as the rest of continental Europe transferred itself to its new single currency in January 1999. There was a fear that we would lose out to other European cities – particularly Frankfurt and Paris – and I felt that it was 'very important to let the world know that even though Britain would not be a member of European Monetary Union, London remained the biggest international financial centre.'[1] Speaking at the time, I said: 'I want to use my year to ensure the City of London can be as great an asset to the country in the years ahead as it has been in the last 800 years.'[2]

The inaugural event to celebrate the appointment of the Lord Mayor is the Presentation Dinner. This is normally given, in honour of the incoming mayor, by his own Livery Company. The Presentation Dinner had always been held on the day that the new Lord Mayor had visited Buckingham Palace to be knighted by The Queen. However, when John Major was Prime Minister, between 1990 and 1997, he had decided – quite rightly in my view – that people who, in the past,

1   Hilary Clarke, 'The new lord of London,' *The Independent on Sunday*, 13 September 1998.
2   Bernard Josephs, 'Lord Levene is London's Lord Mayor,' *Jewish Chronicle*, 2 October 1998.

automatically received an honour for holding a specific post should only get one if and when they had been seen to do a good job, and not before. So knighthoods for Lord Mayors would only be granted once they'd done the job, not before they had started. This caused a huge row in the City, but in my case none of this mattered, as I had already received my knighthood in 1989, when I was Permanent Secretary at the MOD. As my Livery Company, the Carmen, doesn't have its own hall, my Presentation Dinner was held in the Armourers' Hall in the City, with about eighty guests.

In the lead-up to my inauguration as Lord Mayor, the Chief Rabbi, Jonathan Sacks, said to me: 'Look, Peter, the Lord Mayor's Show is on a Saturday, which would not be a very good advertisement for the Jewish faith, because you're not supposed to ride on the Sabbath. Could you hold it on another day? Perhaps you could do it on Sunday?' So I said: 'Of course I can't do that, it's always been held on a Saturday. And anyway, I've been in the show since I became an Alderman in 1984, so I can't suddenly announce that I've become so orthodox that I can't ride on a Saturday. It's out of the question.' 'Well,' said Jonathan, 'how about you walk beside the coach, rather than riding in it?' 'No,' I replied, 'the whole point of the show is the Lord Mayor in his coach, waving his hat from the window. If I don't do that, it will be ridiculous.' However, we did think about his concerns and came up with a solution.

Each new Lord Mayor takes office on a Friday, during what is called the Silent Ceremony, in the Guildhall. The outgoing Lord Mayor parades in, with all the Aldermen, and then transfers the mayoral insignia – the seal, purse, sword and mace – to the incoming Lord Mayor, in complete silence. Then the new incumbent processes out, to be greeted by the State Trumpeters of the Household Cavalry in their gold-embroidered uniforms. Their attendance, usually reserved only for the monarch, is granted in recognition of the fact that in the seventeenth century, when King James II was particularly short of money, the Lord Mayor paid for new uniforms for his trumpeters.

As Lord Mayor, I had a Church of England chaplain, Malcolm Johnson, who was also the Rector of St Boltolph Parish Church for Portsoken. Malcolm proved to be both a good friend and colleague, especially in taking his share of Iris Samuel duties. In fact, Malcolm often went beyond the call of duty in appearing as her escort in clerical garb at formal dinners at the Guildhall – although, secretly, I think he enjoyed them.

I was also given a Jewish chaplain, Abraham Levy. So, bearing in mind what Jonathan Sacks had said to me, I suggested to Abraham that, following the Silent Ceremony in the Guildhall, we might all go to the Bevis Marks Synagogue for the Friday evening service. Then after that, the new Lord Mayor and all his retinue would walk from the synagogue to the Mansion House, for a traditional Jewish Friday-night dinner. Abraham thought this was a brilliant idea. Then about two weeks before this event, I received a telephone call from Jonathan. 'Look, Peter,' he said, 'I'm sure you know what I mean by a royal command. On the night of your Bevis Marks service, His Royal Highness the Prince of Wales is celebrating his 50th birthday, and is holding a reception at Buckingham Palace. I have received an invitation to this event, so therefore I must attend it.' 'Why?' I said. 'Because the invitation says it has been sent 'by royal command', and therefore I have to go,' he replied. I said: 'Well, it's up to you. The Prince of Wales will have 200 or 300 people at his cocktail party. He's not going to notice or worry about the fact that you're not there. I'm

11. With my two chaplains – on the left Rev Dr Malcolm Johnson and on the right Rabbi Dr Abraham Levy.

the first Jewish Lord Mayor for forty years. I would have thought you could come to my service.' 'Well, don't worry,' said Jonathan, 'I'll go to the Prince's party. Then, as it will by then be the Sabbath, I'll walk from Buckingham Palace to the Mansion House, and join you for your dinner there.' And that's what he did. I thought it was a strange choice of priorities. None of this changed our plans, and on the day of the Silent Ceremony, Wendy and I walked from the Mansion House to Bevis Marks Synagogue, with our mayoral chaplain, Rabbi Abraham Levy, where we attended a special Erev Shabbat service. There were about 600 people there, of whom about two-thirds were not Jewish, and most of them had never been in a synagogue before. I had become the eighth Jewish Lord Mayor.

After the service, we walked back to the Mansion House for our dinner, with about two dozen guests. I had said to Abraham: 'Will you please say the prayers for Friday night?' And he replied: 'No, in the Mansion House, this is *your* house. You are the master, so you say the prayers.' I agreed. But when I got up to speak, I was totally overcome. I just couldn't get the words out. In the end, I managed to say what I had planned, which was to mention that I was the first Jewish Lord Mayor for forty years, that I was there with all my family and friends, and that many of my ancestors had lived in the City of London. It was an extraordinary and poignant moment.

On the day after the Silent Ceremony, always the second Saturday in November, the Lord Mayor's Show takes place. The origins of this event go back to the creation of the office of Lord Mayor in 1189, when the establishing charter required that the mayor should present himself to the senior judges, in order to take an oath of loyalty to the sovereign on taking up his post. This annual procession or 'show', originally from the City to Westminster, had become firmly established by the sixteenth century, although it was shortened in 1882 when the Royal Courts moved to the Strand. Much of the journey was covered originally on a barge along the River Thames, hence the name 'float' still associated with the mobile exhibits that accompany the mayor on these parades. But barges were discontinued after 1856, partly because the enormous width of the river reduced the spectacle of this popular procession.

Traditionally, the Livery Companies participate in the Lord Mayor's Show, either as of right or by invitation, together with the so-called privileged regiments of the City of London, such as the Honourable Artillery Company and the Royal Fusiliers. My show, on 14 November 1998, included 6,000 participants, 2,000 military personnel, 200 horses, 70 floats, and 20 carriages.[1] For the first time in over a hundred years, there was a float from the United States, provided by The Cloister, a resort located on Sea Island off the coast of Georgia, where we had owned a holiday home for many years.[2] The Lady Mayoress had her own carriage riding with our daughter Nicole, and with an escort of the Light Cavalry, accompanied by a float from HMS *Argyll*. In recent years, the Lord Mayor's Show has changed a lot, largely because of the huge expense involved in creating a float. Many of the organisations taking place nowadays are representatives of charities, youth groups and marching bands. As an Alderman, I had attended the show many times, but to experience it as the Lord Mayor was almost an out-of-body experience. Suddenly I was inside the eighteenth-century golden State Coach, leaning out of the window, waving my hat, and realising that hundreds of thousands of people along the route were cheering for me. It was a fantastic day and great fun.

During the Lord Mayor's procession, there is a traditional stop at St. Paul's Cathedral, where the new incumbent is blessed by the Dean. John Moses,[3] who held that post when I became Lord Mayor, had asked me what I wanted to do, and had kindly offered every possible scenario, from not stopping at all to the full ceremony. He was extremely sensitive and accommodating. I decided that I would stop, because St. Paul's is an integral part of the City of London. John Moses offered to meet me at the top of the steps leading into the cathedral, where the choir sang 'I will lift up mine eyes unto the hills,' which is a Jewish psalm. Then the Dean made a speech and presented me with an Old Testament in English and Hebrew and used the priestly blessing: 'May the Lord bless you and keep you.'[4] It was an incredibly moving experience.

Just after that, as I was about to get back into my coach, somebody

1   Patrick Sawer, 'The Lord of all shows,' *Evening Standard Metro*, 13 November 1998.
2   Anon., 'Sea Island represents US in London's Lord Mayor's Show for first time in over 100 years', *Savannah Business Journal*, January 1999.
3   Very Revd. John Moses, Dean of St. Paul's, November 1996 – August 2006.
4   Jenni Frazer, 'Jewish links to the fore for new Lord Mayor,' *Jewish Chronicle*, 20 November 1998.

said to me: 'Wait a minute, look up there.' He pointed at a neighbouring building and I saw two figures abseiling down its façade in morning dress. 'Who are they?' I asked. And they said: 'Don't you recognise them? Wait till they get a bit closer, and then you'll know who they are.' All I could see was two pairs of striped trousers descending, but once they got to the pavement, I realised it was my sons, John and Tim. They had never let on to me that they were going to do this, and they did it for charity.

From there we rode to the Law Courts in Fleet Street to take the oath where, by an amazing co-incidence, I was formally introduced at my installation by Judge Michael Hyam, the first Jewish Recorder of London, to Lord Woolf, only the second Master of the Rolls of that faith.[5]

Two days later, on the following Monday, the Lord Mayor's Banquet took place in the Guildhall, attended by the great and the good, including the Prime Minister, Tony Blair, the Archbishop of Canterbury, and the Lord Chancellor. The banquet is preceded by a very formal ceremony whereby all those invited would be seated in the Old Library, and then the most important guests were announced and one by one would process through to be formally introduced to the new Lord Mayor. While this was happening, everybody sitting there had to clap, so the clapping went on for well over an hour, which was very tedious for everyone. It was outdated, and fortunately all that has changed now, in favour of a less formal reception in the Art Gallery, where guests can actually mingle and talk to each other.

As Sheriff, I had been entitled to a flat in the Old Bailey, but as it was really only a bed-sit, we didn't live there. I think I only slept there five or six times, and Wendy never spent the night there. The Lord Mayor, on the other hand, has a magnificent apartment in the Mansion House. It includes a sitting room, a private dining room, and a bedroom with a huge four-poster bed, although I didn't get much time to enjoy all this because I was always too busy. There was a house manager and a butler, I had three valets and a chauffeur and Wendy had a lady's maid, which all meant zero privacy, as the staff were in and out of the apartment all the time.

The principal officer at Mansion House was Air Vice Marshal

5   Jenni Frazer, 'Jewish links to the fore for new Lord Mayor,' *Jewish Chronicle*, 20 November 1998.

12. Our furniture arrives at the Mansion House

Mike Dicken, who was a wise and helpful advisor, and a constant source of reference by me during the year. Of the domestic staff, the principal steward was Colin Tucker, a Scots lawyer by background and who still fills the post today. Colin did a superlative job in running the House and remains a very good friend. He will be very hard to replace when he eventually retires.

When I started at Canary Wharf, there was a concerted attack from some elements of the City of London on me because they believed that in running Canary Wharf I was a major threat to the real estate market in the City of London. I tried to explain to them on many occasions that the addition of some 5 million square feet as a financial district to add to the nation's capital, was a huge advantage and of a size that could never been replicated within the square mile, simply through lack of room. Fortunately, my prophecy proved correct and the City and Canary Wharf now work more happily in tandem. However, the City Corporation used one of their public relations staff, Nigel Szembel, to attack me in the press, which he did with some gusto. Subsequently, when I arrived as Lord Mayor, the Head of PR told me that he was assigning Nigel to act as my personal press advisor and spokesman. I said there was no way that I wanted him to work for me because of the history. The Head of PR then spoke to Nigel who said would I at least talk to him to discuss the issues. When I met Nigel, I told him my views and he said: 'I was only doing my job but if I am working for you, I am your man and if you are not satisfied, you can get rid of me.' So I took him on and he did a tremendous job and we never looked back. In fact, it was he that masterminded the idea of the Achievers' Lunch, which is referred to later in this chapter. Subsequently, Nigel came to work for me at Bankers Trust and Deutsche Bank and then had a very successful career in the City working for Terry Smith. Nigel now runs his own PR consultancy business in Cambridge.

When I arrived at the Mansion House, I asked how much the Mayoralty cost to run in these amazing surroundings. When told the answer, I said we should try to get more bang for the buck. I am just one person, so let's use the Lady Mayoress a lot more. If I can't attend a function, we should offer the Lady Mayoress. This was very often gratefully accepted, and Wendy did a great job incorporating some of her own ideas for 'themed' lunches which were extremely popular.

A great institution at Mansion House was Anni Gale, the Diary Secretary. She had a formidable reputation and an extraordinary memory for events and was paid constant tribute by the Livery Companies who knew that she, and only she, was the gatekeeper if they wanted to fix a function at the Mansion House. Anni also acted as a kind of personal private secretary to Wendy, a role which she has never given up and they continue to work happily together right up to the present day.

Just before we moved in, Wendy said she thought the paintings in the Lord Mayor's apartment were pretty boring and asked me if we could replace them. As I knew the Corporation has a huge collection of pictures, much of which is in store, I told the staff that Wendy would be coming to choose some replacements for the ones in our apartment. 'Oh no, you can't do that,' they said, 'those paintings have been there since time immemorial.' When I said that was no reason for them not being changed, they then argued that it was impossible because they had just redecorated the whole apartment, and if the existing pictures were moved, they would leave dirty marks on the walls. 'Fine,' I said, 'I tell you what; we will deliberately pick paintings that are larger, so if there is a dirty mark, you won't be able to see it.' There were curses.

Anyway, when we moved in, all the pictures we had chosen were up on the walls and everything looked fine. The Corporation had a great director of works by the name of Bill Row, and I said to him: 'How did you manage to do this? They told me it was going to cost tens of thousands.' 'Well, gov, it was easy,' he replied, 'I was out there with my paint pot and brush, and I just touched up round the edges.'

Four days after we had moved into the Mansion House, I went to attend a Livery dinner without Wendy. When I got back, at about half-past ten, the whole place was surrounded by fire engines and vehicles with blue-flashing lights. 'What's happened?' I cried, as I rushed through the door. 'Don't worry,' the staff said, 'we've just saved a minor disaster.' Upstairs, Wendy had left a bath running in our apartment, not realising that it had an extremely powerful tap which caused it to overflow very quickly. Water was pouring through the ceiling of the Salon and had narrowly avoided one of the many seventeenth-century Dutch masterpieces presented to the Mansion House in the will of (Lord) Harold Samuel, following his death in 1987. We found out later that this wasn't the first time that particular bath had overflowed, so that painting has now been replaced by a print – just in case it ever happens again.

Harold Samuel, founder of Land Securities, one of the largest property companies in the UK, had bequeathed his collection of eighty-four seventeenth-century Dutch and Flemish paintings to the Mansion House, on condition that it would be shown in the public rooms. It includes the famous painting by Frans Hals of *The Merry Lute Player*, painted in 1624–28. One day I had a visit from one of the European Commissioners, Fritz Bolkestein, a Dutchman. When he saw the painting, he said he thought it was a fine copy, but when I told him it was the original, he was incredulous. When I was Lord Mayor, Lady Samuel was still alive, and she came on a visit to the Mansion House, with her daughter, to view the collection. She was appalled by the lighting of the pictures and thought they should all be re-lit. I agreed with her and authorised the staff to spend some money sorting this out. Some of the paintings were going to need picture-lights above their frames, which meant drilling through the walls. There was then a huge row because this was going to cost an untold fortune. My response was: 'I don't care. We have to do it. We've got this incredible collection, and we need to show it properly.' Wendy and I then went off on our summer holiday. When we got back, it had all been done. 'How much did it cost?' I asked. 'Well,' they said, 'actually it didn't cost very much. We thought we were going to have to drill through the wall, but we found that the main wall was hollow. There was a trap-door at the bottom, and all we had to do was open it and poke the wire through.'

Once a month, we were able to have a private dinner party in the dining room of our apartment, when we could entertain our own choice of guests. We would gather for drinks in the drawing room, known as the Lady Mayoress's Parlour, and I'd say: 'Would you like to see the Lord Mayor's Dressing Room?' In there we would find all my clothes laid out by the valets for the following morning: vest, pants, socks, trousers, shirt and – because I used to go and swim early in the day – swimming trunks and goggles.

The dressing and undressing became a serious issue and was a nightmare. The lowest form of dress for the Lord Mayor was a short black jacket and striped trousers; at all other times, you had to wear a morning suit, or get dressed up in the full finery. Before I became Lord Mayor, I had got to know Robin Janvrin well,[1] who became The Queen's Private Secretary in 1999. Before I took over as Lord Mayor, he said to me: 'Peter, I've got to tell you something. At the Mansion House, you all dress up in different outfits all day, every day. But if you come to the Palace, you won't find Prince Philip or me dressed up in morning suits. We wear normal clothes, unless we have to go to a special event. Can't you just dumb it down?' I agreed, so most of the time I would wear a lounge suit, to the horror of the staff at the Mansion House, who thought this was complete sacrilege.

For the Lord Mayor's Show, The Queen loans a number of carriages which are included in the procession. The following day, the Private Secretary at the Mansion House told me that I had to write and thank various people, including Her Majesty for the loan of her carriages. When he asked me if I knew how to write such a letter, and I assured him that of course I did, he replied: Are you sure? It has to be drafted in a precise way. You see, it must start: "Madam, my humble duty ..."

---

1   Robin Janvrin, Lord Janvrin (b.1946), Private Secretary to HM The Queen, 1999–2007.

and conclude, "I remain your Majesty's most humble and obedient servant."' 'Fine,' I said, 'I will write it.'

When I became Lord Mayor, the financial City was going through a very rough patch. Just days after I had taken over, Robin Janvrin phoned me up and said: 'Look, The Queen has decided that she'd like to cheer people up a bit and, as you know, she's coming on a visit to the City. But she'd like to see the business side of things, and we don't want everybody dressed up in formal costume.' The Lord Mayor traditionally meets the Monarch and any other members of the Royal Family whenever they come to the City. At the time, I was chairman of Bankers Trust, which meant that I had my own office in the City, so I suggested to Robin that The Queen might be driven there, where I would meet her dressed in a suit, and we would therefore avoid all the pomp and ceremony. He thought this was an excellent idea.

It all worked perfectly. The Queen and the Duke of Edinburgh came on 18 November. After opening the new Financial Services Authority offices in Canary Wharf, she then came on to meet me, before visiting Merrill Lynch and Electra Investment Trust. The Duke went off to visit Lloyds TSB and the Stock Exchange. We all convened for lunch at the *Financial Times*, and then rounded off the visit with a trip to see the Governor of the Bank of England.[1] Later that evening, The Queen hosted a cocktail party for 600 people at Buckingham Palace, to which all the City movers and shakers were invited. That was also a great success. I remember saying: 'Your Majesty, it's so good that you have done this; everybody has been really boosted, and you couldn't have done more to cheer them up.' And she replied: 'Well, I'm delighted.' The next day, Robin rang and asked me if I'd meant what I had said to her. When I said: 'Yes, of course I did, it was a really good idea and it went down very well,' he responded by saying: 'Would you mind writing her a letter to tell her that?' So I said: 'Of course I will, but do you want me to include all this 'Madam, it's my humble duty' stuff?' After a moment, he replied, 'No, don't worry about any of that.'

Shortly after I became Lord Mayor I was approached by the Polish

1   Robin Young, 'Why The Queen is visiting her counting house,' *The Times*, 18 November 1998.

Ambassador who said to me 'We have seen how every year the people of Norway send a Christmas tree to the British people, which is erected in Trafalgar Square, as a token of thanks for all of the support the UK gave to Norway during the Second World War. In Poland, we would like to do the same thing and we would like to know if the City would agree for us to send a Christmas tree to be erected outside St Paul's Cathedral and we will arrange for a choir of Polish children living in London to sing beneath the tree.' I replied that I thought that would be an admirable idea and the Polish Ambassador set about making the arrangements.

Not long afterwards, I was in my office at Mansion House and received a visit from the City Corporation Head of Parks and Gardens. He said: 'I have come to speak to you, Lord Mayor, about the Christmas tree from Poland.' I said: Has it arrived and is it okay?' He replied: 'Yes and no. Unfortunately, the tree had lost all of its pine needles en route and is now just a bare trunk.' 'However,' he added 'don't worry, we have cut an identical tree down in Epping Forest and that will be erected outside St Paul's Cathedral and no one will know the difference.' The Christmas tree was erected, the Polish children sang around it and no one was the wiser.

There are usually three State Visits every year. Although they have relaxed the protocol a little now, during my time as Lord Mayor they all followed a very precise programme. Each visiting head of state would arrive on a Monday. They would either be met at Heathrow Airport or, for some odd reason, be asked to land at Gatwick, and then be put on a train to Victoria Station, where various members of the Royal Family would greet them. Then they were driven to Horse Guards, to be received under a great awning by The Queen, the Duke of Edinburgh, the Lord Mayor, the Prime Minister, the high command of the Armed Forces, and other notables. On the Tuesday evening, The Queen would give a magnificent state banquet at Buckingham Palace for about 200 guests. On the following day, the Lord Mayor would give a state banquet at the Guildhall for 750 guests. Then, on the third and final night, the visiting head of state would give a return banquet, usually in his country's ambassadorial residence in London, or if that was not smart enough, in a hotel.

On the first state visit that I presided over as Lord Mayor, the principal guest was Roman Herzog,[1] the President of Germany. So off we went to the German embassy. I knew the Ambassador quite well, and when we arrived I told Wendy that I was going to sneak a quick look to see where we were sitting, so we knew what to do. I discovered that The Queen was sitting at the top table, with me opposite her. Now, I had frequently had the protocol drummed into me, that you should never start a conversation with the Monarch but wait until you are spoken to. We sat down to dinner, and initially she talked to the German president, who was sitting next to her. But as he didn't speak English, everything had to go through an interpreter and The Queen was finding this somewhat tiring, so turned to look at me. I remember wondering what I was supposed to do, whether I should say something, and would I get my head chopped off if I did. At that time, I was responsible for sorting out the mess of making sure that the Jubilee Line reached the Millennium Dome in time for the celebrations at the start of 2000. After an uncomfortable silence, suddenly The Queen said to me: 'Well, are you going to get the Jubilee Line fixed on time or not?' It was a huge relief, because we had broken the ice. I spoke to Robin Janvrin about my quandary afterwards, and he said: 'Oh, don't worry, you don't have to adhere to those rules anymore, quite unnecessary.'

In June 1999, the President of Hungary, Árpád Göncz, came on a state visit. At that time, although they have revised the protocol since, the Lord Mayor would receive the visiting head of state in the Old Library at the Guildhall. Everybody was dressed up and there would be a lot of clapping. Then after the reception, which lasted about half-an-hour, we would move into the Great Hall for dinner. As it took at least another thirty minutes to move and seat all the 750 assembled guests, we decided to entertain the President by taking him into the Art Gallery, which we had just rebuilt and reopened, following its destruction during the Second World War. This new building included a wall rising the height of two floors, which had been specially designed to display John Singleton Copley's vast painting, *Defeat of the Floating Batteries at Gibraltar, 1782.* The picture had been taken down for safety in 1941, and had remained rolled up in storage ever since, because

---

1   Roman Herzog (1934–2017), President of Germany, 1 July 1994 to 30 June 1999.

there was no wall large enough to display it. Now it had at last been restored and returned to the Guildhall, and I explained to President Göncz that I was going to take him into the Art Gallery, where he would see this amazing painting and hear all about its restoration from Vivien Knight, who was the head of the Corporation of London's paintings collection. 'I'd love to do that' he said. We walked through into the Art Gallery and stood on the balcony in front of this enormous picture, and I said: 'And here is our curator, Vivien, who is going to tell you all about this painting.' But when I looked round, she wasn't there. We had rehearsed all this in advance, but on the night,

13. With President Göncz of Hungary, while showing him the art gallery I have to become the instant art historian.

she just didn't turn up. It was hilarious. All I could say was: 'Well, here we have … um, this very big painting.' Vivien was a very strange lady. Sadly, she died of pancreatic cancer in 2010.

The Hungarian Embassy in London is not large, so they decided to give their return banquet at The Compleat Angler hotel in Marlow, on the banks of the River Thames in Buckinghamshire. It seemed a strange choice, until they explained that Marlow Bridge, near the hotel, had been designed by William Tierney Clark and built between 1829 and 1832; and the Széchenyi Chain Bridge, spanning the River Danube in Budapest, was also designed by Clark as a larger version of the Marlow Bridge, and was opened in 1849, thus the connection was made. We had drinks before dinner on the hotel's lawns, overlooking the river. Of course, everybody there – including the Hungarian President, The Queen and Prince Philip – was in formal dress, being evening dress or uniform and decorations for the men and long dresses and tiaras for the ladies. Meanwhile, there were tourists gliding past downstream on their boats, all doing a double-take at this extraordinary sight.

In October 1999, President Jiang Zhemin of China came on a state visit. After the usual Buckingham Palace and Guildhall dinners, he held a return banquet at the Chinese Embassy in Portland Place. Wendy and I found ourselves sitting on the top table with the President and his wife, The Queen and Prince Philip, and various other members of the Royal Family. After the second course, President Jiang, who spoke very good English, stood up to make an announcement: 'Your Majesty, I wish to serenade you, so I'm going to sing.' He then performed a Chinese love song for The Queen, accompanied by the band of the Welsh Guards! Some of the Royal Household seemed horrified by this but the Duke of Edinburgh was very amused. Then the President announced that he was also going to sing, in English, *If You Were the Only Girl in the World*, but that he would need somebody to accompany him. Up stood Baroness Betty Boothroyd, then speaker of the House of Commons, who had worked in the Tiller Girls dance troupes in the 1940s and 1950s. It turned out that President Jiang and Betty Boothroyd had been rehearsing with the band that afternoon, so he could deliver his love song and they could then perform their duet. It brought the house down. The Queen and Prince Philip loved it.

The night before, when President Jiang Zemin came to the Lord Mayor's dinner in the Guildhall, I, as the host, was sitting next to him. Just before his visit, there had been a lot of anti-China demonstrations in London. When we sat down, he said to me: 'Look, you know we were concerned about demonstrations here, and I know people have been demonstrating. They've tried to cover them up, but I can see what's going on. Actually, I understand what they're demonstrating against. And, as a matter of fact, I don't blame them.' I told him that I had visited China many times. 'Well, if you've been there,' he said, 'what do you think of it?' I said that I thought he and the Chinese were doing an amazing job. 'Exactly,' he replied, and then went on: 'We have 1.3 billion people in China. Do you think I can keep tabs on what they all do every single day? Of course I can't. And are some of them doing things that I wouldn't approve of? Yes. Can I stop them? No. But do you think we're getting it more right than wrong?' I replied: 'Yes, absolutely.'

In 2011, the Duke of Edinburgh celebrated his ninetieth birthday. If the Lord Mayor is unable to attend an important event because he is committed elsewhere, Mansion House will appoint someone to stand

1. In the Great Hall of the Old Bailey with Brother Sheriff Kenneth Ayers and Chelsea Pensioners, 1995.

2. Introduction to the House of Lords with my two sponsors. *Left* Field Marshal The Lord Vincent, *right* The Lord Weinstock.

3. Elected Lord Mayor in September 1998, with Wendy.

4. The Lord Mayor of London and his Lady Mayoress.

5. On Lord Mayor's Day, I am greeted by the Dean of St Paul's, John Moses, November 1998.

6. One of my first overseas trips as Lord Mayor was to China. Here I meet the then Mayor of Dalian, Bo Xilai, who subsequently had a spectacular fall from grace.

7. 'Who has the finer fancy dress?' St Paul's Cathedral with Bishop of London, Richard Chartres, and the Dean, John Moses.

8. Dinner at the Mansion House in honour of the Royal Logistics Corps with the Director of Logistics, Brigadier Tony Dalby Welsh and their Colonel-in-chief HRH The Princess Royal.

9. The python, an innovation of Wendy's, was a popular extra guest at the Mansion House's annual children's fancy dress party.

10. Celebration of Achievement lunch, November 1999. *From left* Alderman and Sheriff Robert Finch, self, HM The Queen, Wendy, HRH The Duke of Edinburgh, Sheriff Pauline Halliday.

11. With Guo Shuqing, Chairman of the China Construction Bank, when I was first appointed to the board in 2005.

12. Visting Real Madrid Football Club, insured by Lloyd's of London.
Left to right self, David Beckham, Ronaldo da Lima, a Spanish broker.

13. With *left* Darragh Gray of Lloyd's Communications team, and *centre* Jonathan Gross, CEO Lloyd's Israel.

14. Visiting Mexico in 2010 as Chairman of Lloyd's and meeting Carlos Slim, who was at the time reckoned to be the richest man in the world.

15. The Governor of California, Arnold Schwarzenegger, meets me in his special tent where he smoked his cigars.

16. Signature of Lloyd's Reinsurance Licence, London. *Left to right* President Hu Jintao, Prime Minister Blair, Deputy Prime Minister Prescott and self.

17. Receiving Honorary Citizenship of Rio de Janeiro from the Mayor, Eduardo Paes and Governor Sergio Cabral

18. HRH the Prince of Wales visits the Underwriting Room at Lloyd's, 2006.

19. At Auschwitz with Nigel Szembel. Wendy and I look at the remains of the gas chambers which the Nazis failed to destroy completely.

20. The next generation, our grandchildren at Sea Island in 2016. *Left to right, back row* Luc, Nicholas, Dylan, Georgia; *front row* Amelie, Charley, AJ, Oscar, Thomas, Jack.

in for him, usually the Senior Alderman (the longest serving past Lord Mayor who is still in the Court of Aldermen). The rules for this are somewhat abstruse, in that if he is abroad, his replacement becomes the Lord Mayor *locum tenens*, whereas if he is in the country but merely at some more pressing engagement, his stand-in is known as a 'representative Lord Mayor'. Prince Philip is a member of countless Livery Companies, and so, when he reached the age of ninety, they all wanted to give a birthday party for him. However, he said: 'Look, it's very good of you, but I don't want to attend umpteen parties, so why don't you all get together and give one?' The senior Company of which he is Liveryman is the Fishmongers', so they decided to give a black-tie dinner in their Hall at London Bridge, and as the Lord Mayor was away, I was asked to stand in as Lord Mayor *locum tenens*.

Prince Philip was, naturally, the guest of honour and some of the guests were his personal friends, and he brought along his partner as well, who was none other than The Queen. Of course, this threw the protocol people in the City into meltdown, because they couldn't think of how to cope with an event to which The Queen was coming, but not as the principal guest. In the end, the Prime Warden of the Fishmongers' hosted the dinner, seated between The Queen and Prince Philip, and I sat on the Duke's other side. When they arrived, there was a choir singing a welcome at the top of the main staircase in the Fishmongers' Hall. As we reached the top, I said: 'Would you

14. I stand in as Lord Mayor *locum tenens* with the President of Chile in 2010, the day after the dramtic rescue of the trapped Chilean miners.

mind stopping for a moment your Royal Highness, as they are now going to sing *Happy Birthday*.' But by then he had spotted all his friends enjoying pre-dinner drinks in an adjoining room, so he said 'I am off to see my friends'. Actually, he was in a very good mood that evening, and later made a brilliant speech, off the cuff, with no notes.

Another person who was a great speaker was the Queen Mother. When I was Lord Mayor, she was invited to unveil a memorial on the north side of St Paul's Cathedral, which had been erected in memory of the civilian victims of the Second World War blitz. She arrived in her car, which had been cleverly adapted, so when the door opened, a foot-rest slid out from underneath, onto which she could step. The car parked on the south side of the cathedral, and I then had to walk her round to the north side. I was terrified because she was, by then, in her late-nineties, and I feared that she might fall over. Anyway, we managed to get her safely to the memorial, where Lord Rothermere made a speech. The Queen Mother then looked at me, so I said: 'Your Majesty, please don't worry, you're not expected to make a speech.' She replied: 'I may not be able to see very well now, but I do know what I'm doing, and I know what I'm going to say.' And she then made an absolutely brilliant speech. She was a truly remarkable lady.

If you look at the Court Circular in the newspapers, you realise what The Queen and other members of the Royal Family have to do, sometimes attending six or seven different events every day, year after year. It seems extremely tedious. I did it on a small scale as Lord Mayor, but I only had to do it for a year. In my case, it wasn't taxing on the mind, but it was incredibly tiring physically. You have to attend countless functions and be nice to everybody all the time. The Livery Company dinners, which are essentially all very similar, are generally held at the Mansion House, and are attended by the Lord Mayor, unless he's otherwise engaged. One night, shortly after I had been appointed, I found myself standing in the Mansion House, waiting to go into the Egyptian Hall, listening to the usual music, and I said to Wendy: 'You know, this is the third time this week that I've stood on this floorboard, waiting to do exactly the same thing.' Wendy turned to me and said: 'Shut up, you've got to understand that, for the Master of this Livery Company, this event is probably the greatest thing that's ever going to happen in his life. So you must tell him that it is the finest dinner you've ever been to, and that you'll never forget it.' Of course, she was quite right. Lord Mayors need to be put in their place from time to time because, being treated like God all the time, they sometimes start to believe it and become absolutely impossible.

The people who attend Livery dinners tend to be clones of each other. Although the Lord Mayor sits next to the Master of the Livery Company, as Sheriff I would generally find myself sitting next to the wife of the senior past Master, who was inevitably rather elderly and sometimes hard of hearing. It's actually quite difficult for anybody to hear anything at those dinners. Anyway, you develop a standard patter, along the lines of: 'Where do you live? Do you have any children? Do you have a dog?' One night, at a very tedious dinner, I sat next to a lady and asked her the usual questions. She turned to me and said: 'Yes, I do have a dog, and you have a dog, whose name is Charley Brown; and we had exactly the same conversation when you sat next to me three weeks ago.' At that point, I flipped, and said to her: 'Well, thank you very much. Look, I have to do this every night, and I simply can't remember every conversation.' I didn't add: 'And by the way, you all look the same as each other.' She shut up like a clam. However, many of the Masters were fascinating characters who greatly enlivened these dinners for me.

This sort of experience brought something home to me. One of my greatest friends at university was Costas Strongylos, a Greek who had been at school with King Constantine[1] of Greece and became his lifelong friend. When the monarchy in Greece was abolished in 1973 and the King went into exile in London, my friend joined him and was subsequently appointed as his Private Secretary. In 1999 Constantine's daughter, Princess Alexia, married Carlos Morales Quintana at St. Sophia Cathedral, the Greek Orthodox church in Bayswater. Wendy and I were invited to a dinner the night before the wedding, which was part of these mega-wedding celebrations. Sitting at our table were some fairly vocal Americans and the King of Sweden. One of the Americans half-recognised him, and said: 'Hi, how are you? How's life? What are you up to now?' And the KIng replied: 'Still the same old thing.' 'Oh,' said the American, 'what's that?' 'Well,' said the Monarch, 'I'm still King.' My neighbour at the table said to

---

1 King Constantine II (b.1940).

me, 'I had the most terrible experience today.' I asked what had happened. She replied: 'Our own aircraft had developed a fault and so I had to fly back commercial from the south of France – it was ghastly.' I replied: 'You are very brave to have come through it!' The following day we went to the wedding itself, followed by a party in the Orangery at Kenwood, where I was seated next to the charming Queen Sofia of Spain, who is King Constantine's sister. While chatting to her, I explained that I was the Lord Mayor and that I found myself constantly having to attend events day after day. And she said to me: 'Look, you've got to do it for a year; for us, it is a life sentence.'

During that year, I attended at least 600 formal lunches and dinners, and made 750 speeches. Some of my predecessors ended the year rather overweight. As Sheriff, I had managed to lose twenty pounds; if you know you are going to be stuffed with food, it's important to make it clear that you only want small portions. When I became Lord Mayor, I was warned early on to avoid drinking wine, because there are so many calories in it, and to be careful what I ate. As I'm a chocaholic, Wendy ordered the staff to give me fruit whenever chocolate desserts were served. I drank water at every event, until one evening when I was very tired. As the wine is always excellent, I decided on that night to drink some. Then of course I had to stand up to speak, and I didn't have the faintest idea what I was doing, it was absolutely terrible. Although we had a speech-writer at the Mansion House, we didn't get on and I didn't like what he wrote. I remember on one occasion saying to Wendy: 'I can't spout all this stuff, it is complete garbage.' When she asked me what I proposed to do instead, I said: 'Don't worry, tonight I know what I'm going to say. I'm just going to speak off the cuff, it will be brilliant, you'll see.' There was an informal rule at the Mansion House that nobody should speak for more than seven minutes. One of the Lord Mayors had even had a giant hour-glass made, and with a great show he'd deploy it when people started speaking, and as it ran down he would start tut-tutting. Anyway, on this particular night, I got up and made what I thought was a brilliant speech, entirely off the cuff. Afterwards I said to Wendy: 'You see, I told you, I don't need this guy writing platitudes for me.' 'Oh, don't you?' she replied, 'Do you know how long you spoke for? You went on for thirty-five minutes.' I never did that again.

I'm afraid that from time to time I would rebel against the relentless programme of ceremonies. There are now 110 Livery Companies, all of which are ranked in a strict order of precedence. The Merchant Taylors and the Skinners have long argued over the sixth and seventh place in this list, because they both received their charter in 1327, but with no surviving proof as to which was granted first. This quarrel is the origin of the saying that everything is 'at sixes and sevens.' Anyway, after decades of squabbling, they decided in 1483 to consult the then Lord Mayor, in the hope that he could settle the argument. He, using the judgement of Solomon, said: 'Look, this is what's going to happen. The Merchant Taylors will be number six this year and the Skinners will be number seven. Next year, you will reverse places.' They thought this was brilliant. So every year since then they have held a ceremony, at which the masters of the two Livery Companies appear before the Lord Mayor in his office, in order to go through this rigmarole. On the day they came to see me, I was feeling facetious. They arrived all dressed-up, but I had been so busy that I hadn't had time to change, so was just wearing a business suit. Once we had assembled, a member of my staff announced: 'Lord Mayor, we have before us today the Masters of the Skinners and the Merchant Taylors, and they are here before you to settle this dispute, as to who is number six and who is number seven.' I was supposed to say: 'Well, as all this was discussed in 1483 by Lord Mayor Billesdon,[1] this is what we're going to do.' But I didn't do that at all. Instead I said: 'This is a load of rubbish. You're all grown men. How can you argue about something like this?' They all looked absolutely horrified, and then I said: 'Only joking!'

As Lord Mayor I attended St Paul's Cathedral frequently and, on one occasion, I processed in with the sword and mace, accompanied by the Sheriffs and two of the household officers. They were supposed to sit on chairs placed for them just in front of the Lord Mayor's official pew. But when we got there, we realised that the cathedral staff had forgotten to put the chairs out. So these two officers, with great presence of mind, turned very slowly and bowed to me, then turned sideways and bowed to each other two or three times, and so

---

1   Sir Robert Billesdon, Lord Mayor in 1483 (Haberdasher).

allowed time for somebody to realise they had no chairs and bring some forward for them to sit on.

Richard Chartres had become Bishop of London in 1995, three years before I became Lord Mayor. I met him at a dinner, at the City University, shortly after he had been appointed. I sat next to his wife, Caroline, and she made me laugh by telling me funny stories. It was a great relief, as, in our time, we had all attended countless such dinners, and subsequently we became great friends. On my appointment Richard presented me with an icon, and said: 'It's alright, Peter, you can keep this one, because it's Elijah.' On the back, it has an inscription saying: 'To Peter the Mayor, from Richard the Bishop.'

As Sheriff of the City of London, I had been invested as a Commander of the Order of St John, a chivalric order first constituted by Royal Charter from Queen Victoria in 1888. In 1998, as Lord Mayor, I rose to become a Knight of the Order. It's a strange set-up, in which the various officers have archaic titles like the Grand Prior, the Prelate, the Sub-Prelates, the Bailiff of Eagles, the Hospitaller, and the Priory Esquires. Every year they hold an investiture for the lower orders at the Priory of St John in Clerkenwell. However, for the higher orders, including the investiture of knights, they arrange a major ceremony at St James's Palace, which I think takes place about once every five years. All the officers turn up in extraordinary costumes, with pages holding their robes. It looks just like the final act of *Cinderella*. About two years after I had been Lord Mayor, I was invited to one of these official investiture ceremonies. The Duke of Gloucester, as Grand Prior of the Order, was presiding. I attended with John Chalstrey and two other friends who, like me, had all served as Lord Mayors. I don't know what happened, but we all got the giggles. Most of the other people there saw this as the pinnacle of their lives, but we saw the funny side of it all.

In 1999 Olusegun Obasanjo was elected President of Nigeria. I had first met him many years earlier on one of my first visits to Lagos, when he was a Colonel in the Nigerian army and United Scientific were selling them mine-detectors. Shortly before he took up office as President, I received a letter from the Nigerian High Commission, to say that Obasanjo would be coming to London, had heard that I was the Lord Mayor, and wanted to come and see me. His predecessor had stolen huge sums of money from the Nigerian people, and as they reckoned much of it was stashed away in banks in London, he hoped that I might be able to help them get some of it back. Obasanjo came to London and I helped him as much as I could. Then he invited me to go on a return visit to see Abuja, the new capital of Nigeria, which had been built largely in the 1980s.

British Airways was one of the very few airlines that flew to Abuja, so I travelled with them. But the British High Commissioner in Nigeria told me that, as Lord Mayor, I would really have to go to Lagos as well, because that was where all the business was still located. However, he was adamant that I could not fly internally on a Nigerian airline, because their planes dropped out of the sky with great regularity. He solved this problem by arranging for me to fly in a private plane chartered and run by Shell, who operate on a massive scale in Nigeria. So I arrived in Abuja, where I was entertained by the Minister for the Federal Capital Territory – equivalent to the Mayor. He insisted on driving me from the airport, in his official car, through their equivalent of the Wellington Arch at Hyde Park Corner, which nobody but The Queen can drive through. In Abuja only the Minister could go through the middle of their special gate.

Then it was off to Lagos in the Shell plane, where I was due to host a large dinner. We had been warned never to use credit cards in Nigeria, because they would be instantly cloned, so everything had to be paid for in cash. The exchange rate for their currency, at that time, was about 100 naira to the pound and the bank notes had never been changed, so if you wanted to pay for anything, you needed suitcases of this money, all of which was absolutely filthy. Nigel Szembel, my extremely able Press Officer who worked for me in the Mansion House, had been given the responsibility of providing the money for this dinner in Lagos. He paid for it in US dollars, but they brought back the change in two bricks of very dirty naira. I remember saying to him: 'Here you are, Nigel, you're lumbered with that.' And he said: 'No, don't worry, I'm not.' Then he called the waiter over and said: 'Here, my friend, this is for you!'

There were countless annual events at the Mansion House, including Livery Company dinners, official banquets for judges and bishops, and the Easter banquet for the Diplomatic Corps. My term of office ran from November 1998 for a year, so my final events took place at the end of 1999, just before the new millennium. I decided that we should do something memorable to mark the end of the twentieth century, so Nigel Szembel, planned the Achievers' Lunch. The idea was that 300 guests would be invited, based on outstanding achievement in every sphere of British life, from politics, performing arts and media, sport, fashion and design, industry and commerce, education, banking, science, and public service. It would include the widest possible range of people, from country dancers and chess players to footballers and philosophers. I enquired whether The Queen would be prepared to attend, which she said she was happy to do, and, of course, I agreed with her request that she wouldn't have to make a speech.

When we started planning this event, I suggested that I would draw up the guest list. Immediately I was advised that this was a bad idea, because the event would obviously feature in all the newspapers and could therefore attract a great deal of criticism over who had and had not been invited. The solution was to write to every organisation in the country, such as the Football Association, the British Medical Association, and the Law Society, asking each of them to nominate three people. We also asked the editor of every national newspaper to put forward names, which included them in the whole process and therefore stopped them from criticising the list. We received a total of 1,766 nominations, which then had to be cut down to a final shortlist of about 350. In order to do this, I chaired a selection committee made of up The Bishop of London – Richard Chartres, a former Lord Mayor – Sir Alexander Graham, Max Hastings – editor of the *Evening Standard*, John Holroyd – Appointments Secretary at Downing Street, Lord Hurd – the former Foreign Secretary, Dame Sheila Masters – Director of the Bank of England, and the Olympic athlete – Tessa Sanderson.

The event took place in the Mansion House on Tuesday, 2 November 1999, and was described as 'The Lunch of the Century'. The guest list included three former Prime Ministers (Sir Edward Heath, Sir John Major and Baroness Thatcher), captains of industry and commerce, national sportsmen and women, Nobel Prize winners, surgeons, scientists, film stars, composers, writers, explorers, and war heroes, many of them household names. But we also invited people unknown outside their own community, like charity and community workers, disabled athletes, and lifeboat skippers. From the world of sport came footballers Sir Bobby Charlton and Sir Geoff Hurst; rugby's Bill Beaumont and Martin Offiah; jockeys Lester Piggott and Richard Dunwoody; athletes Colin Jackson and Mary Peters; cricket's Mike Brearley, Fred Trueman, Basil D'Oliveira and Dickie Bird. Stage, screen, television and showbusiness were represented by Lord Attenborough, Ronnie Barker, Sir Peter Hall, Sir Nigel Hawthorne, Sir Jonathan Miller, Trevor Nunn, Dame Diana Rigg, and Emma Thompson. Singers included Shirley Bassey, Dame Cleo Laine, and Dame Vera Lynn. The arts, including music, literature and the media, provided Lord Lloyd-Webber and Sir Tim Rice, Sir George Martin, Sir Robin Day, Sir David Frost and Sir Jeremy Isaacs, Sir Neville Marriner, Dame Alicia Markova, Dame Janet Baker, Beryl Bainbridge, and Malcolm Bradbury. Two holders of the Victoria Cross and two RAF wartime flying aces, both holders of the DSO and the DFC, contributed to the armed forces category.[1]

We lunched, of course, on British beef. I made a speech in which I said: 'I doubt very much that on any single occasion quite so many people of such distinction have come together at the same time. By recognising your achievements we celebrate the achievement of all who have, though their individual efforts and sacrifices, made this country what it is today. It is not a matter of the 300 or so of us in this room. It is not a matter of 3,000, or 30,000, or 300,000. Everyone, old and young, played his or her part in creating the success and wealth of this nation.[2]'

In order for people to be able to enjoy the lunch as much as possible, we decided to restrict the speeches to two only. I would make the first and, as we had agreed we would not expect The Queen to speak, my task was to find someone to reply to my speech. I looked through this incredible list of guests and my attention was caught by the name of Sir Robin Day, who was the famous political broadcaster and commentator. I had never met him but I called him up and said 'Look, I wonder if I might be able to persuade you to make the speech at the

15. **Sir Robin Day delivers a brilliant speech at the Achievers' Lunch.** *Left to right* **Lord Rothschild, Trevor Nunn, Sir Robin Day, self, HM The Queen, The Bishop of London – Richard Chartres**

Mansion House lunch'. He replied: 'Oh, you don't want me. I am an old fogey.' I said: 'On the contrary, you are by far the best person to make the speech.' And so he agreed. On the day, he followed up my speech with an absolutely brilliant one of his own and right at the end said: 'Having been invited to attend this excellent lunch today, I wondered to myself, who in fact should deserve the accolade of "highest achiever of the century?"' At this point, I became slightly nervous because we had tried very hard to avoid raising anything along those lines, but Sir Robin went on to say: 'It occurred to me that there is one person here who unquestionably stands head and shoulders above all the others and deserves that title and it is, of course, the lady sitting on my left.' (The Queen). This produced thunderous applause from all the guests and I could see that The Queen was very touched.

I had invited Abe Beame,[1] who had been Mayor of New York City in the 1970s. He had been born in London and was the only Briton to have held that position. We flew him over on Concorde a few days

1   Abraham Beame (1906–2001), Mayor of New York City, 1 January 1974 – 31 December 1977.

16. I wait for my walk-on part in The Golden Bowl, filmed in the Mansion House.

before the lunch, as he was in his nineties by then, and invited him to stay at the Mansion House. Over the weekend before the lunch, I was sitting in my office when Wendy phoned through to me and said: 'Can you hear that banging noise? There's nobody else here on a Saturday, but I can hear someone banging.' It turned out that Abe had locked himself into the bathroom, couldn't get out, and was hammering on the door with a bath-brush. We had nearly killed him.

During my year in office, the Mansion House was used as a location in the film, *The Golden Bowl*, which was based on Henry James's novel, and which was produced by Ismail Merchant and directed by James Ivory. It was released in France and the United Kingdom in 2000, and in the United States in 2001. The cast included Kate Beckinsale, James Fox, Angelica Huston, Nick Nolte and Uma Thurman. Of course, they told us that they hoped we would agree to appear in it, so we all dressed up in costumes. When I first saw the finished film, I could barely spot either of us. I think I appeared twice for a matter of seconds, once with Wendy and once on my own. The film company was in the Mansion House for about four days, with hundreds of people and vans all over the place. If I had known in advance how much mess they were going to make, I would never have agreed to it.

I travelled extensively when I was Lord Mayor, visiting thirty countries. My first trip, in December 1998, was to Israel and the West Bank and Gaza, where I met the Palestinian leader, Yasser Arafat.[1] The Palestinians showed me round and told me what was going on. I thought they were actually trying pretty hard, although Arafat himself was regarded by many as a very difficult man. Then I returned to Tel Aviv, where I was due to attend the Balfour Dinner, an annual event commemorating the Balfour Declaration of 1917, which had announced British support for the establishment of 'a national home for the Jewish people' in Palestine. This dinner, which alternated between the UK and Israel with an equivalent guest speaker on each side – such as Chief of Defence Staff or Minister or Mayor, was held along with about 300 leaders of Israeli society. When I stood up to make my speech, I said: 'This morning I went to Gaza. It takes about forty-five minutes by car. In this room, hands up all those who have ever been there?' Not one person responded. I went on: 'Do you know what? I know everybody here believes this situation is impossible to resolve. But we had this problem in Northern Ireland, and I never believed that would be resolved in my lifetime. But it has been, and today it's 95% fine there now. And it was achieved to a great extent by money. The Protestants had money and jobs; the Catholics had no money and no jobs, so they resorted to violence and petrol bombs. Bill Clinton did a deal with Tony Blair, together they poured money and jobs into Northern Ireland, and it worked. I think you could do the same thing here.' Sadly, that hasn't yet worked out in the West Bank and Gaza.

Early in my term, in January 1999, I was asked by the Government to go to as many European capitals as possible, in order to explain that although the UK was not adopting the new Euro currency, the City of London would be very much at the centre of Euro trading. In the space of about three weeks, I visited Vienna, Lisbon, Dublin, Frankfurt, Stockholm, Copenhagen, Milan, Zurich, Paris, Madrid, Helsinki and Amsterdam. On one of my first stops, in Milan, I was

1   Nicky Blackburn, 'City 'finally' recognizes Israel business potential,' *Jerusalem Post*, 16 December 1998.

entertained to lunch by the chairman of a large Italian bank. I explained why I was there. And he said: 'I don't know why you're wasting your time. You don't need to explain any of this to us. Let me tell you why. If on Monday morning, I call in two of my brightest young guys and tell them that I'm posting them to London, they will say: 'What time is the plane?' If, by contrast, I tell them they're going to Frankfurt, they would say: 'What did we do wrong?'' On reflection, I think these trips proved helpful, and I was able to come back and report that the message had been well received. But now with Brexit on the near horizon, the final result is largely unknown.

On another visit, I went to Riyadh and Jeddah in Saudi Arabia, and then on to Beirut in Lebanon. As this was one of the trips on which Wendy was to accompany me, and I knew that she would be unlikely to comply happily with the dress requirements for ladies in Saudi Arabia, we agreed that she would join me later in Lebanon. I was travelling with Douglas Hurd, who at that time was chairman of British Invisibles. We had some fascinating meetings and discussions with the Governor of Riyadh, Prince Salman, who later became King of Saudi Arabia in 2015. He showed us round his palace, which was enormous, with numerous audience chambers. I had never seen anything like it in my life. Then we were introduced to the Speaker of the Saudi parliament, who said that he would show us round the 'Consultative Assembly' meeting hall, in the Al Yamamah Palace in Riyadh. This was larger than the United Nations General Assembly hall at the UN Headquarters in New York. As I knew they didn't have a democratic parliament, I said to our guide: 'This is very interesting. What sort of things are discussed in your parliament? And how often does it meet in here?' 'Well,' he said, 'it hasn't actually met yet, but the hall is here, just in case it meets. Now, let me take you through here.' And we went through a side door into what we were told were the private quarters of King Abdullah. 'Does he live here?' I asked. 'No, this palace is here just in case he comes to visit the Assembly, so he has somewhere to sit down. He lives over there.' We looked in the direction in which he was pointing, and there was another palace, much larger than the one we were standing in. The Saudis were very keen to show how much progress they were making in the development of their economy and their image of a modern society. Our visit was very ceremonial, and they were extremely hospitable to us, but I realised afterwards that I hadn't seen a single female during our entire two-day visit. They just didn't seem to exist, so I was very pleased that I hadn't taken Wendy with me.

We then left Saudi Arabia and flew on to Lebanon, where Wendy joined me. They were just starting to rebuild Beirut after their devastating civil war, and a whole new district in the centre was under development. We stayed in a wonderful hotel, which retained a lot of French influence, with excellent service and food. However, conditions were still somewhat fragile, and I felt very sorry for the Lebanese. Beirut clearly had once been the playground of the Middle East, but it had been very badly damaged.

The British ambassador had arranged a fascinating visit for me to meet the Lebanese politician, Walid Jumblatt, who led the Druze Progressive Socialist Party. In Lebanon there are Christians, Moslems, and the Druze. The latter live up on the hills, outside Beirut, with their own army, and have no allegiance to their country's government at all, except through this man. In order to reach him, we had to be driven out of Beirut and up into the hills, where we exchanged our Lebanese army military escort for a Druze one. Eventually, we reached Mr Jumblatt's headquarters at the top of a mountain. He laid on a magnificent meal and made us extremely welcome. After lunch, he took me into his study, which was decorated with framed photographs on the walls, each one of which had a black border. These turned out to be various members of his family who had all been assassinated. There was also a very large painting of General Georgy Zhukov riding victorious through the streets of Berlin in 1945, with his horse's hooves trampling Nazi insignia to the ground. When I asked Mr Jumblatt why this particular painting had pride of place in his study, he replied: 'When I really need it, the Russians are there to help.' Walid Jumblatt was extraordinary. When I met him, he wore a tweed suit, smoked a pipe, and walked around with two wolfhounds.

One of my early official trips was to China and we landed at Dalian, a city in the north of the country, where we were met by the Mayor, Bo Xilai. He was waiting for us on the tarmac at the airport, with an enormous stretched white Cadillac. As I walked down the steps of the plane, he came up to me and said: 'Welcome to California!' He spoke perfect English. His father, Bo Yibo, had been one of the so-called Eight Elders of the Communist Party of China, who had held substantial power during the 1980s and 1990s. Bo Xilai entertained Wendy and me in Dalian for two days, with wonderful parties. It was the start of his move to become a major international figure. However, years later, in 2012, his political career came to an abrupt end when his wife, Gu Kailai, was convicted of murdering the British business-man Neil Heywood. She was given a suspended death sentence, which was later commuted to life imprisonment; and her husband was stripped of all his political positions. The following year, he was found guilty of corruption, deprived of all his assets, and also sentenced to life in prison.

In June 1999 the final of the cricket World Cup was taking place in London. The City Corporation, encouraged by its many cricket supporters, had arranged a banquet at the Guildhall which the Duke of Edinburgh had agreed to attend. So far so good, but on the day in question, June 18th, it had proved to be one of the hottest days of the year, and a group had organised what they called a 'Carnival of Resistance' or 'Reclaim the Streets' for the same day. The City of London Police were worried about the event, fearing it might lead to serious rioting in The City, but in a briefing the night before, they assured me that everything would be well under control.

The day started off peacefully enough with a long tail of cyclists riding round and round in front of the Mansion House and the Bank of England, slowing down traffic, but not much else. But at lunchtime, reports were coming in of serious trouble at Liverpool Street and on London Wall a woman who had clambered on top of a police vehicle fell off and was then injured when the vehicle reversed. She was taken to hospital where, reportedly, they found a long knife concealed in her boot.

The rioting escalated with a carefully planned attack on LIFFE (The Futures Exchange) at Cannon Street which developed into a battle between the rioters and some pretty focussed traders. The rioters clearly did not know their enemy and picked the wrong City institution to attack. The traders won what became a pitched mediaevalesque battle – with scaffolding poles used as battering rams and lances to breach the LIFFE building. Pretty soon it seemed that the Police had lost control of large parts of the City as some of the worst rioting ever seen within the Square Mile continued unabated. Whilst all this was going on, I was in the Mansion House and told to stay inside whatever happened as there was a pretty unfriendly crowd outside keeping their eyes open for me.

I was asked if I could go as soon as possible to the TV studio at Millbank to be interviewed. It was important to get the message out that the City would be back at business on the next working day, indeed contingency planning was already underway in Guildhall to ensure that it did. It was an important message to get out especially as news of the rioting was all over the global media. But no cars could move and the streets were largely under the control of the rioters. However, someone came up with the idea of ordering a taxi bike to take me, and suggested that if I dressed down to a tee shirt, jeans, trainers and a motorbike helmet, I could escape unrecognised. Happily, the ruse worked and I was able to turn up at the studio. I managed to return to the Mansion House only to be asked when I would be going to the Cricket Dinner at the Guildhall. I had already heard that the Police had advised Prince Philip not to attend, and so I had assumed that the banquet would be cancelled as most of the guests would be unable to get there. But the Cricket aficionados of the City wouldn't hear of it and insisted that I must attend.

By this time we were all pretty shattered, so I was more than a little irritated, but eventually I agreed and said that I would reluctantly go, however I was not prepared to change into full Lord Mayoral evening dress and they would have to put up with me in my 'motorcycle' outfit. They were horrified but I said it was that or nothing. I did turn up, to a Guildhall only about a quarter full, but to be fair they gave me a rousing reception.

At the end of my term of office, Nigel Szembel, who had throughout the Mayoralty acted as my very successful 'Collaborateur in Chief', very generously commissioned a brilliant cartoon showing me on the motorbike, and that is how the cover of this book came to be produced.

When you are travelling around the world as Lord Mayor, you are given lots of presents, some of which are rather tacky. So, we had to take gifts too, but we made sure we gave decent presents. One member of staff from the Mansion House travelled with us, with the job of carrying a suitcase full of the gifts we were giving away. Sadly, it never got any lighter for him, because it gradually filled up with all the gifts we were given. We usually gave pieces of silver to our senior hosts abroad. For all the Livery Companies, I commissioned watercolours from the artist David Gentleman, who had painted banquets taking place at the Mansion House or the Guildhall. We kept his originals, and issued limited numbered and signed prints, which were rolled up in a golden tube for presentation as gifts.

On our trip to Brunei in 1999, we travelled there as guests of their Royal Family. I was invited and entertained by Sultan Hassanal Bokliah, and Wendy was entertained, sequentially, by his two wives. Brunei is tiny and has a population of only just over 400,000 people, but it is an immensely wealthy country because of its petroleum and natural gas deposits. The Istana Nurul Iman, which is the Sultan's official residence and the seat of the Brunei government, is considered to be the world's largest residential palace, covering over 200,000 square metres, with an estimated seventeen floors, including those underground. It was completed in 1984 at a cost of US$1.5 billion. Along with its contents, it was mind-boggling. What looked like vases of flowers on first sight turned out not to be flowers, but huge diamonds and pearls. The British High Commissioner took me to see the Sultan, who spoke to me very quietly in Malay, through an interpreter, although I suspect that having graduated from Sandhurst, his English is as good as mine.

Wendy was accompanied by the High Commissioner's wife, who took her to see the Sultan's two wives. The first one asked her if she had ever visited Brunei's amusement park, Jerudong Park, which had been built and funded by the Bruneian government at a cost of US$1 billion and had opened in 1994. It is the largest and most expensive amusement park in South East Asia, and is currently still larger thanPhase 1 of Hong Kong Disneyland. Until recently all the rides were free. When Wendy replied that we had never been there, the Queen of Brunei said: 'Well, you must go there this evening.' 'But Your Majesty,' said the High Commissioner's wife, 'it's not open on Tuesdays.' And The Queen replied: 'Then we shall open it.' We were due to attend a state banquet that night, so off we went, dressed up for dinner, to visit the amusement park. When we arrived there was an astonishing musical display of fountains. The manager, who like many of the people working there, was British, said to us: 'It's a great honour for us that you have come here. We're so delighted to see you. But I'm terribly sorry to tell you that, because we only knew late on that you were coming, we haven't been able to switch on all the lights. We have two million lights here, but I've only managed to get about three-quarters of them switched on.' It was still an incredible sight, and we were the only people there.

Shortly before our visit, the Sultan's brother, Prince Jefri Bolkiah, who had been the country's finance minister from 1986 to 1998, initiated a number of very costly projects. One of these was the creation of the world's most expensive hotel, now known as The Empire Hotel & Country Club, which he decided would be the first seven-star hotel. It has 518 guest rooms, suites and private villas, all surrounded by gardens and lagoons, with views over the ocean and the resort's golf course. When we were taken to see it in 1999, it was unfinished and parts of it were still a construction site. But even then, it was already an astonishing place. The lobby was absolutely enormous; the regular rooms were the equivalent of a super-suite in any other hotel; and the suites were so big, you could happily live in them. Then, of course, there was the presidential suite, which outstripped everything we had seen before, until they showed us the royal empire suite, which had a full-size Olympic swimming pool in the bathroom. The Sultan of Brunei has the largest collection of Rolls Royces in the world, and if you took one of the villas at this hotel, it came with a Rolls Royce, a Ferrari, or a Lamborghini.

As Lord Mayor, I made more than thirty overseas visits in the year, as part of my main task of promoting both the London and UK financial services industry around the world. Not surprisingly, these included the United States, where I was told that the British Consul General in San Francisco had managed to secure a speaking slot for me at Bohemian Grove. I had never heard of Bohemian Grove. It turned out to be a private 2,700-acre estate at Monte Rio in California, owned by the all-male Republican membership of the Bohemian Club, which is based in San Francisco. In mid-July every year they hold a two-week, three-weekend retreat at Bohemian Grove, which is attended by prominent business leaders, government officials, former US presidents, senior media executives, and famous artists and musicians. They all camp in tents or wigwams, hold numerous discussions, and lay on two or three speeches, the most important of which is the Lakeside Address, which I had been allocated.

At about this time, David Osborne and Ted Gaebler had published a book in America called *Reinventing Government: How the Entre-preneurial Spirit is Transforming the Public Sector.* I had read this book, and found it said that government should be run a lot less bureaucratically and along more commercial lines, and that a lot of its work could be privatised and contracted out. Of course, we had already started doing this in the UK and were miles ahead on these ideas, so I wrote a speech entitled 'We reinvented Government before you did.' It went down very well.

The British Consul General in San Francisco drove me out to Bohemian Grove which was in the middle of a forest, and surrounded by guards, who rode around in trucks. As one of the guest speakers, I was given the VIP suite, which was in fact a garden shed with bunk-beds. Although it was mid-July, they gave me an electric blanket, because they said I might find it got cold at night. How right they were. On the first night, I woke up at two o'clock in the morning, and it was absolutely freezing, so I was very glad of that electric blanket. All the tented camps on the estate had strange names, like Hiawatha; and all these important guests seemed to revert to being little boys, on their childhood camping holidays. As everybody slept in tents, or a garden shed, and there were no women there, it was *de rigeur* for all the men to pee in the bushes, which was just part of the ethos. However, they imported the best chefs from San Francisco and the finest wines, and there was much competition between the camps as to who produced the best food.

You could wander from camp to camp, to hear different talks. On one day, I found myself sitting next to the Director-General of the Smithsonian Institution on my right and a Nobel Prize winner on my left. To increase the bizarre nature of the whole place, on Saturday night they organised a musical show, in which a boat was rowed into the middle of the lake. Once it got there, they would set it on fire, in a ceremony called 'the 'Cremation of Care,' representing the burning of all 'dull care.' The motto of the Bohemian Club is 'Weaving spiders come not here,' implying that outside concerns are to be left outside.

Nobody was allowed to talk business, mobile phones were forbidden, and it was in an area where there was no reception. However, people had discovered that if you climbed to the top of a nearby hill, you would get a signal. I remember going up there one day myself, and finding a lot of other men chatting on their mobile phones.

During a Lord Mayor's period of office, there is always a visit to Sheffield, where there used to be a thriving industry in silver and silver-plate. The city even has its own Livery Company, known as the Company of Cutlers in Hallamshire, which is the other name for that part of Yorkshire, and distinguishes it from the Cutlers' Company in the City. I met their Master Cutler at a dinner in London, where he told me about their amazing collection of Sheffield plate. They had managed to acquire a piece for every year since the company's foundation in 1624, with the exception of anything from 1847, for which they had searched for many years but without success. Once I knew I would be attending one of their great dinners, I said to my brother: 'Listen, if you can find me a piece of Sheffield plate hallmarked in 1847, I want it and I'll buy it.' Half-an-hour later, he rang me back to say: 'I've got one on my shelf, it's an inkstand.'

So off I went to this banquet in Sheffield, where there were about 700 guests. They presented me with a huge silver sword. I remember thinking how glad I was that I'd thought to bring something for them. When it was my turn to speak, I stood up and said: 'Master Cutler, thank you so much for this wonderful gift. I hope that you will accept this small present from me. I have a piece of old Sheffield plate to give you, which was made in … 1847.' The place went into uproar, men were crying! They had been looking for a piece from this date for decades, so that they could complete their collection, and I had suddenly turned up and given it to them. Although the sword had been presented to me personally, I decided that I should give it to the Mansion House. On my return to London, I went to hand it over to Robert, the plate-man, and told him the story. '1847?' he said, 'hold on a minute.' And he went off to a drawer and unearthed a whole canteen of Sheffield plate cutlery, all dated 1847, which nobody else had realised was there.

There had been a longstanding tradition that outgoing Lord Mayors would present a piece of silver to add to the plate collection at the Mansion House. Although this custom had largely fallen away, primarily because of escalating cost, I felt that I must honour it in commemoration of our family business. So I commissioned a scale model in silver of a pikeman of the Honourable Artillery Company, which was modelled based on somebody then serving in the regiment. It was so realistic that his friends could recognise him. Having lived in the Mansion House for a year, I knew that the huge plateroom downstairs was full of silver that never saw the light of day, except on high days and holy days, so I presented my pikeman with an engraving on it saying: 'To be kept in the Venetian Parlour', which is the Lord Mayor's office. That ensured that it wouldn't be stashed away in the basement; and, happily, my successor, Sir Clive Martin, who had been a pikeman himself, commissioned a matching musketeer, so now they both are displayed as a pair in the Venetian Parlour.

So that was my year as the Lord Mayor of London. It was absolutely exhausting, and I think if you had to do it any longer, it would kill you. Apart from anything else, some of what happens repeats itself, so the routine can become quite numbing. All the Livery Company dinners feature the ancient ceremony of a loving cup, where a goblet of wine is passed round the table, and there is always a toast to The

17. Handing over. The Lord Mayor's Banquet in 1999 with incoming Lord Mayor, Clive Martin, and Prime Minister Tony Blair.

Queen. Even today, although I have now retired as senior Alderman, I could participate in one of those events with my eyes closed. You know exactly when there will be a bang, at which you all stand up. I became a sort of automaton. Sometimes, when we finished events, Wendy would ask me: 'How was that? What did you talk about?' And I'd say: 'I haven't got the faintest idea and I can't remember.' When my year came to an end, people said: 'I bet you're sorry it's finished. Wouldn't you like to do it again?' 'No way!' was my reply but I wouldn't have missed it for the world.

CHAPTER TEN

Chairman of Lloyd's

IN 2001 Sir David Walker, for whom I had worked at Morgan Stanley, contacted me to say that he had been asked to make recommend-ations for a new Chairman for Lloyd's of London, and asked if I would be interested. When I pointed out that I didn't have any previous experience in the insurance industry, he assured me that they actually wanted primarily a representational head for the business. So, I said that I would be interested in that role, and in June 2002 I was elected as Chairman, with instructions to take over from my pre-decessor Sax Riley in November. It was the first time Lloyd's had made such an appointment from outside the insurance market. Following the terrorist attack on the World Trade Center in New York on 11 September 2001 (9/11), Lloyd's had just reported losses of £3.1 billion. It was the largest deficit in their 314-year history, and they had not been in profit for five years.[1] My lack of experience in insurance was not universally looked at with approval from all quar-ters in Lloyd's, but Robert Hiscox, Chairman of Hiscox, remarked: 'Not knowing about the market is an absolute asset. Lloyd's is the only mutualised market in the world and anyone who comes from outside and says 'this is odd' is a good thing. Lloyd's has been incap-able of recognising that it is part of the insurance world. Its failure to change almost killed it.'[2]

Unlike a number of my friends, I had never been a Lloyd's Name, the term applied to private individuals who had committed them-selves as underwriters for the market's insurance policies. However, I

1   Katherine Griffiths, 'Outsider Levene to be named as the new chairman at Lloyd's of London', *The Independent*, 12 June 2002; and Andrew Bolger, 'Levene takes leading role at Lloyd's', *Financial Times*, 12 June 2002.
2   Michael Loney, 'The troubleshooter', *Reactions*, April 2003.

had, many years previously, been introduced to an underwriter at Lloyd's, who had told me, over a very good lunch, why it would be a great idea for me to become one of the Names. In a nutshell he explained that, following an interview with Lloyd's, and assuming I had a reasonable slug of assets, I would then sign a piece of paper. Every year after that, I would get a large cheque and a tax rebate. I remember saying: 'Is that all there is to it?' When he said that it was, I replied: 'It all sounds a bit too good to be true. You've been so helpful explaining how wonderful it all is, but can you give me any reason why I wouldn't want to do this?' He paused and then said: 'Well, you built up your own business; you made money out of that. You ran the business and you knew what was happening. If it was doing well, it was down to you; if it was doing badly, you had to sort it out. If you sign up for Lloyd's, you will commit all of your assets to that business. You won't really have any control over what they're doing, nor will you probably understand very much of it. And if it does well, you will get a big fat cheque. But if it doesn't, you could find yourself in hock for every penny you've got, every penny your wife has got, and you might lose the lot. How does that grab you?' And I said: 'Well, you know what? Maybe I won't.' He replied: 'I don't blame you.'

Following the Lloyd's crisis in the 1990s, when 34,000 of these individual Names lost substantial sums of money, Lloyd's had decided to establish a new construct for running their business by setting up a Franchise Performance Board. The idea was that this would take a much more active role in vetting the performance of the individual companies that collectively made up the Lloyd's insurance market. Prior to this, there had been no policing of these firms, but this new board would actively review their performance in future. Furthermore, those who were not doing well would in future be given a warning, and if they didn't improve, they would be removed from the Lloyd's market.

When I first joined the organisation, I quickly realised that there was a very close analogy between the situation facing Lloyd's and the scenario that I had walked into at Canary Wharf. By the time I took over at the latter, back in 1993, a lot of solutions to the problems associated with the infrastructure were being addressed or had already been solved, such as the DLR, but nobody had managed to change the failed perception of Canary Wharf in the eyes of the public. In other words, if you give a dog a bad name, everybody continues to think it is terrible. Lloyd's had a similar problem. It had a terrible reputation that was worse, in its day, than that, subsequently, of RBS. But when I got there, I realised that they had actually done a very good job in setting up the structure to initiate the new Franchise Performance Board to police the individual syndicates in the market. Lloyd's should have been at the top of its game again, particularly because it had this world-famous name. This had come home to me soon after I'd joined when we were on holiday in Vietnam, where we had an official guide. When he asked what I did, and I told him, he replied: 'Oh yes, Lloyd's is the biggest name in insurance in the world.' I remember thinking that if a young man in his twenties, in this ultra-Communist country, knew all about Lloyd's, then it clearly had the most amazing brand name. Even more so than Canary Wharf, it was something that was just waiting to have its reputation rebuilt. So over the years, between 2002 and 2011, that's exactly what I did. I told my colleagues: 'Look, I'm not an expert on insurance, but we've got more than enough people here who know about that. I want to help rebuild the Lloyd's brand, by being a spokesman and front man for it.'

I saw it as my job to travel the world and change the prevalent negative perception that people had about Lloyd's at that time. It was something that I had already been trained to do, because as Lord Mayor I had spent a year travelling to the same places to promote the City of London. I warmed to this new task, partly because I never had to explain what Lloyd's was; wherever I went, people had already heard of it. It was also an exciting challenge which former Chairmen had not really addressed, mainly because they had been too busy trying to fix a broken product and nobody really wanted to mention in polite society that they had anything to do with Lloyd's. In fact, I remember when my Chairmanship was first announced in the press, a number of my friends phoned up and said, 'Congratulations! Or should we say commiserations?' Once this had happened several times, I retorted, 'Now look, shut up. If I didn't think I could fix the Lloyd's reputation, I wouldn't have taken it on. You may remember that when I went to sort out the Docklands Light Railway, they said, 'What does he know about trains?' But I seemed to fix that alright.

And when I went to Canary Wharf, they said, 'What does he know about real estate?' And I don't seem to have done too badly there either. So maybe you should give me the benefit of the doubt with Lloyd's?'

When I became chairman of Lloyd's, the Chief Executive was Nick Prettejohn, a brilliant man. We had two completely different skill-sets, but we got on very well. When I got the job, I remember saying to him, 'Look, I'm now the chairman; you've been the Chief Executive here for some time. We ought to discuss who does what.' And he replied, 'I'll run the machine; you get us the right image.' That was the one and only discussion we had on the subject. He ran and looked after the market, which he knew inside-out; and I acted as the promoter. Under this arrangement, we never once fell out. Not long after my appointment, Lloyd's was hit by the aftermath of Hurricane Katrina in 2005, which was the costliest natural disaster in the history of the United States, with damages estimated at $108 billion. It brought Lloyd's close to collapse, but somehow it managed to survive.

* * *

Lloyd's is currently occupying its third principal home. Having originated in a coffee-house in Tower Street in the 1680s, and quickly outgrown subsequent premises in Pope's Head Alley, in 1774 the society rented space in the Royal Exchange, where they remained for over 150 years. The first purpose-built building for Lloyd's, designed by Sir Edwin Cooper, was built in Leadenhall Street between 1925 and 1928. A large extension in Lime Street, linked to the main building by a bridge, was added in 1950–, to the designs of Terence Heysham. At that time, the owners of Bowood House in Wiltshire, faced with massive repair costs, had decided to demolish a part of their property, including the Great Room, which had been designed in 1763 by the famous Scottish architect Robert Adam. Terence Heysham had been looking for a fireplace to install in the new committee room of his extension, and persuaded Lloyd's to buy not only Adam's magnificent marble mantelpiece, but to acquire his entire room at auction, with a view to installing it as the new council chamber. There was only one problem. When it arrived in Lime Street in 1956, the Adam Room was found to be too long, so they chopped a slice out of the middle, joined it up to make a slightly shorter room, and incorporated the spare eighteenth-century plasterwork into an adjoining vestibule. In 1979, following a decision to redevelop the site, Lloyd's was demolished and a new building was commissioned from Richard Rogers, which opened for business in 1986. He was told that, as part of this job, he was expected to incorporate the Adam Room, *in toto* and restored to its original length, into this new premises. Initially, he is reported to have said, 'If you think I'm going to put some eighteenth-century monstrosity in my icon of the twentieth century, forget it.' But when Lloyd's replied by saying they would then have to look for an alternative architect, he agreed, and it was then very cleverly incorporated. The finished impression was best summed up by my good friend, Richard Chartres, the Bishop of London. When he came to see it, he said, 'Oh Peter, this is magnificent; this is the piece of Fabergé in the Conran shop.'

I found I was the chairman of two bodies: the Council of Lloyd's, which had been in existence since time immemorial; and the newly minted Franchise Performance Board, which had been created to watch the performance of the market. Before I formally took over, I was invited to attend the last Council meeting under the Chairmanship of my predecessor, Sax Riley. I found myself in Adam's magnificent dining room, where an enormous table had been installed. The council members and the permanent staff of Lloyd's sat on one side, the insurance industry members sat on the other, and everyone had a microphone and a name-plate in front of them. It was like a scene from the United Nations. After that first meeting, I said, 'This is the most ridiculous thing I've ever seen. It looks like an encounter between the bosses and the unions, and I don't like it.' I suspected all the little cliques were ganging up together, so I decided that when I chaired my first Council meeting, I would arrange the *placement* for the table, and nobody would sit where they used to. 'Are you sure you can do that?' I was asked. 'Yes,' I replied, 'that's exactly what I'm going to do; and furthermore, we're taking away the microphones.' I wasn't sure how this was going to go down, but at the end of the next meeting, a number of those in attendance came up to me and said quietly, 'It's such a good idea that you did that.' I then said, 'And we're not going to meet in the Adam Room anymore. We're going to build a very boring, twenty-first-century conference room, with a modern table and chairs, and that's where all future meetings will be held.' From that time onwards, the Adam Room was reserved for dinners and other formal events.

Shortly before I was due to take over as Chairman of Lloyd's, I received a visit from Evan Greenberg, now Chairman of Chubb, who is a son of Hank Greenberg, accompanied by Brian Duperreault, who is now President and CEO of American International Group [AIG] – the American multinational finance and insurance conglomerate, which Hank Greenberg had previously built into the largest insurer in the world. They came to visit me and said: 'Listen, we are very dissatisfied with the way that Lloyd's has been run, it is unsatisfactory financially and has developed an unwelcome reputation.' I replied: 'Look, you know I have not yet started this job and as Lloyd's is effectively a mutual and you are important members of that mutual, instead of coming to complain to me and telling me what I should do, why don't you help us develop and improve the Corporation from within.' They were some- what taken aback but then agreed that what I had said was reasonable and they did really help to restore Lloyd's' reputation.

One of the first things that happened when I arrived at Lloyd's was the recruitment of a director for the new Franchise Performance Board. His role was to act as a policeman and to watch, like a hawk, all the syndicates in the market. We chose a German by the name of Rolf Tolle, who was a great guy and an absolute tyrant. He and his staff looked at the business plans of all the businesses working in the Lloyd's market, and then said one of three things: 'We think it's fine;' or 'We have one or two questions which we'd like you to answer;' or 'We don't like it and we'll tell you why.' With the latter position, the next step was to say 'We'd like you to take it away, think about what we said, and come back and tell us what you feel.' How long that took, and how many chances they had to reform, varied in each case, depending on what the issues were.[1] Once Rolf had gone to work, I was asked, 'What are you going to do when he finds somebody who isn't toeing the line?' 'We'll throw them out,' I replied. I don't think

---

1   Lisa S. Howard, 'Lloyd's Chairman outlines Challenges', *National Underwrit- er*, 7 April 2003.

they believed me, but very shortly after I started, we did chuck one firm out, and it all changed after that. Rolf did a great job, it made a big difference, and after not too long – although I don't claim any credit for them – we started to get very good results, with an immediate gain of £834 million for 2002, against the loss of £3.1 billion in the previous year.[2] Speaking to the Association of Insurers and Risk Managers at the Institute of Directors in January 2003, I was able to explain that one of the reasons for the growing confidence and strength of Lloyd's had been its willingness to reform and modernise:

> 'Change is never easy. It takes courage and foresight. And it is often more painful the older an organisation is. But although Lloyd's is more than 300-years-old, the history of our market is one of constant change. Our reputation rests on our flexibility, our ingenuity and entrepreneurial spirit. Lloyd's strength is that it is a genuine market in which innovation sparkles, not an organisational behemoth that suffocates fresh thinking.'[3]

I spent a lot of time at Lloyd's concentrating on developing our international business and reputation and decided that I wanted someone to head up the international business development side who wasn't British and who could speak other European languages. I succeeded in recruiting Jose Ribeiro, much to the annoyance of his boss Joe Plumeri, who was then the Chairman of the Willis Group. However, Joe forgave me for what I had done and later became a close friend and colleague in the insurance world.

*   *   *

As previously mentioned, while I was Lord Mayor, I had acquired an unbelievable collection of assorted international *objets* from my travels around the world. On taking over as Chairman of Lloyd's, I opened the cupboards in my new office, and all the same things fell out, no doubt given to previous Chairmen on their trips abroad.

2   Antonia Senior, 'Market in profit for first time in six years', *The Times*, 3 April 2003.
3   Lloyd's press release, 'Lloyd's is certainty in an uncertain world – Levene', 29 January 2003.

Whereas, in the 1990s, Lloyd's had once been a watch-word for disaster when many of the Names were losing everything they had, we had now become heroes. Nearly half of Lloyds's business comes from the United States, which might seem odd. But, although the Americans have tried to replicate it, they have never managed to beat Lloyd's at their own game. When the Twin Towers of the World Trade Center in New York were destroyed by terrorists on 9 September 2001, the Treasury Secretary, Paul O'Neill, was astonished to discover that it was mostly insured by Lloyd's. Years later, the then Secretary, John Snow, came over and made a speech at Lloyd's, where he said: 'When it comes to the crunch, Lloyd's stepped up to the plate and took it on the chin.' That disaster actually came close to wiping out the business; by December 2003, two years after the attack, we had paid out £2.4 billion in direct and re-insurance claims.[1] But, remarkably, Lloyd's survived and has gone on to be as strong as ever. Nowadays, you don't find people asking whether or not Lloyd's can survive.

*　*　*

One of the things that Nick Prettejohn and I wanted to achieve was to take it out of its Stone Age working methods. You would see men walking around with leather folders, known as 'slip cases', in which they carried all their paperwork. I had never come across an industry as paper-bound as the London insurance market. It surpassed even the civil service – where I had spent some years – in its volume of paper. Similarly, the underwriters at Lloyd's sat at 'Boxes' in the Underwriting Room, from where they negotiated insurance on vast businesses, such as shipping, property, and oil refineries, and all of it was conducted face-to-face. I thought this was ridiculous and pointed out to my new colleagues that when I had recently worked in an investment bank, everybody sat in front of a computer-screen. 'Yes,' replied the Lloyd's team, 'and look what good it did them. When people want insurance from us, they come and see our underwriters. They know their business, and they will either say 'yes' or 'no'.' 'But you can't work like this in the twenty-first century,' I exclaimed. 'Yes,

1   Frank Kane, 'Selling Lloyd's the Levene way', *Observer*, 7 December 2003.

we can; and yes, we do,' they responded. 'Alright,' I said, 'keep the people, but let's get rid of the paper.' After that, there were attempts to give people iPads, but the amount of paper used was still mind-boggling. Lloyd's has a back-office in Chatham, and in 2006, when Richard Ward succeeded Nick Prettejohn as Chief Executive, he discovered that we were still sending tons of paper there by road every week. He said, 'There's only one way to deal with this,' and took the truck off the road. When people said, 'How are we going to transport all this stuff?' he replied, 'We're not.'[2] When I started, the back-office was employing several thousand people. We subsequently reduced that facility to a small modern building, but Lloyd's working methods are still very paper-based and, to this day, nobody has managed to convert it so that people can work entirely on-line.

I was also determined to tackle the aftermath of the crisis that had overwhelmed so many of the Names of Lloyd's in the 1990s. As soon as I arrived, I said, 'Look, what happened to those people must never, ever be allowed to happen again. So the practice of having Names with personal, unlimited liability is going to stop now. I don't even like using the term 'Names'. If we have people who want to invest in insurance businesses, that's absolutely fine. But they must be able to invest in an incorporated vehicle, so they can hold shares. If it does well, great; if it does badly, that's not so good. But at the end of the day, the worst thing that can happen is that they lose their investment. They don't lose their last cufflink.' So we implemented this immediately by not allowing any new Names to enter the market as individuals.

Once this change started to take effect, I asked, 'Why can't these investors, who have built up insurance businesses in their own name, now turn themselves into limited companies, which would solve the potential threat of the sort of catastrophes we saw in the recent past?' My staff at Lloyd's explained that, although my suggestion was correct, it was impossible because the Inland Revenue would not allow these individual investments to be transferred into a business, which would thereby allow the investors to carry forward any losses they had incurred and off-set them against future tax. 'Right,' I said, 'if the

2   Andrew Cave, 'Measured rage from the market leader', *Sunday Telegraph*, 7 June 2009.

181

Inland Revenue won't allow it, I will go and talk to the Chancellor of the Exchequer.' So off I went to see Gordon Brown, where I explained, 'Look, I've never had anything to do with insurance or Lloyd's in the past. But it is an important British institution, which fell on very hard times. Its name turned to mud, and my job now is to try and refurbish it and get things right again. Many people lost all their money as Names. If in future we could allow investors to turn their interests into limited companies, so they could carry forward their losses, this would make all the difference in the world.' 'Is that what you're asking me to do?' said the Chancellor. 'Yes,' I replied, expecting an immediate refusal but, to my astonishment, he agreed immediately and said it was the right thing to do. The announcement was made in his spring Budget in 2003 and introduced in the Finance Act the following year.[1]

Thus, interestingly, Lloyd's owes a huge debt of gratitude to two people, one of them being Gordon Brown; the other one is Ed Balls. Lloyd's is not a limited company; it is a corporation, under the old-English sense of the word, which means that it is a body corporate and unlimited. It operates under its own Act of Parliament, the Lloyd's Act,[2] which lays down very precise terms under which it should be governed and run. In 1992 the government published *The Report and Code of Best Practice*, known as the 'The Cadbury Report' after its author Sir Adrian Cadbury, which brought in new model guidelines and rules for the governance of listed companies. It was all perfectly sensible, except that we did not – and could not – comply with any of this, because of our existing structure as a corporation. When Lloyd's quite rightly received criticism over this, I said, 'I agree with you entirely, but I can't do anything about it unless we can amend the Lloyd's Act.' The Treasury's response to this suggestion was, 'Look, forget it. You would have to take that through parliament, which would take up an inordinate amount of their time. We have better things to do than fiddle around with your archaic structure.' So that was that, for the time being.

Unsurprisingly, Lloyd's was very involved in the long-standing

1   Anon., 'Lloyd's to limit names liability', *Guardian*, 10 April 2003.
2   The Lloyd's Acts which are currently in force were passed in 1871, 1911, 1951 and 1982. The 1982 Act is the unofficial consolidated version which incorporates the later amendments made by the Legislative Reform (Lloyd's) Order 2008. [Source: Lloyd's website]

discussions about climate change because of the potential damage that could be caused from natural disasters which had been caused by various climate change phenomena.

One of the leading proponents of the fight against global warming was HRH The Prince of Wales. He was also very concerned to try to preserve the Amazon rainforest. At the time of the G20 conference, held in London in April 2009, he had asked me if I would join the organisation known as Climate Wise when he would address the world leaders coming to London on the subject and seek contributions from them to help to preserve the rainforest. Although it was not part of the official programme, at very short notice, Prince Charles organised a meeting at Clarence House (his official residence) to which he invited the most extraordinary audience. On page 184, you can see the seating plan, together with a photograph which shows very clearly the back of my head! I say the meeting was extraordinary because sitting there were the Prime Ministers of Australia, Norway and Italy, together with the President of France, the President of the European Commission, Prince Saud of Saudi Arabia, the German Chancellor, Secretary of State Hilary Clinton, the Canadian Finance Minister and the President of the World Bank. I am not sure quite how much this meeting raised financially but it was certainly an unusual experience, particularly as it was not part of the official programme and it illustrated the extraordinary pulling power of one of the most senior members of the British Royal Family.

Moving forward, I had initially been appointed as Chairman in 2002 for a three-year term, which had then been extended for a second term. As I was coming up to the end of that, they asked me to serve for a third term, which I said I would be happy to do. However, under the Lloyd's Act, no Chairman could serve for more than two three-year periods. I pointed out that if we amended that particular clause in the act, we could take the opportunity to incorporate all the other amendments we wanted at the same time. Once again, when I approached the Treasury, they weren't interested. At that time, Ed Balls was Economic Secretary and I pestered him, trying to explain repeatedly why all this was necessary. Then suddenly, on 28 June 2007, the very day he left the Treasury to become Secretary of State for Children, Schools and Families, he signed off a letter to me saying that he had

Seating plan

	His Excellency Ban Ki-moon United Nations	His Excellency Celso Amorim Brazil NOT SEATED	
The Rt Hon Ed Miliband Secretary of State for Energy and Climate Change			The Honourable Kevin Rudd Australia
The Rt Hon Hilary Benn Secretary of State for Environment, Food and Rural Affairs			His Excellency Jens Stoltenberg Norway
The Rt Hon Douglas Alexander Secretary of State for International Development			His Excellency Taro Aso Japan NOT SEATED
The Rt Hon David Miliband Secretary of State for Foreign and Commonwealth Affairs			His Excellency General TNI (Ret) Dr H Susilo Bambang Yudhoyono
His Royal Highness The Prince of Wales			Her Excellency Dr Angela Merkel Germany
His Excellency Silvio Berlusconi Italy			His Royal Highness Prince Saud Al-Faisal Saudi Arabia
Secretary of State Hillary Rodham Clinton United States of America			His Excellency José Manuel Barroso European Commission
The Honourable Robert Zoellick World Bank			His Excellency Nicolas Sarkozy France
The Honourable James Flaherty Canada			The Honourable Samuel Hinds Guyana

ClimateWise

His Excellency Ali Bongo Ondimba Gabon	The Lord Levene of Portsoken ClimateWise

18. The impressive seating plan for the Climate Wise Conference.

19. The Prince of Wales and the Climate Wise Roundtable Conference at Clarence House.

considered everything I had said and would agree to the amendment to the Lloyd's Act. Presumably, he then fled the building, because the Treasury were furious. They had to get the new legislation through parliament, and we had to get all those in the Lloyd's market on side. But eventually it went through under the Legislative Reform (Lloyd's) Order of 2008, which allowed chairmen to serve for three terms and included all sorts of other sensible changes. In December that year, I made a point of going to see Ed Balls in his new department. 'Ed,' I said, 'I've brought you a Christmas present.' And I handed him a framed copy of the Legislative Reform Order. 'What is this?' he asked. I replied, 'This is what you did.' 'Did I?' he said, 'I don't remember.' So I told him, 'You became the saviour of the Lloyd's market, and I'm giving you this as a souvenir to thank you.'

*   *   *

Lloyd's, historically, has always sat on a huge amount of cash, which was managed in an extremely conservative manner, most of it being invested in government bonds and blue-chip companies. At one stage, all sorts of investment bankers would come in to see us, and they all said, 'Look, you're living in the Dark Ages. You've got all this money, and we can make a fortune for you.' And I always used to reply, 'That's really nice of you to come and talk to me about this, but I prefer to be very, very safe.' When they told me that was boring, I said,

STATUTORY INSTRUMENTS

2008 No. 3001

REGULATORY REFORM

The Legislative Reform (Lloyd's) Order 2008

Made - - - - -	*18th November 2008*
Coming into force - -	*19th November 2008*

The Treasury, in exercise of the powers conferred by section 1 of the Legislative and Regulatory Reform Act 2006(**a**), makes the following Order.

For the purposes of section 3(1) of the Legislative and Regulatory Reform Act 2006, the Treasury considers that the conditions under section 3(2), where relevant, are satisfied.

The Treasury has consulted in accordance with section 13(1) of that Act, and has laid a draft order and an explanatory document before Parliament in accordance with section 14(1) of that Act.

Pursuant to section 15 of that Act, the affirmative resolution procedure (within the meaning of Part 1 of that Act) applies in relation to the making of the Order.

In accordance with section 17(2) of that Act, the draft has been approved by resolution of each House of Parliament after the expiry of the 40-day period referred to in that provision.

Citation and commencement

1. This Order may be cited as the Legislative Reform (Lloyd's) Order 2008 and shall come into force on the day after the day on which it is made.

Interpretation

2. In this Order "the Act" means Lloyd's Act 1982(**b**).

The Council

3.—(1) Section 3 of the Act (the Council) shall be amended as follows.

(2) In subsection (2)(c) omit the words ", whose appointments shall not take effect unless and until confirmed by the Governor for the time being of the Bank of England".

(3) In subsection (5), paragraphs (ii) and (iii) shall cease to have effect.

(**a**) 2006 c. 51. Section 32(1) of that Act defines "Minister of the Crown" for the purposes of the Act. Sections 1, 4, 11, 13, 24 and 27 of that Act have been amended by S.I.2007/1388.
(**b**) 1982 c. xiv.

20. My Christmas present to Ed Balls. The Legislative Reform (Lloyd's) Order 2008.

'Well, you know what? Boring is beautiful.' As a result, when the great financial crash took place in 2008, Lloyd's was fine, although there was one Friday during that crisis, when everything was collapsing and I became very concerned. That evening, I phoned Richard Ward, our Chief Executive, and said, 'Look, I'm really worried. What's happening with our money?' He assured me that I didn't need to worry, because all our money was in the bank. 'Yes, Richard,' I responded, 'but *which* bank?' It was the first time in my business life that I realised that it was all very well having money in the bank, but what would happen if the bank failed, which at that moment looked highly likely. Thereafter, I tried hard to get them to spread these billions of pounds of reserve cash around a bit more widely, although it proved impossible and too complicated because various trust funds specified how and where it was deposited.

In the years when Lloyd's was at its lowest ebb and the Names had been facing huge bills, there were very serious doubts as to whether it could survive. Enormous efforts were made to keep it afloat and led by its Chairman at the time, David Rowland, they developed the concept of a vehicle into which all of the bad or questionable business would be moved, leaving only viable business within Lloyd's. This vehicle was called Equitas and was chaired by Hugh Stevenson.

After I had been in the Chair at Lloyd's for a couple of years, I was attending the annual insurance conference at the Greenbrier Hotel in West Virginia. This hotel is remarkable in that the US Government, at the height of the Cold War, had built, in total secrecy, an enormous bunker under the hotel into which the members of the Senate and Congress would be moved in order to continue the government of the nation in the event of nuclear war. Fortunately, the bunker had never had to be used for that particular function and became something of a tourist attraction for visitors staying at the hotel.

On the second morning, I woke up to find a note had been pushed under my door. It read as follows: 'The Chairman of Equitas called and asked you to call him back urgently. PS: it is good news.' The PS, of course, was enormously significant and reassuring since, if the Chairman of Lloyd's was asked to make an urgent call to the Chairman of Equitas, the worst might be feared. In any event, I phoned Hugh Stevenson who told me: 'I have very good news for you. We have done a deal to sell Equitas.' This was very good news and would defy the critics who said that eventually Equitas would go bust and the erstwhile Lloyd's Names would face enormous bills. Equitas had been sold to Warren Buffet, probably the only possibly buyer. In the event, since he took it over, it has flourished, the Names are no longer at risk and Lloyd's has had the Sword of Damocles removed from over its head.

During the banking crash of 2008, I did say on a number of occasions that a better solution for the troubled banks would be to follow the Equitas model and shift their bad assets into a special purpose vehicle. That way, it would no longer be in the public domain and so would be able to manage its own affairs and get on with the job of sorting it out quietly.

*　　*　　*

Lloyd's periodically came under attack from the Burma Campaign UK, an organisation that works for human rights, democracy and development in what is now called Myanmar. Their argument was that Lloyd's was insuring exports from there in contravention of the United Nations embargo. In fact, when we checked this out, it transpired that our total business there was about £50,000, which out of an annual budget of £30 billion just didn't register on the scale. Eventually, these public attacks wore off. Then one day I was invited, with others, to join Gordon Brown on an official trip to promote the UK in India and China. On the morning of our flight out of Heathrow, the *Observer* published an article on the front page of their business section headlined: 'The Baron who holds Burma's purse strings.' They had targeted me in the past about Lloyd's business there, but their campaign had also run out of steam. Now they had suddenly twigged that not only was I chairman of Lloyd's, but I was also a director of the French oil and gas company Total. And as Total is one of the largest investors in Myanmar, they argued that I was directly responsible for funding their military regime.

Gordon Brown was a great supporter of the Burmese pro-democracy politician, Aung San Suu Kyi, who was then under house arrest in her own country. During our flight to India, he started reading the *Observer* article, realised that it was about me and that I was on the plane, and summoned me into his presence. 'What's all this?' he said. I replied: 'Yes, I am a director of Total, and I have talked to them about their involvement in Myanmar. They are indeed one of the largest foreign investors in that country, and they employ a lot of people there. But they have also assured me that they make a point of looking after their staff. They have built schools, clinics and hospitals. They have also said that if Total leaves Myanmar, the company's investments will be taken over immediately by the Chinese, and they will not look after their staff in the same way. So we have no intention of leaving Myanmar.' 'I don't believe all that,' retorted Gordon Brown. 'Look,' I said, 'if you want me to resign from Total, I will. But it won't make the slightest bit of difference. Instead of haranguing me, I'm sure I could ask the Chairman of Total to come and talk to you.' 'Yes, you do that,' he responded. I subsequently tried three or four times to set up such a meeting through his office, but it never happened. Sometime later, a new natural gas terminal was opened in the north of England. The opening ceremony was attended by Gordon Brown and – as Total were a major investor in this project – the company's Chairman had come over from Paris. He approached Gordon Brown and said: 'Peter Levene tells me that you're concerned about our investment in Myanmar.' To which Brown just replied: 'Oh, don't worry about all that.'

*   *   *

Being both Chairman of Lloyd's and a board member of the oil and gas company Total, I went to some odd places. One of the strangest was the tar sands of Northern Alberta in Canada, where vast deposits of crude oil were being extracted using open-pit mining methods. This involved digging out the sand with vast hydraulic power shovels and burning it to extract the oil. It has always been controversial, because the process produces a lot of pollution. When I went there, I was told that only two months of the year are tolerable, because the climate is so cold; and at that time they had a negative income tax, in other words people were being paid to live there. Once the enormous shovels had extracted the sand, it was dumped into hauler trucks and driven to a hopper, where the oil was burnt off. The tyres of the trucks were higher than the ceilings of any average room and were the single largest expense because they quickly wore out on the snow and ice. The men who worked there were on month-on, month-off shifts, because there was nothing to do. And rather like the North Sea oil rigs, the canteens served superb food, in an effort to keep the employees happy. But no women were allowed on site, and at the mine I visited there were big notices everywhere warning the workers about the perils of drug and alcohol abuse. As part of our tour, we were taken into the control room, from where all the truck-drivers were co-ordinated to dump their loads into the hopper. There was one man in there, with a skinhead hair-cut, sitting at a computer and surrounded by weight-lifting equipment. He was running the whole operation. 'Hey,' he cried, when we arrived, 'watch this!' And he pressed a button, which speeded up the whole process, so all the truck-drivers had to race at high speed to get round.

Before joining Lloyd's, I had also become Chairman of the UK arm of the defence company General Dynamics, and so, on their behalf, I went to Algeria, where we were trying to sell some new equipment. At that time, Algeria was one of the most dangerous places in the world, and I was advised that the only safe place to stay was the British Ambassador's residence in Algiers, which had a machine-gun post on the roof manned by British soldiers. We were picked up at the airport by an armoured car. Fortunately, the trip was relatively uneventful, except that there were occasional explosions, when our escorts would say, 'Oh, don't worry, that's just the government bombing some of the rebels in the mountains.' While I was there, I was told that the Algerian Energy Minister had heard about my visit. He knew that I was also Chairman of Lloyd's and wanted to know if he could come and see me on his forthcoming trip to London. They had recently had a very bad accident when a natural gas plant exploded, killing many people, and he was hoping that Lloyd's might be able to give him advice on safety procedures to prevent this happening again. I said that I would be delighted to see him.

When I got back to London, I said to my colleagues, 'Look, the Algerian Energy Minister is coming in two weeks' time, and I want you to get a couple of underwriters to talk to him about safety in gas plants.' 'Well,' they replied, 'we could do that. But don't get underwriters to talk to him, it would be much better if you ask a couple of the brokers.' 'I don't want the brokers,' I said, 'I want underwriters, who actually deal with this type of risk, to talk to him.' 'That's not a good idea,' they said. We went on arguing like this, until eventually I said, 'Look, I've decided I want the underwriters, so that's what we're going to do.' Two weeks later, the Minister arrived, we sat down with the underwriters, and he started asking them questions. Their answers were so inadequate and hopeless that the British Ambassador, who was sitting there, said to me afterwards, 'If I'd had a revolver, I would have pulled it out and shot them.' My colleagues later explained to me, 'Look, you've got to understand, underwriters are experts, but they're not used to talking to humans, because they only talk to each other. If you speak to the brokers, you actually get people who are slightly more attuned to the real world.'

Lloyd's insured many unusual risks such as the football clubs Real Madrid and Barcelona in Spain, and the Ferrari factory in Italy, and I much enjoyed visiting quite a few of them. We also had considerable business in California, so I was invited to go and meet the Governor, Arnold Schwarzenegger. The Governor's residence is in Sacramento and when we arrived there, I was told that he would be meeting us in his tent, which seemed a bit odd. It turned out that, since smoking had been banned in all public buildings in California, he had taken to holding his meetings in a tent that he had pitched in the grounds, so he could continue smoking his cigars. I also often went to visit Sérgio Cabral, who served as Governor of the State of Rio de Janeiro from 2007 to 2014. He too lived in an official Governor's residence, the vast and ornate Palacio Laranjeiras. He was very helpful and instrumental in getting Lloyd's established in Brazil and was the speaker at one of our Lloyd's annual City dinners. He went on, as the Governor of Rio, to play a major part in helping Rio win the opportunity to host the Olympics in 2016. Sadly, since then he was caught up in various political scandals in Brazil and is now *hors de combat*.

* * *

One of the most prominent individual Names when I joined Lloyd's was Rona Delves Broughton, who ran the High Premium Group.

They were the really high-rollers, with large sums to invest. Rona and I met often and we got on very well. When I left Lloyd's, she and the rest of the High Premium Group organised a lunch and gave me a very kind gift because they said I had saved the institution for them. When I started at Lloyd's in 2002, there had been a huge divide between the Names, who represented the old guard and made up about 10 per cent of the business, and the big corporates, who accounted for the other 90 per cent of the market. There was total enmity between these two groups. Nick Prettejohn warned me that it was awful, and that he had vowed to fight the Names to the death. Early on I had to address the Association of Lloyd's Members, which included all the old-and-bold. When I stood up and said, 'Look, I have to admit, I don't know very much about insurance, but I'm doing what I can,' one man rose to his feet and replied, 'Well, you said you didn't know very much about insurance, and that is abundantly obvious.'

I also had several confrontations with Michael Deeny, who was another of the high investors and Chairman of the Association of Lloyd's Members. When we were trying to make some changes to established practice, he and others just didn't want to talk. In the end, I organised a peace conference, which included him and another good friend, Bronek Masojada, who runs Hiscox. Once we started talking, one of them would say something, and the other would say something else. And I would say, 'Look, remember I don't understand all this. But it seems to me that you're not really very far apart on these issues.' At the end of the day, we brokered a deal, and there was a sudden outbreak of peace. When I started, it was like thermo-nuclear war. Now the Names are still there, but it's just not an issue anymore. I think I had a huge advantage that I didn't come with any precon-ceived position. I was therefore able to say, 'What's the problem? Why are you doing that?' It was not unlike the situations I had found myself in at the MOD, DLR and Canary Wharf, where I also came in from outside and was able to ask similar questions.

*   *   *

Early on I was told that I had two main tasks, which were to win for the Corporation licences in India and China. I said that I thought we would succeed with the former, but that the latter would be a bit more difficult. So off I went to China, where I met Mr Li Kemu, the Vice Chairman of the China Insurance & Reinsurance Commission, which is their regulator. As with all meetings in China, the usual procedure ensued. You sit in a chair with a microphone in front of you, and your interlocutor sits next to you with another microphone in front of him. Between you is a big vase of flowers and the interpreters on each side, through whom you speak. The Chairman said, 'It's very good to see you. Of course, we know all about Lloyd's here in China. How can I help you?' When I explained that we wanted to get a licence to write re-insurance for the Lloyd's market in China, but had been told that it would be very difficult, he replied, 'Well, all you have to do is make an application. I will get someone to bring us an application form, and I will read through it with you, so you can see what has to be done.' When the form arrived, he looked at it and asked me: 'Question one: what is the name of your company?' Well, of course Lloyd's is not a company, so I had to say, 'Ah, that's a bit difficult.' 'Yes,' he said, 'I thought it was. I'm terribly sorry, but under Chinese law we can only give licences to insurance companies.'

I returned to London and explained what had happened. There I was told that, as China was now in the World Trade Organisation [WTO] and subject to its rules, they could not discriminate against us on the basis of legal form. Back I went to China to see Mr Li again. 'Very nice to see you,' he said, 'how can I help?' and I replied, 'Well, I came to ask you if we could get a licence, and you told me that we couldn't because we're not a company. But now I'm told that, under WTO rules, to which you are now subject, you cannot discriminate against us on the basis of legal form.' 'How interesting,' he replied, 'and what else would you like to tell me?' Returning to London, I reported to my colleagues, 'Look, that's not going to work. We'll have to form a company.' 'But Lloyd's isn't a company,' they retorted. 'Read my lips,' I said, 'go and form a company called Lloyd's China Reinsurance Limited. It will take twenty-four hours and it will cost £100. Just get on with it.' Once that was done, I got back on a plane to Beijing to see Mr Li again. 'Very nice to see you,' he said, 'what have you come to tell me this time?' 'Well,' I replied, 'you told me to form a company, so we have formed one, and it's called Lloyd's China Reinsurance Limited.'

'You've done *what*?' he exclaimed. 'Does that change things?' I asked. 'Well yes,' he said, 'it certainly does.' By this time, Mr Li and I had developed a very good working relationship. I took him, as a gift, a copy of Adam Smith's *The Wealth of Nations* in Mandarin and he gave me a copy of Marshal Sun Tzu's *The Art of War* in English.

After that, we made our formal application. At that time any deal with the Chinese state had to be done on a government-to-government basis, so we had to submit our application through the British Embassy in Beijing. They helped us work through the whole process, which took three years. While all this was going on, there were two important visits. The first involved Tony Blair going to China in July 2003, where he saw President Hu Jintao. I was part of the trade delegation that travelled with him. When he emerged from his meeting with the President, he said to me, 'It will work, you're going to get your licence.' 'When?' I asked. 'Soon,' he replied. That was then followed up with the state visit of President Hu Jintao to the UK in November 2005. Shortly before he arrived, the British Ambassador in Beijing said to me, 'Look, I'm told you're going to get your licence when the President comes to London. He has various goodies that's he's going to give out during his visit.' As usual, there was a state banquet at Buckingham Palace. After dinner, Tony Blair came up and asked me if I had received the licence for Lloyd's. 'No,' I said, 'and tomorrow morning I'm in a party of luminaries that is being sent to meet him, and I don't know what to say.' Anyway, the next day I went into the office early, at about eight o'clock, and found an e-mail from the British Embassy in Beijing. It said, 'Very pleased to tell you, you've been granted your licence in China, which is attached.' That was a turn-up for the book, I thought, and off I went to meet Hu Jintao. 'Mr. President,' I said, 'I come to thank you. I'm the Chairman of Lloyd's, and we've just …' 'I know, I know,' he replied, 'when I left Beijing on Monday, as I was going up the steps of the plane, I asked if they had sent Lloyd's their licence. When they said, 'No, Mr. President,' I said, 'Well, you had better get on with it." Of course, that's what he told me. The truth was that he knew there might be public demonstrations against him in London, and he wanted to see how bad they were before he made his final decision. In the event, they weren't that bad, so he said, 'Right, you can send Lloyd's their licence.'

Then we had to set up Lloyd's in China and had to decide in which city it should be based – Beijing or Shanghai. I went to visit the mayor of Beijing, who wasn't very engaged on the issue, but then met the mayor of Shanghai, who was falling over backwards to secure our new office in his city. They did us a fantastic deal: they found us the space, which wasn't easy; subsidised the costs of our office and sent the Mayor along to the official opening. I made a speech, and decided to deliver one paragraph in Mandarin. The only way I could do that was to learn it parrot-fashion, so after I started the speech in English I then switched into Mandarin – they were delighted. We quickly became very friendly with the people in Shanghai. When we first got the licence, the insurance market In London were a bit sceptical about China. When we had the office opening, I said to four of the market barons, 'Look, do me a favour, just come with us'. 'No,' they replied, 'we can't waste our time.' 'But you've only got to come for a couple of days,' I explained. 'Have two days in Shanghai and two days in Beijing, we'll get them to show you round, and then you can tell me if I've wasted your time.' So they came out to Shanghai, were shown round, and after lunch on the first day, they came up to me and said, 'OK, you win.' Now, of course, it's a growing market for Lloyd's. We started off with four syndicates and premiums of just a few million Renminbi but by 2017, there were 30 syndicates, over 100 people and premium income of 2 billion Renminbi.

Sometime later, I went to see the regulator, Li Kemu, who was by then my good friend, and he said, 'You remember we talked about having a licence for direct insurance, rather than just re-insurance?' 'Yes,' I replied, 'and you told me that wasn't possible.' 'Well,' he went on, 'ask me again.' 'What do you mean?' I asked. 'Ask me again,' he said. So I asked what would happen if we requested a licence for direct insurance, and he answered, 'We'll give it to you.' 'That's amazing,' I cried, 'can we announce it?' Yes,' he said, 'but you know what? I'm going to let you make the first announcement. Would you like to do that?' I told him that the following day I was going to the World Fair in Shanghai, where I would be visiting the British pavilion. 'Fine,' he said, 'why don't you make a speech there, to say that Lloyd's has just been given its licence for direct insurance.' I did just that, and it brought the house down. After that, the whole market was able to work throughout China.

As I said, I was also asked by Lloyd's to get a licence in India. I went there twice, once with Tony Blair and once with Gordon Brown. We never got anywhere; they were the most impossible people to deal with. On both occasions, the Indian Prime Minister promised us that he would fix it, but nothing happened. I was subsequently told that there are seven families in India who actually run the country, and if you're not in with them, it's pointless to waste your time. I found the Chinese to be very tough to deal with but, once we'd done the deal and got our licence, there was nothing they wouldn't do for us. Whenever they promised to do something, they would do it without question.

However, my successor as Chairman of Lloyd's, John Nelson, did manage to finally obtain a licence in India, which is now available for use by the Market.

* * *

Sometime after we got our initial licence in China, I saw the Chinese Foreign Minister and said to him, 'You know, I've got to tell you, we're absolutely delighted. Everybody in the Chinese government has been incredibly helpful to us, and we're really grateful. And I just wondered if there was anything that Lloyd's could do to thank you?' He told me, 'In China we're not ashamed to admit that, amongst all the wealth and development, we still have a considerable amount of poverty. Every government department has been allocated one province to work on, where we are instructed to help the people solve their problems. The Department for Foreign Affairs has been given the province of Yunnan, in the south-west of China, on the border with Vietnam. It would be really good if Lloyd's would pay for a new school there.' Yes, I thought, I'm sure it would. 'So how much would this school cost?' I asked. 'Well,' he said, 'we already have a design for it. There will be two storeys, with a playground; it will take 250 children; and it will cost about £50,000.' 'So,' I responded, 'if I give you a cheque for £50,000, you will build the whole school?' 'That's it,' he replied. 'Done,' I said.

Thus in 2007 we funded the construction of Lloyd's Primary School in Laomeng village in Yunnan province. The school opened

21. The Lloyd's Primary School in Laomeng, Yunnan province, China.

in 2009 and has supported 280 children from the village and surrounding areas since then. Once it was completed, I wanted to see it, so I decided to go to the opening ceremony. The Chinese assured me that I would be most welcome, but pointed out that I would have to fly to Kunming, which is the capital of Yunnan. I assured them that I'd been there before, and that it wouldn't be a problem. 'Yes,' they said, 'but once you get to Kunming, it's a two-day drive by jeep into the hills. The whole area was devastated during the war in Vietnam, and there aren't really any decent roads up there.' In the end, I sent some of our staff, who were working in Shanghai, and they sent back photographs of this beautiful school.

Recruiting the teachers seemed a potential problem, because it's really in the middle of nowhere. But, of course, the Chinese went to their teacher-training college, selected the people they wanted, and just directed them where to go. Shortly after the school opened, I was told there was a more serious issue. Many of the children, some as young as five, were spending up to three hours a day walking to and from school in this mountainous region, so the authorities had decided that it would be better if they boarded at the school from Monday to Friday, and just went home at weekends. 'Where do they sleep?' I asked. 'They sleep on the floor,' they told me. When I objected

22. School children at the Lloyd's school.

to this, they went on, 'You don't understand, sleeping on the floor in the school is probably better than where they sleep at home.' 'It doesn't matter,' I said, 'we'll have to build a dormitory.' So Lloyd's and five managing agents – Catlin, Travelers, Starr, ACE, and Navigators – contributed an extra £50,000 to construct the new dormitory. Since then, the school has been the most phenomenal success.

*   *   *

In January 2009, while on a visit to New York, I noticed that all the billboards were running a story about a plane that had crashed in the Hudson River. Back in my hotel, I switched on the television and discovered that Captain Chesley 'Sully' Sullengerger had successfully landed his US Airways passenger jet on the river, after a bird strike had caused his engines to stall. All 155 passengers and crew on board survived and had been safely evacuated. When I got back to London, one of my colleagues at Lloyd's said to me: 'Look, that Captain saved the Lloyd's market an untold fortune. If his plane had crashed 400 yards to the left or right, it would have been facing the equivalent of 9/11. He is a great hero. In the past, when Lloyd's was primarily ensuring

23. Presentation in New York of Lloyd's Gold Medal to Captain Sullenberger by HRH the Duke of York.

the merchant fleet, we instituted a Gold Medal for saving life at sea, and I think we should consider giving this pilot one.' I thought this was a great idea, so I got in touch with Captain Sullenberger and asked if he would be prepared to accept a Lloyd's Gold Medal if we came over to New York to present it to him. He said he'd be happy to do that. I then contacted HRH Prince Andrew, the Duke of York, and asked him if, as a fellow pilot, he would be prepared to make the presentation. He too agreed, and on 23 June 2009 Captain Sullenberger was the guest of honour at our annual Lloyd's New York City Dinner, where the Prince handed him his Gold Medal. 'Sully', as he was known, said that he would 'gratefully accept this deep honour on behalf of my crew, my passengers and all the first-responders who performed so admirably and courageously during the evacuation that day.'[1]

* * *

Lloyd's has an extensive collection of letters and silver related to Horatio, Viscount Nelson, all of which is on display in special cases in

1   Staff writer, 'Capt. Sullenberger gets Lloyd's Life Saver Medal', *NU Online News Service*, June 24, 2009.

the Underwriting Room. The organisation was always deeply aware of the debt it owed to Nelson and the Royal Navy in helping to establish Britain as the world's greatest trading nation. And Lloyd's played a leading part in underwriting the war effort against France during the late-eighteenth and early-nineteenth centuries. When I was chairman, we celebrated the 200th anniversary of the Battle of Trafalgar in 2005. As part of those celebrations, we held discussions about lending our collection for a temporary exhibition, so more people could see it. Initially, we talked to the National Maritime Museum at Greenwich, but they weren't very helpful. Then I had a call from St Paul's Cathedral to say that they were thinking of mounting an exhibition. 'Why St Paul's?' I asked, 'you haven't got anything of Nelson's.' 'Well,' they replied, 'we thought you might say that. We have got one thing actually. We've got his body!' I knew St Paul's quite well, from my days as Lord Mayor, but I had completely forgotten that he was buried in their crypt.

CHAPTER ELEVEN

Director and Chairman

W HEN MARGARET Thatcher reluctantly resigned as Prime
Minister in 1990, there was a succession battle between John
Major, Michael Heseltine and Douglas Hurd. Major emerged as the
winner and became Prime Minister in November of that year. He
sensibly said that he didn't want to fight with Michael Heseltine in
future, so he immediately appointed him Secretary of State for the
Environment, followed by promotion to President of the Board of
Trade and Secretary of State for Trade and Industry in 1992, and
finally First Secretary of State and Deputy Prime Minister in 1995.
Michael in turn asked me to be his Personal Adviser both at the
Department for the Environment, between 1991 and 1992, and again
at the Board of Trade, between 1992 and 1995. By 1992 I had already
been appointed as John Major's Adviser on Efficiency and Effectiveness, on the recommendation of the Cabinet Secretary, Sir Robin
Butler, but as the Prime Minister was really too busy to deal with
many of the issues that arose, I reported most of the time on those
matters to Michael, as the Prime Minister's deputy.

The day after the General Election in May 1997, which John Major
lost, Michael had an attack of angina and was admitted to the Harley
Street Clinic. Nobody was allowed to talk to him. Fortunately, our
housekeeper Linda's husband worked as a porter at that hospital, so
he was able to pass messages backwards and forwards, which was
very helpful, as Michael had been talking to me about what I might
do in the future. Once he had recovered, and declined an offer to fight
William Hague for leadership of the Conservative Party on medical
advice, and told me that he planned to return to running Haymarket,
the publishing business he had established in the 1960s. By that time
the company was making an annual profit of over £10 million and

employed about 1,000 people. Michael asked me to join the board of Haymarket as a director, which is a role I continue to perform.

Chairman, Bankers Trust International plc (1998 – 1999)

In mid-1998 when I was acting as a senior advisor at Morgan Stanley in London, one day I received a phone call from a head-hunter. I was asked whether I would be interested in being considered for the role of Chairman of Bankers Trust International – the London based international division of the American investment bank Bankers Trust. I said to them that I could be interested but that as I was due to become Lord Mayor of London in a few months' time, it would really not allow me sufficient time to undertake such a role unless, of course, they wanted to wait until my mayoralty was over.

The head-hunter said that they were aware of this and, indeed, this was one of the reasons which had attracted them to me because I was so well known and connected in the City of London. They said: 'Look, if you will start in September, you will have a few weeks to get your feet under the table and then we will support you for the rest of the year whilst you are Lord Mayor. Your involvement in Bankers Trust's matters will be very limited and you can start in earnest at the end of the mayoralty'. On that basis I said I was very interested and went to talk to David Walker, who was the Chairman of Morgan Stanley in London, to tell him what had happened. He said that he would be very sorry to lose me but he thought that the only appropriate job at Morgan Stanley in London for me would be his job and he was not about to leave!

Bankers Trust did make me a very attractive offer and so I left Morgan Stanley and was installed in the Bankers Trust London headquarters in Appold Street in the City.

Then, in November 1998, Deutsche Bank agreed to purchase Bankers Trust which came as a bolt out of the blue to me. So, having just entered the Mansion House, I suddenly found myself Chairman of a Deutsche Bank division in London. Within Bankers Trust personnel, both in London and New York, this acquisition was certainly not universally popular. Frank Newman, the Chairman of Bankers Trust, parted ways with Deutsche Bank shortly afterwards, in June 1999, when he received severance pay of $55m. It is rumoured that subsequently some Bankers Trust staff in New York were seen to be wearing t-shirts which read: 'Frank Newman got $55m and all I received was this lousy t-shirt.'

It seemed that Deutsche Bank had bought Bankers Trust because they wanted to build up a presence in the United States, particularly in New York and they believed that this would be a good way of achieving this quickly. Deutsche Bank had appointed a consultant from McKinsey, by the name of Klaus Droste, to work with them on the acquisition. He came to see me and a number of other people in the bank, and one of his questions was: 'What name would be most appropriate for the merged entity of Deutsche Bank and Bankers Trust?' I said that it might be a good idea to try and reduce the name to initials which had been successfully achieved by CSFB (Credit Suisse First Boston), BZW (Barclays de Zoete Wedd) and DLJ (Donaldson Lufkin & Jenerette). I continued that if we shortened Deutsche Bank/Bankers Trust to DBT, this might be a good solution for what everyone hoped would become an international investment bank. Other people were consulted as to their opinion on names and, in due course, a decision was made that the merged entity would be known as Deutsche Bank – so much for the value of consultation.

24. HM The Queen visits Bankers Trust, November 1998.

The Bankers Trust headquarters in London moved into the new Deutsche Bank building in London Wall and I moved with it. For some reason, as part of my remit, I became Chairman of Deutsche Bank Scotland and Deutsche Bank South Africa. The franchise in South Africa was very successful and they decided to hold an event to which their major clients would be invited with their partners, and Wendy and I were also invited. It was a ride on a private South African train called Rovos Rail. It was extremely luxurious with compartments fitted out not only with double rooms with full sized double beds, but also with bathrooms with a full-sized bathtub. The plan was for all the guests to embark on the train at Pretoria station and then to ride overnight to a safari lodge, called the Royal Malewane, in Kruger National Park where all the guests would be able to view the abundant game. It was an upmarket event as all the guests on the train were required to appear for dinner in evening dress. All went well in our very luxurious accommodation and we gathered in an observation car at the end of the train before dinner. Before we had gone into dinner, Wendy had decided that it would be fun to take a bath in the full-sized bathtub. However, when she ran the water, it wasn't hot and so she gave up on the idea. But after the dinner as there was a telephone in the compartment linked up to the train stewards, I suggested that Wendy should phone them to see if they could fix the hot water. Very quickly, a steward appeared, tested the water, saw that it was not hot and said not to worry, it would be fixed quickly but the train would have to be stopped. I said, 'You can't stop the train with all these people on board.' but he said, 'Yes, I can'. The train duly stopped, two engineers jumped down on the track, and, after a lot of knocking and banging, the hot water was working.

I have never been able to sleep on a train and this was no exception, so when we arrived at the game lodge in the morning, after a 12-hour train journey, I was pretty tired. We were, however, able to go to our very comfortable accommodation and to spend the rest of the day there.

The lodge Manager asked me why we were not staying the night and I explained that we had to go back on the train to Pretoria but, thinking about it, I asked him how far away we were from Pretoria. He told me that it was about 4 hours by road or 45 minutes by plane. Nevertheless, we stuck to the original plan and having enjoyed a very good day at the Lodge, endured another 12-hour return rail journey, disgorging, in due course, a crowd of happy but exhausted passengers.

At the end of my year as Lord Mayor, I moved back to Deutsche Bank to work in the City office. For a number of reasons, I did not enjoy the experience very much and, as recorded in Chapter 9, I moved from there to Lloyd's.

Chairman, International Financial Services London (2000–2010)

British Invisibles was an organisation set up in 1968 to promote UK-based financial services abroad. Originally known as the Committee on Invisible Exports, it was a private-sector body financed by corporate subscriptions and grants from the Corporation of London and the Bank of England. It organised overseas missions, lobbied for free trade in financial services, and compiled statistics. The driving force behind the scheme had been Jonathan Charkham who held the position of Advisor to the Governor and who set up the original committee. The Bank of England were very keen on the group and happy to pay a substantial contribution towards its costs. When I became its Chairman in 2000, shortly after completing my stint as Lord Mayor, I was asked by Eddie George, the Governor of the Bank of England, to review all its functions. The various options ranged from redirecting it to closing it down altogether.

By February 2001, I was ready to make my recommendations for change. The first was to rename the organisation International Financial Services London, usually shortened to just IFSL. I thought the 'British' part in the former name was no longer relevant, because the financial services coming out of London were increasingly being provided inter alia by Swiss, German and American banks based in the City. I also decided that in future, instead of tagging along on the Lord Mayor's trips abroad and also just making promotional visits overseas, IFSL would focus its efforts on organising conferences where they could sell specific areas of City expertise. And, finally, I wanted IFSL to become the focal point in London for visiting foreign dignitaries. Working with the Foreign Office, the Bank of England, and other organisations, we would provide introductions to the City, so foreign heads of state or ministers could have access to the top privatisation experts, investment bankers, traders, and insurance brokers.

A blow to the scheme occurred, however, when Mervyn King took over as Governor of the Bank of England from Eddie George. Mervyn had made it very clear from the start of his tenure in office that he didn't believe that the Bank of England should become involved in promoting the financial City, and should confine its activities more closely to pure central banking issues.

I realised this when I became Chairman of Lloyd's. At the outset of my Chairmanship, I had a meeting twice a year with the Governor for an hour's chat about how the business was faring, with only the two of us present. Incidentally, the Governor had the same arrangement with the Chairmen of the clearing banks in the City. But, as soon as Mervyn King arrived, my PA told me that all the meetings that we had in the diary were cancelled. When I asked if we had new dates, I was told that the Governor no longer wished to have these meetings. Clearly, he didn't feel the need to be so closely involved in what was happening in the City of London!

In the same vein, however, Mervyn made it clear to me that the Bank, which has been so supportive to IFSL, even to the extent of giving them a vacant floor in premises belonging to the Bank of England for the organisation to occupy, rent free, would also be cancelled.

The relationship between IFSL and the Bank of England or, more precisely, between the Governor and myself became more difficult and we found ourselves living very 'hand to mouth'.

Fortunately, the Government decided that an organisation of this kind was desirable to help promote the financial services industry and this resulted in the setting up of the CityUK, a new body that incorporated what was left of IFSL and, has since then, under very good leadership, gone from strength to strength.

Chairman, General Dynamics UK Ltd (since 2001)

General Dynamics is one of the four largest defence companies in the United States. When I was Chief of Defence Procurement at the MOD, they used to woo me because the UK was potentially a major customer. In 1989, I was told that the British Army had decided to buy new tanks. I was slightly surprised by this, because I had previously been told that we didn't need any more tanks, so I questioned the General who was in charge of army procurement. It seemed that the real reason behind this decision was the government's desire to provide work for the Vickers tank factory in Newcastle. When I learnt this, I said: 'Well, I'm not playing that game. If we want to buy new tanks, we're going to have a worldwide competition.'

So we invited bids for the contract. The four bidders were General Dynamics, who were building the M1 Abrams tanks; Vickers, who were offering a new version of the Challenger tank; the German Krauss-Maffei Leopard tank; and the French GIAT Industries (now Nexter) Leclerc tank. We conducted trials on all of these. The American tank came first, the German second, the French third and the Vickers tank – which didn't even actually exist at that point – was rejected as being not good enough. Vickers then lobbied the British Government furiously and persuaded them to invest £90 million in its future development. Meanwhile, General Dynamics contacted the MOD to say: 'Look, we want to sell our M1 Abrams tanks all over the world. If the British Army buy them, that will give us a huge credential. So, if you agree to buy them, we will agree that not only those you buy for the British Army, but all those that we sell outside the United States, will be manufactured under licence in the United Kingdom, and we will give you that licence.' I thought this was a great deal. Vickers retaliated by persuading the Government, partly through the good offices of David Young, who was Secretary of State for the Department for Trade and Industry between 1987 and 1989, that if they were allowed to go ahead with their new Challenger tank, they would be able to sell huge quantities all over the world. As a result, the offer to build American tanks here in the UK was turned down. Since then, 408 Challenger 2 tanks have been delivered to the British Army since 1998, and the sole export sale was a mere thirty-eight to the Royal Army of Oman. To demonstrate the short-sightedness of the UK Government's decision, it seems as if there have been over 2,280 export orders to foreign armies for the Abrams tank.

In the late-1990s, when I was working for Morgan Stanley, I went to see Nick Chabraja, the chairman of General Dynamics. I was in search of new business, but he said: 'I don't want to talk to you about any of your potential deals, but I do need to talk to you about something else. We are currently bidding to supply the British Army with a new tactical radio communications system called Bowman. If we are successful with our bid, we're going to manufacture them in a relatively small factory we own in Britain. It's going to be a huge deal, and we would like you to become the Chairman of this British subsidiary.' I had been out of the MOD since 1991, but I wasn't sure how they would react to this proposal. So I went to see Rob Walmsley, who had been my Military Assistant when I worked there, and had himself risen to become CDP in 1996. I explained to Rob that I had made it clear to General Dynamics that I could not be part of their current bidding process with the British Government, but if they were successful, they had it in mind to appoint me as Chairman of their UK subsidiary. I also suggested that, if they did win the contract, it would be helpful for the MOD to know they had somebody at the top of it whom they already knew. Rob agreed that it was fine, as long as I didn't get involved in the bidding for the Bowman radios. General Dynamics won the contract, and consequently I was appointed as the Chairman of General Dynamics UK Ltd in 2001.

Their first British factory was based in Hastings, on the Sussex coast, one of the more inaccessible towns in the south of England. Once we were awarded the contract for the Bowman radio, they conceived the masterstroke of building an additional plant in Wales, which was a huge success, not least because there are many financial incentives and benefits to locating a business in Wales.

Initially, General Dynamics UK just made communications equipment, but have recently diversified into making light tanks (and just secured a £5 billion contract to supply the British Army with the new Scout armoured vehicles). We bought an existing factory, which had previously belonged to a forklift truck business, so it already had all the production hardstanding for vehicles and heavy cranes that we would need. Our parent company in the United States had long built tanks of every kind, and they also had a subsidiary in Spain, manufacturing tanks for the Spanish army. It was agreed to assemble the first hundred in Spain and then transition assembly to our new plant in Merthyr Tydfil in Wales. This takes me straight back to my days at United Scientific and Alvis.

Director, J. Sainsbury PLC (2001–2004)
I became a Non-Executive Director of Sainsbury's in 2001. By 2004

the business had been going steadily downhill for some time. One of its main competitors, Tesco, had nearly 1,900 stores, while Sainsbury's had only 721. With their higher earning power, Tesco were able to sustain margins at six per cent. Sainsbury's had dropped from its high point of eight per cent, when John Sainsbury was Chairman and Chief Executive in the 1980s, to less than four per cent.[1] Asda and Waitrose were also snapping at their heels. The Chief Executive of Sainsbury's, Sir Peter Davis, who had been appointed in 2000, had attempted a recovery plan, but this had failed. By this time, I was the senior Non-Executive Director, with a role that included keeping in touch with large shareholders.

It was clear that Peter Davis had to go, so, in March 2004, I was deputed to tell him that he must stand down as Chief Executive, and at the same time we had appointed Justin King to take over his job. Sir George Bull, the first non-family Chairman of Sainsbury's, retired and Peter replaced him. but not for long. When he stood down as Chief Executive, we realised that under the terms of his contract, he was very generously compensated. The shareholders, already exasperated by his performance as Chief Executive, now went into revolt over his extremely generous bonus package.

The Sainsbury's lawyers looked at all this and said: 'Well, I'm afraid we can't get out of all this, because of the way his contract has been drawn up.' I was loath to make the payments but the lawyers told me we had no option. By this time, we had decided that we wanted to appoint Philip Hampton as the new Chairman, and indeed he did take over from Peter Davis in July 2004. However, once he too had looked at all the legal arguments over this contract, he said: 'Look, I understand where you're coming from and I think you're right. But Sainsbury's is in such a mess, and we've just taken on Justin King, who is very good, and we must now use all our energy in turning the business round. We haven't got time to have this big fight with Peter Davis, so we must just grit our teeth and pay him.' To this, I found myself saying: 'I think you're right, in terms of Sainsbury's. But I know that I'm right, in terms of being a Director on the board. So, if that's what you're going to do, I'm going to resign, because I don't agree with it. Having said that, I can

1   Judi Bevan, *Trolley Wars: The Battle of the Supermarkets*, (London, 2005), p.204

see that, coming into this afresh, you are doing the right thing in saying that this company doesn't have time to fight this battle now.' So that was it. I resigned and Peter Davis was paid.

While all this was going on, and just after Peter Davis had left, we were fast approaching the date for the Sainsbury's Annual General Meeting [AGM]. Although we had already agreed that Philip Hampton was to be the new Chairman, I felt that it would be very unfair on him to have to start his chairmanship by going to an AGM and be faced by a mob of angry shareholders. Sainsbury's always had huge turnouts at their AGMs, because thousands of their customers, who were also shareholders, came along. The questions would start with the some-what mundane, such as: 'I have always found the marmalade on the fourth shelf on the left in the Cromwell Road store, now it has been moved, and I can't find it anywhere.' Then someone else would say: 'I've bought Sainsbury's mayonnaise for years, and now you've changed the flavour and I hate it.' And as everybody who came got a goody-bag, they all flocked in to get their free food. Anyway, I suggested to Philip Hampton that he should take over as Chairman in July, and I would take the flak at the upcoming AGM. He agreed that was a good idea.

So I chaired the Sainsbury's AGM in 2004, at the Queen Elizabeth II Centre in Westminster. One of the first questions was: 'How can it be that the Chief Executive of Sainsbury's is paid more than the Prime Minister?' To which, in a sudden flash of inspiration, I said: 'Well, that's because the Prime Minister doesn't have to worry about running Sainsbury's.' It was thought by some that the Sainsbury family still owned the business, when in fact, by that time, their shareholding was down to about three per cent. Although, of course, John Sainsbury didn't see it that way. As far as he was concerned, and having been its Chief Executive and Chairman from 1969 to 1992, it was still *his* business. Anyway, he came along to this very rowdy AGM, and at the end of it he came up to me and said: 'I want to tell you that that was the best chaired meeting of Sainsbury's since I left.' Praise indeed.

Chairman, World Trade Centre Disaster Fund UK (2001–2006)
Shortly after the four co-ordinated 9/11 terrorist attacks in America in 2001, the then-Governor of the Bank of England, Eddie George,

phoned me up and said: 'Peter, we must show solidarity between London and New York, because the two cities are absolutely joined at the hip. I want to have a World Trade Centre Disaster Fund to collect British donations, and I've decided that you're going to be the Chairman of it.' Well, if you're told what to do by such a determined Governor of the Bank of England, you just do as you're told.

While we were working on this fundraising, we found out that black teddy bears had been produced as a symbol of mourning for some previous national disaster. Thus, we commissioned our own version, to sell at about £10 each. A few ladies in the Midlands undertook to make them and process our orders, and the black teddy bears were launched on ITV's *Good Morning* programme by my wife, Wendy. Suddenly, we were selling thousands of them, and it got completely out of control, with the little old ladies working twenty-four hours a day packing teddy bears. But it all helped, and after about a month into our fund raising, and backed by some very large donations from the City, we had raised several million dollars.

Then we had to think about how to spend the money, and decided that we would like to help children who had lost their parents, by paying for their education. Most of the school system in New York was free, so they didn't really need our money. However, we discovered that the Roman Catholic Church and the Jewish community ran private schools, so we gave them the money to cover the education of some of their pupils who had been affected by the terrorist atrocity. I never asked to meet any of these children, because I didn't want them to feel that they had been singled out or treated differently in some way.

The Catholic Archbishop of New York was Cardinal Edward Egan. Like a lot of Cardinals, he lived well and, on one of my visits to the city, he invited Wendy and me, as well as our son John, out to dinner, to thank us for all that we had done. Of course, he could walk into any Italian restaurant in New York, and all the staff would instantly prostrate themselves on the floor. He took us to one of the best restaurants in the city, where it was clear that he was very well looked after. He told me that he had previously served as Secretary to Cardinal John Cody, Archbishop of Chicago, in the 1960s. At that time, much of Chicago was run by the Italian Americans. So, whenever there was any trouble, Egan would meet up with the famous

Irish-American Mayor, Richard Daley, and he – together with the head of the Jewish congregation and the Catholics – would sort everything out. Apparently, it worked very well.

Member of the Supervisory Board, Deutsche Borse (2004–2005)

The Chairman of Deutsche Bank, when I first arrived, was Rolf Breuer. A very impressive and charming man whom I got to know quite well and really liked. After he had left Deutsche Bank, he became Chairman of Deutsche Borse, the German Stock Exchange in Frankfurt. He contacted me to ask if I would be prepared to join the Supervisory Board of Deutsche Borse. The German corporate oversight is often formed by a two-tier system consisting of the Supervisory Board, which is normally made up of executives from other companies, and the Executive Board which would run the business. Rolf explained to me that he was keen for the Deutsche Borse to join up with the London Stock Exchange and he thought that my connections and reputation in the City might help to negotiate that tie up. I agreed to join the Deutsche Borse Supervisory Board, and the then Chief Executive of Deutsche Borse was Werner Seifert. He developed a plan with a Canadian banker from Goldman Sachs to achieve a merger of the London and Frankfurt Stock Exchanges. I suggested an alternative plan but Werner proceeded with his version which proved to be unsuccessful. I was not happy with the discussions at the Supervisory Board at Deutsche Borse and, consequently, tendered my resignation. This was at the time not far removed from when I resigned from the Board of Sainsbury's and the question was posed in the press as to whether I was becoming a serial 'resigner'. I responded by saying that I believed working in accordance with my own principles was the right thing to do, and that was the practice to which I would adhere.

Director, Total (2005–2011)

Total is a French multinational oil and gas company, and one of the seven largest oil companies in the world. When I was Chairman of Banker's Trust in London in 1998–99, I became great friends with my French colleague, Bernard Attali. Through him, I met Jean-Pierre Halbron, who in turn introduced me to Serge Tchuruk, who was a

Director of Total. They had traditionally appointed a Briton to their board, and in 2005 Total asked me to take up this role, following the death of Lord Alexander, the former Chairman of NatWest.

The board meetings took place in Paris every other month and were conducted entirely in French. Although I speak that language pretty well, these meetings lasted for hours on end, and eventually I would find myself losing the thread. Most of the people on the board, especially the Non-Executive Directors, knew the oil industry inside-out, but I didn't. They also, unlike Non-Executive Directors in other organisations, got immensely involved in all the detail. I found myself saying: 'I don't know enough about this.' It was so exhausting trying to follow the endless discussions in French that eventually I asked the Chairman if he would mind providing simultaneous translation for me. 'But your French is fine,' he said. 'I know,' I replied, 'but it's tough, you know, when it goes on for hours.' Anyway, he declined my request. I stayed on for about six years, but stood down when I knew that I was going to join the board of Eurotunnel. The Chairman of Total, when I left, was Christophe de Margerie, a brilliant and charming man who tragically was killed when his aircraft was taking off from Moscow in 2014 and hit a snowplough. In Eurotunnel (now GetLink), they do provide simultaneous translation for the British Directors, so you can relax and listen, and follow more easily.

Director, China Construction Bank (2005–2012)

When United Scientific had set up its factory in Singapore in 1974, under what was then called the Pioneer Industry Scheme, the future development of Singapore was being master-minded by their Economic Development Board. I quickly became a proselytizer for the organisation, particularly when they were holding conferences in London to persuade other people to invest in Singapore. They had a well-developed defence industry, a significant part of which was run from 1983 by a remarkable lady, Ho Ching. In 1985 she married Lee Hsien Loong, who became the third Prime Minister of Singapore in 2004, and is the eldest son of the country's first Prime Minister, Lee Kuan Yew. I first met Lee Hsien Loong when he was a young national serviceman, because he used to come to our factory in Singapore to train in using some of the equipment we were building.

By 2005, Ho Ching had become Chief Executive of Temasek Holdings, an investment company owned by the Government of Singapore, and she rang up one day to say that Temasek, the Singaporean government investment arm, had just bought a sizeable share in China Construction Bank, which is one of the four big Chinese banks. She wanted to appoint someone to the bank's board, couldn't appoint a local, and wanted to know if I would take on this role. I asked what it would involve. 'They have a quarterly board meeting in China,' she replied. 'Well,' I said, 'I'm quite busy, and I'm not sure that I can ...' Before I could get any further, she said: 'Listen, you have just succeeded in getting a licence for Lloyd's in China. Whom do you know at the top of the Chinese financial services industry?' I had to confess that I knew nobody really. 'Well,' she went on, 'if you become a Director on the board of China Construction Bank, you will be at the top of that industry, so I suggest that you do it.'

So off I flew to Beijing, where I met Guo Shuqing, the Chairman of China Construction Bank, a charming Oxford graduate who spoke perfect English. Every three months, I would attend their board meetings, which actually rotated around different Chinese cities. I went to places I'd never heard of, and became part of the Chinese financial establishment, which was fascinating. After six years, in 2012, I was told that it would be against the rules for me to remain a Director any longer. However, they appointed me to the board of a subsidiary called China Construction Bank Asia Ltd, which is based in Hong Kong Kong and incorporates the retail branches that formerly belonged to Bank of America and who had sold the business to CCB. That has since grown enormously, because mainland Chinese companies have discovered that it can be much cheaper to borrow money in Hong Kong than in Beijing. Now I attend quarterly meetings in Hong Kong, where all the meetings are partly conducted in English, with simultaneous translation for the Chinese directors. The previous meetings I attended in China were all in Mandarin, with simultaneous translation into English for me and the three other English-speaking Directors. One was Greg Curl, who had been nominated by the Bank of America, because they were the largest foreign shareholder in China Construction Bank. The second was Dame Jenny Shipley, who joined the board in 2012, and the third Elaine La Roche, who had come from Morgan Stanley. I remember thinking that Jenny Shipley's name rang a bell, and sure enough I discovered that, as Prime Minister of New Zealand, she had come to the Mansion House for lunch with me on an official visit when I was Lord Mayor.

When I was appointed to the board of China Construction Bank in 2005, and before I had attended my first meeting, I received a phone call from their offices. It was a Saturday morning and I was at home. 'Terribly sorry to bother you,' they said, 'but would you be able to come to a board meeting tomorrow in Beijing?' 'Of course I can't get to a board meeting in Beijing tomorrow,' I replied, 'what's the panic?' They assured me that it was 'nothing special,' simply that the Chief Executive had resigned, so they needed to appoint his replacement. When I asked why he had resigned, they said: 'Oh, he's just gone off to run another state-owned Chinese bank. It's all perfectly normal, but we just have to regularise all this.' I pointed out that we would need to set about looking for a new Chief Executive. 'Don't worry,' I was told, 'that's all been sorted out, he's starting next Friday.' 'But if I remember rightly,' I said, 'I'm on the Appointments Committee.' 'Yes,' they said, 'that will meet on Thursday.' I quickly discovered that there was only one candidate for the job. Once I started attending the board meetings, I caused a few waves and matters began to improve. I also pointed out that, as the second largest bank in the world by market capitalisation, they should have a base in London, and eventually persuaded them to open a small office here, which has subsequently turned into a sizeable subsidiary.

Guo Shuqing, the first Chairman I worked with, came to England. Lord (Jacob) Rothschild, who is a good friend, wanted to meet him. I agreed to take Guo Shuqing to Waddesdon Manor, the great nineteenth-century chateau in Buckinghamshire, built by Baron Ferdinand de Rothschild between 1874 and 1889. Jacob showed us round and then took us for dinner to his home nearby. I'd warned him that this Chinese banker was a great wine-buff, so of course we drank the finest Château Mouton-Rothschild and had a wonderful time. Shortly afterwards, at one of our meetings in China in 2011, Guo Shuqing told me that he was leaving because he had been appointed to Chair the China Securities Regulatory Commission. He subsequently served as Governor of Shandong province between

2013 and 2017, and has recently been appointed as the Chairman of the China Banking Regulatory Commission and Party Secretary of the PBOC (the Chinese Central Bank).

Once Guo Shuqing had gone in 2011, a new Chairman for China Construction Bank took over. This was Wang Hongzhang, who had previously been head of the Commission for Inspecting Discipline at the People's Bank of China but spoke no English. In spite of this, he and I got on well, and I remained very friendly with him. He also came to London, and I arranged various visits for him, including a dinner at the Mansion House with the Lord Mayor and a trip to Buckingham Palace. I had hoped that Prince Andrew would be able to show him round, but as he was away, the staff at the Palace gave him a tour and took him to see the exhibition of The Queen's diamonds.

On my visits to China for the board meetings of China Construction Bank, once a year I was allowed to take Wendy as a guest. We were looked after by a young lady by the name of Wang Lidan, whose job included taking care of the overseas directors. She had a master's degree in interpretation and was one of the superb team who provided simultaneous translation, from Mandarin to English and vice versa, at our board meetings. One day she said to me: 'I would like to take a master's degree in financial economics. I have heard that the London Business School [LBS] is the best school in the world. If I apply to them, will you act as a referee?' I said that I would do that with pleasure, but I warned her that it was tough to get into the LBS and I couldn't guarantee that she would get a place there. She replied: 'Oh no, if I apply, they *will* give me a place.'

Three months later, she rang up to tell me that she had won a place at LBS. Then she went on to say: 'I've heard that the British Government give out Chevening Scholarships to international students with leadership qualities, to help them with postgraduate studies at universities in the United Kingdom. I want to apply for one, so will you act as my referee?' Again, I agreed, but pointed out that Chevening Scholarships were few and far between. Again, she replied, 'If I apply, I *will* get one.' She had to apply through the British Embassy in Beijing, because the scholarships are funded by the Foreign and Commonwealth Office. When I next visited China, she was still waiting for an answer to her application, although it was expected imminently. So, I rang the British Ambassador and said: 'Look, do me a favour. Can you have a look and see if this lady has got a scholarship?' When he called me back, he was laughing. 'Oh, yes,' he told me, 'she's got her scholarship. She was a brilliant candidate.'

Wang Lidan went to the LBS and got her second master's degree. I attended her graduation in Regent's Park, along with Jenny Shipley, who happened to be in London at the time. A few weeks later, Lidan told me she was going back to Beijing. I asked her what she was going to do there. She said: 'I don't know, because when I came to London, I had to leave China Construction Bank. They said however that they might consider re-employing me, once I had taken my degree.' So she went back to China and approached her former employers. The first thing they said was: 'Well, you say you've got this master's degree, but you haven't actually got the certificate for it yet. How do we know you're telling the truth?' I told her that she could tell them that I had been at the graduation and witnessed her receiving the degree. Eventually, she was re-appointed, but only to her old job, which consisted of organising flights and hotel accommodation for the overseas directors and translating.

25. Brilliant Chinese scholarship student, Wang Lidan, graduates from London Business School with her second master's degree. *Left to right* Dame Jenny Shipley, Wang Lidan, and self.

A few months later, she told me that her husband, who worked in the IT department of China Construction Bank, was being posted to their branch in Dubai, and that she would be going with him. Unfortunately, there was no role for her in the bank there, so she wanted to know if I could help her find a job in Dubai. I did try, but in the end I had to say: 'Look, if you were moving to London, I would be able to get you a job in about thirty seconds. But I'm afraid there is very limited use for a Mandarin-English interpreter in Dubai.' Fortunately, she had recently acquired written permission from the Chinese authorities to have a baby. Once she knew she was expecting, she asked Wendy and me to choose an English name for the child. It was at the time of The Queen's Diamond Jubilee in 2012, so we suggested Elizabeth for a girl and Philip for a boy. In the end, they had Philip, who now lives with them in Dubai, together with a second child, a daughter named Elizabeth.

Chairman, Defence Reform Group (2010–2011)

When the Coalition Government was formed in 2010, Liam Fox was appointed Defence Secretary. He had decided that significant reforms were needed throughout both the MOD and the Armed Forces and he set up a Defence Reform Steering Group to oversee this work. After he had assembled the group, he then contacted me to ask if I would chair it. I did think that forming a group without the Chairman having a say in the selection of its members was not the best route. However, after discussion with Liam Fox, I agreed to take it on and so found myself back in the MOD building some 20 years after I had left it. I said that I would prefer to leave procurement out of our remit, as I had very entrenched views on the subject, but would concentrate on other areas. In fact, I was not very comfortable with one or two of the members, but managed to add George Iacobescu to the fit to help with the review of the MOD's real estate.

One of the most important issues which we addressed was the status and inter relationships of the Chiefs of Staff – that is the CDS (Chief of the Defence Staff), CNS (Chief of the Naval Staff and First Sea Lord), CGS (Chief of the General Staff), and CAS (Chief of the Air Staff). I had discovered early on in the MOD to my surprise, that the three service Chiefs did not report to the CDS but were in fact on a par with him. When I enquired further as to whom they formally reported, I found to my surprise that their ultimate reporting officer was in fact Her Majesty The Queen!

I felt that we should try to establish a more conventional structure by having the three Chiefs report in to the CDS, but I knew that any move to apparently demote them would be received very badly. So, in order to avoid that, I suggested that they should remain as they were but that a new group should be set up to include The Defence Secretary, the CDS and others but not to include the other Chiefs. Unsurprisingly this was not well received in some quarters, but it was put into effect and is still in place. It led also to the realisation that the Chiefs could be more effective if they were primarily co-located with the Service which they headed, rather than being based in the MOD Main Building. Some commented that they were being 'rusticated', but the majority view of the Chiefs was more along the lines: 'Now I can spend more time actually running my service.'

Chairman, NBNK Investments plc (2010–2012)
In 2010, when I was approaching the end of my chairmanship of Lloyd's and wondering what I was going to do next, my sister-in-law phoned me up one day and said: 'Look, my cousin has asked me to find out if you'd be interested in becoming Chairman of a new bank? I think they said they've got £1 million to spend on it.' My immediate response was: 'They won't get very far with £1 million in a new bank, but let me talk to your cousin.' So I rang him. It transpired that he was working with a group backing a start-up business aimed at creating a new British high-street challenger bank. Its main target was to bid for 632 branches that Lloyd's Banking Group was being forced to sell by 2013 under European Union competition laws. The new vehicle was to be floated on the London Stock Exchange, and had attracted investment from some of the largest institutions in the City – including Aviva, Invesco, Foreign & Colonial, and Baillie Gifford – who had committed up to £2 billion to pay for the acquisition. They had also agreed to hand over a cheque immediately for £50 million to fund our bid and all the associated set-up costs.

Initially, Sir Brian Pitman, the former Chairman and Chief Executive of Lloyd's Bank, was lined up to chair it, but he died suddenly in

March 2010, so they asked me to become the Chairman. I agreed, and we started to put together our board of directors. These were Sir David Walker, Chairman Morgan Stanley in the UK, and who had written a report for the Government on banking reform; John McFall, a Labour peer and former Chairman of the Treasury Select Committee; Dan Brennan, a distinguished QC and member of the House of Lords, who also sat on the Labour benches; and Michael Forsyth, a Conservative peer who had served as Secretary of State for Scotland in John Major's Cabinet. We then recruited Gary Hoffman as the Chief Executive. He had formerly worked at Barclay's for twenty-six years, ending up as Vice-Chairman, and had more recently been Chief Executive of Northern Rock. Describing his appointment to a journalist in January 2011, I said: 'Gary is a star. He is a really tough, focused operator. He is not a glitzy banker; he is a roll-up-your-sleeves and get-to-work type of banker. He is not going to run a suave bank with fish tanks and plasma screens.'[1] We were all aiming to create a customer-friendly, transparent retail bank. One of our first tasks was to settle on a name but, until we were up and running, we were not allowed by the regulator to use the word 'Bank' in the title. So, in the interim, we used 'NBNK' short for New Bank, but we all got used to it – as did the press – so that interim name stuck.

We thus set about putting together all the infrastructure that would enable NBNK to bid for these 632 Lloyds branches and establish itself as a new bank. By 2011 we had made our first bid of £730 million as an upfront payment. There was one other rival bid, from the Co-op Bank, which offered £350 million upfront, followed by £400 million dependent on business performance over the next fifteen years. In December we were astonished to hear that the Co-op was the preferred bidder. NBNK was being advised by Credit Suisse, who had assured us there wouldn't be any other bidders, so I asked them for their thoughts on all this. They told us that they thought the Co-op Bank was having very severe financial problems and would be unable to finance the offer they had made to Lloyds. They also drew up a risk assessment document outlining their belief that the Co-op's finances

1   Simon Watkins, 'We're ready for a lot of rude letters,' *The Mail on Sunday*, 23 January 2011.

were overstretched and the fact that it was unclear how they were going to raise the funding for the proposed acquisition. At the board meeting of NBNK on 26 January 2012, we decided (and minuted) that we should pass this information on to Lloyds, so the following day Gary Hoffman and I went to see their chairman, Sir Win Bischoff. I said to him: 'We know you're talking to the Co-op and we know this is a competition, but frankly if this all collapses, it's not going to look good for anybody. We have therefore decided to give you this confidential paper, which has been prepared for us by Credit Suisse, and I think if you read it, you will find that the Co-op cannot ever be considered a serious bidder.' He took the paper and replied: 'Thank you very much.'

Lloyds had announced in December that they would reach heads of terms with the Co-op Bank by the end of March 2012, but by April it was clear – as we had predicted – that the Co-op was not going to meet that date. On the recommendation of our investors, and having been invited back into the process, we decided to make a second bid. Then in May, I received a telephone call from the office of the Governor of the Bank of England, Mervyn King, inviting me to go to see him. We had a confidential meeting, at which we discussed NBNK's bid for the Lloyds branches, and he told me that he believed the politicians favoured the Co-op bid and that we would lose; our only solution might be to talk to the politicians. Of course, he was right, and on 27 June 2012, our second bid was rejected. It seemed that Lloyds had come under considerable political pressure to accept the Co-op's bid, not least because one of the goals of the Conservative-Liberal coalition agreement of 2010 was to promote the interest of mutual organisations like the Co-op, which are owned by and run for the benefit of their members. At that stage, NBNK abandoned its plans.

By February 2013 Lloyds were considering a stock market flotation of this side of their business, if their preferred bidder failed to complete on the deal, and indeed in April the Co-op Bank decided not to proceed with the acquisition, having reported losses of £600 million and uncovering the extraordinary background of their then Chairman, who became known as the 'Crystal Methodist'. Two months later, in June, reports emerged that the Co-op Bank had a shortfall in its capital of about £1.5 billion, caused largely by its takeover of the Britannia Building Society in 2009 and poor management. In January 2014 the Treasury Select Committee decided to investigate all of this, and Gary Hoffman and I were amongst those called to give evidence. By that time, Mervyn King had retired from the Bank of England, but – with his prior agreement – I revealed to the committee what I recalled he had told me at our meeting back in May 2012. However, in his evidence to the committee, Mervyn King disputed my account. I also told the MPs that I had hand-delivered the risks assessment document on the Co-op to Sir Win Bischoff in his office at Lloyds on 27 January 2012, and that Gary could confirm this because he was with me. When Win gave evidence, he flatly denied that I had ever given him anything.

I was so angry about this, that I told the Treasury Select Committee that, back in June 2013, I had received a telephone call from *The Times*, who said then that they were putting together a story suggesting that I had fabricated the existence of this document. As I explained to the committee:

'Fortunately for them, before they went to press, they decided to pull that story. I was very angry. I telephoned another director [of Lloyds], Norman Blackwell (since promoted to Chair, Lloyds Bank), and I said: 'If you dare state that, I will throw the book at you.' That to me says a great deal about the Lloyd's thinking on this, because that document clearly did exist. I was not lying, Mr. Hoffman was not lying, our board was not making this up, and their only defence was to say that I had fabricated the whole thing ... Although they may pooh-pooh it now and say, 'Well, anybody could have said that [about the Co-op]', they were obviously worried that they had been given this advice and had ignored it, or he [Win Bischoff] had been given it and certainly had not shown it to his board.'[1]

Gary Hoffman had told me, throughout the bidding process, that he believed that Lloyds real intention was to try to retain the branches, to turn them into a stand-alone bank itself and then to float that off or to sell it. Indeed, that is precisely what happened. The man at Lloyds

1   Transcript of oral evidence given by Lord Levene to the Treasury Committee on 21 January 2014, in answer to Question No. 1591.

responsible for the potential sale of the branches was Paul Pester. Gary's prophecy was, of course, absolutely accurate – a decision to sell the branches to the Co-op Bank rather than NBNK all ended in tears and, therefore, Lloyds Bank was left 'reluctantly' to take over the package itself. These actions were managed by Paul Pester who, subsequently, became Chief Executive of the newly renamed TSB. Not long thereafter, they negotiated the sale of the TSB to the Catalan bank Banco Sabadell who is now its owner. However, another prophecy, which Gary made, was that NBNK would have to make significant expenditure on the IT systems for those branches to make them work properly. At the time of writing, the recent severe problems experienced in the IT field by TSB under Banco Sabadell's ownership have proved only too true, and Paul Pester has had to resign.

Director, Eurotunnel (since 2012)

Eurotunnel, or Groupe Eurotunnel SE, to give it its proper name – most recently renamed as GETlink SE - was formed as a company in 1986, with the aim of financing, building and operating a railway tunnel between England and France. Individual investors were told that if they bought a minimum of £5,000's worth of shares, they could benefit from unlimited passage through the tunnel for life once it opened, which it did in 1994. Wendy and I both took up this opportunity, at £1 per journey. Initially, the service had teething problems, but gradually it improved; and, as we subsequently bought a house in France, we now use it frequently.

When I was Chairman of Lloyd's, the British Ambassador in France organised a lunch for one of our presentations in the Embassy in Paris. There I met Jacques Gounon, the Chairman and Chief Executive of Eurotunnel, who had decided that he was no longer going to put up with 5,000 British shareholders getting free transport to and from France. What he didn't know, when he announced this, was that these shareholders were often senior lawyers and retired judges, and they all rounded on him. When we met, I told him that I too was a shareholder, and then said: 'Look, you've got about 5,000 British shareholders. How many trips a year do you think they will each take? Perhaps one or two. How much will that cost you? Nothing! So if you tell them they're welcome to have these privileges for life, they'll love you.' This all helped in his negotiations with share-holders, who, as a result, subsequently went on to support him in a vital restructuring of the company's finances in 2007.

A few years later, Jacques asked me to join the Eurotunnel board. I agreed and took up this post in 2012, just after I had left Lloyd's. The company and its board are largely French, with only two other British directors apart from me, these being the former Conservative and Labour politicians, Tim Yeo and Patricia Hewitt. Eurotunnel has been through some tricky times, but by 2014 it had an operating profit of £57.1 million. There was a brilliant episode in the BBC TV series, *Yes, Prime Minister*, which was called 'A Diplomatic Incident,' and was first broadcast in 1987. It's all about the negotiations between the French and the British over the future Channel tunnel, and is extremely funny. Years later, I got to know Bernard Emié, the French Ambassador to the United Kingdom between 2011 and 2014, and I gave him a copy of that episode, because I thought it might help him understand the British. He loved it!

In January 2012, the French ferry company Sea France went into liquidation. It had been operating ferry services from Calais to Dover since 1996. When Jacques decided that Eurotunnel should buy their ships, I remember saying: 'Are you sure you want to do this? We're running a successful, high-tech tunnel. Do you really want to get involved with the French seamen's union?' But he was adamant that it was the right thing to do. Inevitably, once Eurotunnel had the ferries, it was referred to the Monopolies Commissions in both the United Kingdom and France. Jacques assured me that he had already spoken to the Commission Chairman in Paris, and there would be no problem from there. However, the Monopolies Commission in London were not at all happy and said that they didn't approve of what Eurotunnel were doing. We decided to appeal, but in the mean-time, the Monopolies Commission said: 'Look, we have already determined that you are running a cartel, and you have to stop.' Jacques' response to this was: 'Says who? How are you going to make me do that?' And they replied: 'That's very simple. Unless you sell your interests in the ferries, we will close the port of Dover to your ships.'

In the end, Jacques realised that we would have to close the ferry operation down. Whereupon, the French seamen's union accused

Eurotunnel of ruining their livelihood and trashed the ferries by slashing the seats with knives. We were now faced with a sizeable repair bill. But somehow Jacques, who has an extraordinary knack of landing on his feet, managed to get them fixed and then sell them in 2016 for a very good price to DFDS, who were the rival operators.

Chairman, Starr Underwriting Agents Ltd (since 2012)

Hank Greenberg was born in New York State in 1925, and is now ninety-three-years-old. His father died when he was six, and his mother subsequently married a dairy farmer. During the Second World War, he served in the United States Army. He took part in the Normandy landings in 1944, during Operation Overlord, and the liberation of Dachau concentration camp in May 1945; he was awarded the Bronze Star and the French Legion d'Honneur for his military service in Europe. After returning home, he gained a law degree, before volunteering as a soldier again during the Korean War of 1950–53, during which he won another Bronze Star.

After all that, he decided to look for a job, and his friends suggested that he look at the insurance industry, much of which was based near Wall Street in New York. So he went to see the recruitment office of one company but was given very short shrift, but, as he was leaving, he saw the office door of the company's head of personnel, walked straight in, and talked his way into a job. By 1960 he was Vice-President of C.V. Starr & Co. Inc., a diversified financial services firm that had been named after its founder, Cornelius Vander Starr (1892–1968), who had created the insurance company AIG (American International Underwriters) in Shanghai in 1919. By 1962 Starr had appointed Hank as the head of AIG's North American holdings, and in 1968, shortly before his death, he picked him as his successor. Hank has remained chairman and Chief Executive of C.V. Starr ever since, and still runs the business in his nineties. He has a conference call with senior staff once a week giving him a close up of the group's operations. His real name is Maurice, but everyone calls him Hank. He looks about sixty, and still runs, walks and skis.

Hank was also Chairman and Chief Executive of AIG from 1968 to 2005. Under his direction, it became the largest insurance company in the world. On one of my first visits to New York as Chairman of

Lloyd's, I was told that I should go and see him, because obviously they had business in the Lloyd's market. But when I tried to set up a meeting, I was told that Mr Greenberg was very busy and rarely met up with anybody. I pointed out that I was only the chairman of Lloyd's of London, and so his staff agreed to try to fit me into his schedule. In the end, he came out of a meeting to talk to me and we sort of hit it off. The first thing he said to me was: 'Look, the Lloyd's market is a diabolical mess, and you've got to sort it out.' As we did subsequently sort it out, he and I got on very well.

In 2005 the New York Attorney General, Eliot Spitzer, attacked Hank on various regulatory and accounting issues. Hank was forced to resign from AIG. He had been the biggest shareholder in AIG, and at one moment had been one of the richest men in the world.

I remember the day Hank was forced out of AIG. I was in New York and rang him up to ask how he was. 'How do you think I am?' he said, 'I'm terrible.' I asked if he'd be free for lunch, and he replied: 'Of course I'm free for lunch, nobody wants to have lunch with me.' We met up and discussed his future. 'What will you do now?' I asked. He said: 'Wait and see.' Anyway, he remained Chairman and Chief Executive of C.V. Starr and turned that from essentially a holding company into an insurance firm. Then, when I left Lloyd's in 2011, he asked me if I would like to become Chairman of their London business, Starr Underwriting Agents Ltd, a post which I accepted in 2012 and hold to this day, and which is a very successful and growing business.

CHAPTER TWELVE

Reflections on a Busy Life

Thanks to my parents, I am very conscious of the enormous advantage I received in being given a good education, particularly at the City of London School. I am a great believer in the value of education and have had the privilege of serving as a Governor of my old school, the City of London, since 1985. I have been joined in this appointment by my younger son, Tim, also an Old Citizen, and who qualifies as he has been recently elected a Common Councillor. I subsequently had the opportunity of giving something back to the education field and, for that reason, was particularly pleased with the decision by Lloyd's to build a school in Laomeng village in Yunnan province, one of the more remote parts of China, to provide a good education to the children who lived there. Closer to home, Wendy and I decided to help fund the new library at the City of London School, known as the Levene Learning Centre, which has proved to be enormously popular.

I always thought that the great benefit which I had received thanks to the education for which my parents had paid, was the most important thing for me to replicate for my own children. I know that, in turn, they think likewise and have had the good fortune to be able to provide a first-class education for their children – our grandchildren, who are taking full advantage of it.

After leaving school and entering the workplace, I owe much to Bennie Linden for giving me the opportunity at an early age to build my self-confidence and self-belief.

Today it is so important to bring young people on by delegating responsibility and empowering them. In a fast-moving world of non-stop innovation, age has proved to be no barrier to entry – after all,

Mark Zuckerberg is only 34! Of course, young people make mistakes through inexperience. The trick is to learn from them and not to repeat them.

As I built up United Scientific over the years, I was able to show that, with the right level of determination and drive, success can be achieved early on. I rather like Sir Richard Branson's quote that 'If somebody offers you an amazing opportunity but you are not sure you can do it, say yes – then learn how to do it later!' I wish I had said it because this sums up my career so well. Without question, the most dramatic change in my life came when I was invited, out of the blue, by Michael Heseltine to go into the MOD with a brief to reform the Dockyards. And, even more so, when I was then appointed as a Permanent Secretary in the MOD to take responsibility for an £8bn procurement programme. Never having been a civil servant, my appointment created a tremendous uproar at the time.

When I first met Michael at the lunch to which he had invited me, I was initially overwhelmed. But as our conversation developed, I realised that here was a very successful businessman turned politician, who, on becoming Defence Secretary, had immediately realised that the Government was paying through the nose for its defence procurement. Since I had been in the defence industry for 20 years, I knew this to be true and realised that I would be able to help him, and so it proved. Looking back, so much of what I did subsequently was at his behest – the DLR, the Dome, Canary Wharf – and all had the same challenge of the unfamiliar and of learning on the job. I relished it.

I certainly was not the first businessman to be conscripted by the British Government – both Lord Rothermere and Lord Beaverbrook became key players in wartime Governments. Later Lord Rayner came straight out of the business world from running Marks and Spencer into the MOD where he established the Procurement Executive which I subsequently took on. Thereafter two Lords Sainsburys (John and then David), came in separately to work for governments of two different colours. They brought their experience to bear on numerous problems faced by successive Governments. My success at the MOD in taking on a very commercial post was symbolic of the start of building a bridge between the private sector and the huge

Government bureaucracy which was staffed by extremely able people, but with few of them having a commercial background except in some of the nationalised industries. I suppose also, and in a strange way, not understanding at the outset too much about what civil servants were supposed to do was actually rather helpful – ignorance can be bliss. In many ways, I was an unwitting trailblazer for the Public Private Partnerships of the late 80s and 90s.

Over the years one does come to adopt certain attitudes. One of the earliest ones that I learned from an older and wiser colleague was that 'people do business with people and not companies.' How many times does one call up to ask for someone who is known to you, and if they are not available, you are asked if you would like to speak to someone else and you reply 'no thank you, I will wait until they are back'. This propensity to deal with people we know is I think much stronger than just going to the name of a company because it happens to be well known.

Before anyone may think that everything I touched turned to gold, there were certainly one or two failures in between. I would not have counted my involvement in the Millennium Exhibition at the Dome as one of my greatest achievements, although it did indirectly lead to the redevelopment of the Greenwich Peninsula. The Dome itself, albeit not the greatest success as an exhibition, is now a superb centre of entertainment with an excellent transport connection through the Jubilee Line. To me, the biggest failure was our inability to create NBNK as a new challenger bank, although as I have written, I still believe that we were the victims of an appalling political misjudgement.

Running United Scientific, working in the MOD, serving a year as Lord Mayor of London and acting as Chairman of Lloyd's, sent me on endless journeys around the world to some extraordinary places. The majority of those journeys involved flying with British Airways which now has a fascinating website feature which regularly updates the distance that their Executive Club members have travelled. When I consulted this at the time of writing this chapter, it recorded that I have travelled 1,896,275 miles on British Airways flights, spent 22 weeks in the air and travelled the equivalent of 7.8 x the distance to the moon.

Through all these journeys, I developed over time an approach for dealing in different countries, and as that approach became refined, it enabled me to have some success in negotiating some important agreements. I learnt at an early age that understanding the modus operandi of different countries enabled me to make rapid progress, and not to make the mistake of treating each market as if it were just the same as the UK. Trade may be universal but the niceties of doing business abroad encompass a whole range of political and cultural sensitivities apart from the obvious differences in cuisine and language.

Had the subjects I studied at School and University been a significant factor in my success? Other than the benefit of a first-class education, and the mind training and discipline that this brings, I think not except learning foreign languages. Sadly, today in the UK, enthusiasm to learn other languages is on the wane, partly because English is used so widely around the world. But that means that you lose out on becoming close to people and their families, and understanding how other countries and people culturally tick. I have no doubt that my fluency in French enabled me to establish a much better and quite different relationship with my colleagues in the French MOD – somehow it seems that people feel that if you can converse with them in their own language you have a greater affinity. The severe downturn in numbers learning a foreign language in the UK at GCSE is a worrying sign for the future.

All of our grandchildren bring me tremendous pleasure and satisfaction and I am always eager to hear of their latest exploits.

Our youngest grandchild in New York, now aged 10, has been educated there since the age of 3 at a bilingual school. She now speaks, reads and writes Mandarin fluently. Having tried at a much later age to master a smattering of the language, and having totally failed, I am full of admiration for her. She certainly can look forward to an especially bright future.

Technology, as everyone knows, has changed the world enormously. There is today talk of little else but the continuing IT and oncoming AI revolutions. However, I fondly remember a rather earlier technology revolution and that was in telephony. When I first started to work at United Scientific in the early 1960s, if I wanted to place a telephone call to Nigeria, I had to call the overseas operator and book my call perhaps three or four days in advance. It might then come through on the due date although rarely at the due time and the quality of the call made it often very difficult to hear what was being said. Then came the progressive introduction of IDD (International Direct Dialling). Calling someone on the other side of the world by merely pushing a few buttons on the phone made a tremendous difference and I could virtually measure the increase in business that we could achieve in each country as their telephone network was joined. Little could we have imagined at that time being able to do exactly the same thing from a thin device which slips into my inside jacket pocket, and being able at the press of a key to have the whole world of information available from the same device, through sources like Wikipedia.

The seamless link between my career at United Scientific, my work at the MOD and as Chairman of Lloyd's was the business of managing change. Whether it was in response to restrictive working practices, entrenched commercial attitudes, structural inefficiencies, product complacency, a lacklustre corporate image or boardroom obduracy, I have always enjoyed challenging the status quo for unless you are one step ahead of the competition and the technological curve, change has a nasty habit of leaving one behind by which time it's often too late to catch up.

In an astonishing short space of time by historical comparisons, communication and technology have changed and continue to develop at a dramatic pace. This was brought home to me when I was appointed to the House of Lords Committee which produced a report on Artificial Intelligence (AI). Some of the leading experts in the UK came to give evidence to us and we visited some of their facilities – I was amazed by what I heard and saw. But this time it will not be me but our children and grandchildren who will have the challenge to manage these changes and enjoy the benefits derived from them.

ACKNOWLEDGEMENTS

I HAVE BEEN fortunate in having a group of remarkable and resilient personal secretaries on my close staff. Somehow they all managed to put up with my quirks and foibles and without them, there is no way that I could have achieved what I did. In particular, Sharon Yardy who worked for me for many years at USH, Jill Matthews who came to work for me in the MOD, stayed on to work for my successor, Malcolm McIntosh, and subsequently left to work for GKN. And two others that put up with me for a long time: Liz Crichton who had worked for me, then went off to live in the Middle East, who came back again and re-joined me at Deutsche Bank before retiring to live with her husband in Cyprus and who, very sadly, died recently. And last, but not least, my present PA, Barbara Addison, who followed me out of Canary Wharf into nine years at Lloyd's, the short spell at NBNK and is currently at Starr, and whose help in the preparation of this book has been invaluable.

My family have all been extraordinarily supportive. First, I have to mention the role played by my wife Wendy who has supported me throughout, even when she may have thought some of my ideas to be crazy. In particular, she played a critical part when I was in the MOD. On many of my foreign trips there would be a dinner organised to which spouses would be invited. She would invariably be seated next to the host, my opposite number, and developed the technique of working into their conversation his view on what he thought about our discussions earlier in the day – a very revealing and invaluable source of information. Her support continues undiminished.

In addition to Wendy, my three children and 10 grandchildren all persuaded me to write this book and I am immensely proud of all of them. They are totally uninhibited in talking to me and help me to understand their world today, which is so very different from when I grew up in the 1950s and 1960s. Throughout my busy and at times frantic business career, my children have given me much succour and pride. My eldest, John, is now a partner at Goldman Sachs in New York; my daughter, Nicole, after working for Margaret Thatcher's favourite PR advisor, Sir Tim Bell, now runs her own PR consultancy; and the third of the trio, Tim, is running his own very successful investment fund having just floated an IPO of the first Fintech fund on the London Stock Exchange.

Having toyed with the idea of writing a book for several years, it was through an introduction from my friend and colleague, Chris Joll that I met Samantha Wyndham that I found a collaboratrice who had the patience to sit with me, hour after hour, while I disgorged rather random memories. So, much of the credit for the final production of this book must go to her along with the very professional team of Anthony Weldon, as publisher and Alan Ogden, as editor.

My undying thanks to them all.

INDEX

Whitmore, Sir Clive, Permanent
  Secretary 42, 51, 98, 107
Whitmore, Dr Patrick 9
Willesden 4, 5, 6
Withers, Gary, Imagination 111
Woolf, Lord, Master of the Rolls 141
World Trade Center, 11 September 2001
  attack 173, 180
World Trade Center Disaster Fund UK,
  PL as Chairman 210–12
World Trade Organisation (WTO) 193
Worshipful Company of Armourers 124
Worshipful Company of Carmen 124,
  137
Worshipful Company of Fishmongers
  151–2

Worshipful Company of Merchant
  Taylors 155
Worshipful Company of Shipwrights 100
Worshipful Company of Skinners 155

Yeo, Tim, MP 224
Yes, Minister television series 55, 60, 224
Young, David, Secretary of State for
  Trade and Industry 207
Younger, Hon. George, MP, as
  Secretary of State for Defence 67, 70,
  72, 73, 77, 83
  and launch of HMS *Argyll* 99

Zain Hashim, General Tan 123
Zoulfikar, Mahmoud 35